Thinking German Translation

Thinking German Translation is a comprehensive practical course in translation for advanced undergraduate students of German and postgraduate students embarking on Master's translation programmes. Now in its third edition, this course focuses on translation as a decision-making process, covering all stages of the translation process from research, to the 'rewriting' of the source text in the language of translation, to the final revision process.

This third edition brings the course up to date, referencing relevant research sources in Translation Studies and technological developments as appropriate, and balancing the coverage of subject matter with examples and varied exercises in a wide range of genres from both literary and specialised material. All chapters from the second edition have been extensively revised and, in many cases, restructured; new chapters have been added—literary translation; research and resources—as well as suggestions for further reading. Offering around 50 practical exercises, the course features material from a wide range of sources, including:

- business, economics and politics
- advertising, marketing and consumer texts
- tourism
- science and engineering
- modern literary texts and popular song
- the literary canon, including poetry

A variety of translation issues are addressed, among them cultural differences, genre conventions, the difficult concept of equivalence, as well as some of the key differences between English and German linguistic and textual features.

Thinking German Translation is essential reading for all students seriously interested in improving their translation skills. It is also an excellent foundation for those considering a career in translation.

A Tutor's Handbook offers comments and notes on the exercises for each chapter, including not only translations but also a range of other tasks, as well as some specimen answers. It is available to download from www.routledge.com/9781138920989.

Margaret Rogers is Professor Emerita in Translation and Terminology Studies at the University of Surrey; **Michael White** is Lecturer in German at the University of St Andrews. The two co-authors of the second edition, **Michael Loughridge** and **Ian Higgins,** as well as the originator of the *Thinking Translation* series, the late **Sándor Hervey,** are all former colleagues at St Andrews, the former both with extensive experience of professional translation.

Thinking Translation

Thinking German Translation

A Course in Translation Method:
German to English

Third Edition

Margaret Rogers and Michael White

**with material from the second edition by
Michael Loughridge and Ian Higgins
based on an original idea by Sándor Hervey**

Routledge
Taylor & Francis Group

LONDON AND NEW YORK

Third edition published 2020
by Routledge
2 Park Square, Milton Park, Abingdon, Oxon, OX14 4RN

and by Routledge
52 Vanderbilt Avenue, New York, NY 10017

Routledge is an imprint of the Taylor & Francis Group, an informa business

© 2020 Margaret Rogers, Michael White, Michael Loughridge,
Ian Higgins and Sándor Hervey

First edition published by Routledge 1995
Second edition published by Routledge 2006

British Library Cataloguing-in-Publication Data
A catalogue record for this book is available from the British Library

Library of Congress Cataloging-in-Publication Data
Names: Rogers, Margaret, [date] author. | White, Michael James, author. |
    Loughridge, Michael, author. | Higgins, Ian, author. | Hervey, Sándor G.
    J., author.
Title: Thinking German translation : a course in translation method :
    German to English / Margaret Rogers and Michael White ; with material
    from the second edition by Michael Loughridge and Ian Higgins based
    on an original idea by Sándor Hervey.
Description: Third edition. | Abingdon, Oxon ; New York, NY : Routledge,
    2020. | Series: Thinking translation | Includes bibliographical references
    and index.
Identifiers: LCCN 2019050757 (print) | LCCN 2019050758 (ebook) |
    ISBN 9781138920972 (hardback) | ISBN 9781138920989 (paperback) |
    ISBN 9781315686264 (ebook)
Subjects: LCSH: German language–Translating into English.
Classification: LCC PF3498 .H46 2020 (print) | LCC PF3498 (ebook) |
    DDC 438/.02—dc23
LC record available at https://lccn.loc.gov/2019050757
LC ebook record available at https://lccn.loc.gov/2019050758

ISBN: 978-1-138-92097-2 (hbk)
ISBN: 978-1-138-92098-9 (pbk)
ISBN: 978-1-315-68626-4 (ebk)

Typeset in Times New Roman
by Apex CoVantage, LLC

Visit the eResources: www.routledge.com/9781138920989

**With grateful thanks to our own translation teachers
and colleagues**

Contents

Preface to the third edition

In introducing the second edition of *Thinking German Translation* (2006) our colleagues noted that the original 1995 edition had been completely revised and rewritten. We have maintained that tradition, taking into account developments over the intervening years as well as incorporating some refinements based on earlier years of translation scholarship, not to forget our own classroom experiences over time. The important link with St Andrews is maintained, acknowledging the origins of the course in the early 1990s and the original idea of Sándor Hervey. We are particularly grateful to Michael Loughridge and Ian Higgins, co-authors of the second edition, for the wealth of material with which we have been able to work in our attempt to fashion a new edition. Thanks are due to students in St Andrews who have trialled much of the material and many of the exercises set.

In terms of structure, we have kept the idea of sections, of which there are now four: Overview and Basic Concepts; Some Key Issues; Formal Properties of Texts; and The Translation Process and Translation Specialisms. The introduction provides a preliminary orientation to contextualise the course within the current Translation Studies landscape and in the practice of translation. Each section also has its own brief introduction, which can be used by the tutor and/or the students to decide where to focus their interest and attention if they need or wish to be selective in pursuing the course.

Many of the topics and some material from the second edition have been carried over into the new chapters, with many revisions and additions, bearing in mind the time gap between the second and third editions. We have also split two chapters (one on translation as a product and one on grammatical and sentential issues), combined two chapters (literal and connotative meaning), and added two new chapters (research and resources; literary translation). In our efforts to accommodate these changes, we have incorporated some of the topics and material from the second edition section on Contrastive Topics and Practicals in the chapters on Formal Properties of Texts. The number of exercises has been increased to almost 50 and we have attempted to broaden the range of exercises to include tasks other than but still related to translation, such as research, analysis and evaluation.

Our focus remains that of the original course, namely, written translation rather than, for example, the fast-developing area of multimedia or audio-visual translation. That would require another book. We have continued to work with examples from a range of text genres, both literary and non-literary or 'specialised', and dating from the middle ages to the present, in order to root the discussion in each chapter in practice, and because we believe that the different forms of textual study and production which inform Translation Studies and modern languages more broadly are mutually informing. The final section of the course applies the essential points of the previous chapters to the translation process from research to revision, with a chapter on each of three specialisms: consumer-related texts, science and technology, and literature.

One new feature is a Further Reading section at the end of each chapter, which we hope will help both tutors and students to pursue further any particular points which interest them and to build up an inventory of key literature and resources.

Responsibility for the changes made since the second edition, sometimes radical, remains, of course, our own, including our reorientation of a central theme of the second edition—translation loss—towards translation as a more creative and, we hope, exciting activity, namely, translation as a process of decision making and text production. And that is how we open this new edition.

Margaret Rogers, University of Surrey
Michael White, University of St Andrews
August 2019

Acknowledgements

In acknowledging the help and support we have received during the production of this course, we think not only of our personal contacts, but also of the good-natured helpfulness of many employees of large and small firms and other institutions whose texts we asked to use. But at the very least we would like here to say thank you publicly to the following friends and colleagues: Professor Sabine Braun for her valuable advice and insights on some of the German material used in this book and Eyvor Fogarty for her professional advice on the Postscript. We would also like to thank colleagues at Routledge—Camille Burns and Claire Margerison—for their efficiency, helpfulness and patience in providing editorial assistance.

The authors and publisher would like to thank the following people and institutions for permission to reproduce copyright material. Every effort has been made to trace copyright holders, but in a few cases this has not been possible. Any omissions brought to our attention will be remedied in future printings: Cambridge University Press for extracts from the Authorized Version of the Bible (The King James Bible), the rights in which are vested in the Crown, are reproduced by permission of the Crown's Patentee, Cambridge University Press; Wolf Biermann for permission to cite the song 'Kunststück'; The Random House Group Ltd. for permission to reprint ©1994: extracts from *All Quiet on the Western Front* by Erich Maria Remarque. Translated by Brian Murdoch. Published by Jonathan Cape; The Random House Group Ltd. for permission to reprint ©1963: an extract from *Cat and Mouse* by Günter Grass, translated by Ralph Manheim published by Martin, Secker and Warburg; The Bundesverband der deutschen Industrie, for material from its *Für ein attraktives Deutschland* programme (1994); Verlagsgruppe Random House GmbH ©2003 for permission to reproduce the poem 'Todesfüge' by Paul Celan. Published by Suhrkamp; Georg Thieme Verlag for material from Diwok et al. 'Superoxiddismutasenaktivität von Ginkgo-biloba-Extrakt', *Zeitschrift gesamte Inn. Medizin*, Vol. 47, 1992; Professor H. Feldmeier of the Charité University Medicine Berlin, for part of his *Die Welt online* article on malaria research ('Neuer Impfstoff bremst Vermehrung von Malaria-Erregern'); *Lufthansa Magazin* (2000) for extracts from the in-flight publication. Reprinted with permission from Lufthansa Magazin; *Germanwings Magazin* (November 2014) published on behalf of Germanwings by Ink for extracts from their magazine; Niederrhein Tourismus for an extract from their website; Alfred Kröner Verlag for permission to reproduce extracts from *Lexikon der Sprachwissenschaft* by Hadumod Bußmann, 1990, 2nd edition; Taylor & Francis Group for permission to reproduce extracts from *Routledge Dictionary of Language and Linguistics* by Hadumod Bussmann, translated and edited by G.P. Trauth and K. Kazzazi, 1996; Tourismus und Stadtmarketing Husum GmbH and Husumer Bucht—Ferienorte an der Nordsee e.V. for an extract from a Husum tourist board brochure; C.H. Beck for permission to reproduce an extract from *Königsallee. Roman* by Hans Pleschinski, 2013; The *Frankfurter Rundschau* for permission to reproduce 'Selbst linke Querdenker werden umgarnt' by J. Schindler published on 11 September 1998. © Frankfurter Rundschau. All rights reserved; Reckitt-Benckiser for permission to reproduce the Calgon slogan; The British National Corpus Consortium for data extracted from the British National Corpus, distributed by Oxford University Computing Services on behalf of the BNC Consortium. All rights in the texts cited are reserved; Oxford University Press for permission to reprint an extract from *Faust Part One* by J.W. von Goethe. Translated by David Luke. Oxford University Press. 1987; Berliner Forum für Geschichte und Gegenwart e.V. for permission to reprint part of their flyer for Checkpoint Charlie; Oxford University Press for permission to reproduce 'Blaue Hortensie/Blue Hydrangea' from *Selected Poems with parallel German text*, by Rainer Maria Rilke, translated by Susan Ranson and Marielle Sutherland. Oxford University Press. 2011; The Modern Humanities Research Association for permission to reproduce an extract from *An Impossible Man*, by Hugo von Hofmannsthal, translated by Alexander Stillmark. MHRA. 2016.

Introduction

In the years since the previous edition of this course book appeared, and certainly since the first edition of 1995, much has changed in the translation world, both in theory and in practice. Translation Studies as a discipline is becoming increasingly interdisciplinary. This development reflects not only the ways in which translation as a practice is embedded in many aspects of our lives, including socially, politically, economically, educationally, medically, legally and last but certainly not least, creatively; it also reflects new ways of analysing a whole range of translation issues from new disciplinary perspectives and using new methods. Translations have also increasingly come to be valorised as 'rewritings' based on the creative expertise of the translator in refashioning texts for new situations and new readerships in a different linguaculture. The dominant narrative has been shifting away from translations as largely derivative, involving unavoidable loss, towards translations as new texts with often creative solutions to complex problems. While it is certainly the case that source texts differ in their degree of difficulty—e.g. pulp fiction *versus* literature from the canon, or a parts list *versus* a learned article on ground-breaking science—*all* texts pose difficulties of one kind or another, whether these are generic, terminological, textual or cultural. There is, of course, also the unavoidable fact that a text in the original language serves as a starting point for the translation, but translations are not the only kind of text to have certain derivative qualities, as our first chapter will argue.

As a practice, translation in the professional world is becoming ever more connected with technology. The translation of many texts is today supported to varying degrees by suites of interlinked tools ranging from 'memories' of previous translations, electronic dictionaries or 'termbases', online text corpora and machine translation. While this kind of 'workbench' approach is used now throughout what has become a global industry, online means for researching and solving translation problems are relevant not only for translators of what in German are sometimes called '*Gebrauchstexte*', '*Sachtexte*' or '*pragmatische Texte*', but also for translators of literary texts.

A further change which has gained pace over the last two decades is the spread of translation as a degree subject in many universities, not only within the UK but also throughout Europe and globally. Whilst the dominant pattern in the UK has been to offer specialised three-semester courses at Master's level, building on the linguistic and cultural proficiency attained in a Bachelor's programme, more and more translation-specific courses are now being introduced at undergraduate level; in some cases, even whole degree programmes are offered. This reflects a growing acknowledgement of the role such courses and programmes can play in raising students' awareness of the complex nature of translation and in preparing them to be 'communication brokers'. A certain expediency must also be acknowledged in the response of many modern language departments to recruitment problems exacerbated by a shrinking pool of suitably qualified language candidates. At the same time, the language programmes that students encounter in different universities in the UK and abroad are now extremely varied: where this course was originally written for students (and teachers) with experience of prose and translation as a principal mode of language learning, this can no longer be taken for granted.

Perhaps more than ever, then, this book attempts to speak to an increasingly diverse readership. For students on non-literary degrees or students entering translation courses from different backgrounds, it contains a short chapter on literary translation, as well as an introduction to analysing sound patterns in verse—and plenty of literary texts for translation. For students on more traditional programmes, the scientific and technical aspect of the course has been expanded, in particular in a new chapter on translation resources, but also through the range of examples which seek throughout to balance literary with non-literary texts. The level of difficulty too varies, from sales catalogues and short pieces for discussion, to complex texts which require more detailed knowledge. Our feeling here is that often *seemingly* easier pieces offer productive scope for the full discussion of particular issues, and more syntactically and culturally complex pieces offer a challenge appropriate at honours or Master's level.

This book is not an introduction to theories of translation. There are a number of excellent publications already fulfilling this role, to which we refer at appropriate moments in the course. Rather, it is an attempt to introduce students to some of the key issues in *doing* translation, principally from German into English rather than the reverse, with a strong emphasis on the practice as a decision-making process. It is now accepted that a translator's competence—whether as a qualified professional or as a student—includes the ability to articulate specific reasons for their chosen translation solutions. 'It sounds better' will no longer do. Our aim is to facilitate the identification and classification of translation problems and to open up choice in dealing with them. Key issues here—anticipating the sort of questions that students might have in their minds when setting out, rather than a theory-led agenda—include the ancient story of closeness or freedom, the rather disputed and now relativised notion of translation 'equivalence', the nature of texts (genre and text function), (inter)cultural issues (even between German and English), meaning and translation, and some formal properties of texts and their relation to translation (from text to sound). The section covering the formal properties draws on the three contrastive topics in the second edition, which are no longer presented as stand-alone chapters. Instead, we have opted for greater integration with our key translation issues. Throughout the book, we also introduce a wide range of strategies for dealing with translation problems, and in one case, dedicate a whole chapter to a particular strategy (compensation), in keeping with the previous edition.

The translation process can sometimes be viewed rather narrowly by students as the actual act of writing out/typing a draft translation. To counter this, we have added a new chapter on research and resources, covering what could be viewed either as 'pre-translation' preparation or, depending on preferred working methods, an *ad hoc* activity interleaved with the actual writing activity. The use of online resources is crucial although not exclusive here. The final stage of producing a translation which is fit for purpose is covered by the chapter on revising and editing, including many updates on the second edition version focusing in particular on the clarification of key terms ('editing', 'revising', 'proofing').

While the book is not in itself a study of translation theories, it does refer more explicitly to Translation Studies than previous editions, and contains suggestions for further reading; for us, engagement with scholarship on translation as a linguistic and cultural phenomenon and its practice underpins and supports critical reflection on translation as a practical activity.

Section A

Overview and basic concepts

In this opening section, we lay some of the groundwork on which the book builds, considering translation as text production and the relationship of the translated text to its source text, dealing with issues which often shape the expectations of new translation students such as closeness and equivalence.

Chapter 1 focuses on translation as writing for a purpose, developing the idea of translation as situated textual production in which the translator is a decision maker. Throughout the course we will be introducing strategies which you can add to your translator's 'toolbox' in order to tackle particular issues arising from linguistic, cultural and other differences in both systems and actual texts. Our first two strategies are chosen to raise your awareness of translation as a text-creation task, not simply as an encoding-decoding exercise, including moves that you may not even have regarded as legitimate parts of a translation task. These are the reduction (or even omission) of elements in the source text and expansion or exegesis in the target text.

Chapter 2 takes this discussion a step further but through the lens of a common question posed by students when translating: how close should my translation be to the source text? We aim to show that the translator as decision maker has a number of legitimate methods: literal translation, often seen as accurate or faithful, is not necessarily the default approach, but one of a range of methods from word for word to much more nuanced choices. In order to decide on their overall approach or method, translators therefore need to know what the target text is for, including who it is for, and where/when it will be used or made available.

Asking about closeness raises the issue of equivalence, which is the focus of the third chapter. Although equivalence as a key concept in translation has been challenged from both a cultural and a functional perspective, it is often an intuitive starting point when learning to translate. The chapter focuses mainly on equivalence below the textual or even the sentential level: these topics are dealt with in more detail in later chapters. But common to all is our aim to refine the notion of equivalence and to distance it from a common-sense understanding of 'sameness'. The many examples serve as vehicles to introduce more translation strategies, including cultural and functional equivalents, compensation, transfer/borrowing, substitution and a combination of strategies as a 'couplet'.

1 Translation

A decision-making process

One productive way of thinking about translation is to think of it as a form of rewriting, that is, as a process of composing a text for which there are models and antecedents, contexts and purposes. While many people new to translation tend to have a rather mechanical view of a process in which there is a single, inevitable, 'correct' or 'accurate' solution for every problem encountered, translation is actually a process which involves choices and implications at many levels. And these choices are often interdependent, as well as being dependent on the context in which they are located.

In this opening chapter, we begin by thinking about translation and writing as related processes, and then introduce you to translation by considering two particular **strategies**—'standard conceptual tools of the trade' (Chesterman 2000: 87)—which you may not consider to be translation at all, namely **expansion** (or exegetic translation), and **reduction** or **omission**. Both literary and non-literary—or 'specialised'—texts will be considered, focusing on translation as a situated, decision-making process of text interpretation and production. Indeed, it is one of the primary aims of this course to help you shape your own decisions in an informed way when translating. But before we go any further, it is useful to think about the kinds of skills you have as a linguist already that you can bring to, and develop through, your work on translation.

To put it simply: translations and their sources are texts which originate and function in particular and often rather different socio-cultural contexts. Becoming better at German translation involves, in part, gradually becoming better at managing the inevitable changes and challenges that moving between the two languages *and* cultures causes; but it equally means becoming more aware of the nature of textual production and meaning in general, in other words, how texts are written, how they generate meanings, and how they are read and used.

Translation and (re)writing

All texts have two aspects: they are documents, objects, produced at a given time, by a human being, for a more or less conscious purpose, from the banal to the sophisticated; once written, they are, in a sense, detached from their authors, having both an existence of their own and creating meanings as they are interpreted by their readers. All texts, thus, are always pulled in two directions, their meanings and their significance are governed and created by two different sets of circumstances. This is obviously the case for historical texts, but it is equally a commonplace to observe that contemporary texts such as letters, emails and tweets are often misunderstood because they are ephemeral forms dependent on the moods and immediate situations of the writer and reader, which are often different. Most writing in fact involves addressing and overcoming contextual differences of some kind and anticipating the reader's understanding. As a student, you know this from the written work you produce. When we write essays, if we want to get better at it, we must always ask ourselves two questions: what do I really mean (i.e. in my mind)? And what have I really said (on the page)? Good writing—and good translating—involves being able to be clear about the meaning that needs to be communicated, as well as having the analytical frame of mind to decide what the text in front of you actually communicates, and whether the text meets the expectations or needs of the reader. Good writing involves being able to see the text from the point of view of the reader as well as the author.

The distinctiveness about translation resides then in two things: firstly, the meanings we wish to convey are not primarily our own, though they will of course be the product of our own (hopefully informed) reading; secondly, the language of the text and the cultural context in which our text will have to function as a piece of writing are different from those of the original. Hence, texts which are translations have to be conceived both in terms of their relationship to the source text (ST), a relationship that raises issues of 'equivalence' (more of this in Chapter 3), and their existence and functions as texts in their own right within the linguistic and cultural systems of the target language. The translator interprets the source, formulates the translation, re-interprets the source and reformulates the translation in a continuous process of interaction. And while this interpretive process governs all writing, the successful translator is aware of and manages the potential interpretations of their text by making necessary changes and choices governed both by the resources of the target language (TL) and the purpose of the target text (TT). Translation is thus an exercise in exacting pragmatism.

It is useful to recall, however, how pragmatic most writing is. Many people think of pieces of writing, especially literary works, as stable, unchangeable wholes, written by a single person, with writing being a more or less single act. This is rarely the case. Scientific articles are, for example, often co-written and edited by a team of researchers, but the same is often true even of works of literature: Goethe's great play *Iphigenie auf Tauris*, the most classical of classical dramas, is a case in point. Itself a reworking of classical material for an eighteenth-century audience, Goethe's play was composed and privately performed in Weimar in an early prose version before it was refashioned under the influence of Italy to become the verse classic we know today. Furthermore, in his rewriting in Italy, Goethe even sent the text to his contemporary, the literary critic Herder, giving him scope to amend the text (Goethe 1945/1960: 404). Writing is a process, and texts, including translations, are the outcome of that ongoing process, which involves consideration, evaluation, revision and meeting external constraints. It is not only translation which is a kind of 'rewriting'—as one well-known translation scholar, André Lefevere, has characterised this type of text production (see Asimakoulas 2020: 494–98 for an overview)—it is also so-called 'original' texts, whether literary or specialised.

Starting on strategies

Goethe lived through a period in which translation and the reception of foreign literature were of formative importance for German letters, and his late eighteenth-century novel, *Wilhelm Meisters Lehrjahre* (1795–6), gives us a fascinating insight into the translator's need for pragmatism. On his travels with a theatre company, Wilhelm is given *Hamlet* to read in the prose translation by Wieland. An enraptured Wilhelm decides that the theatre troupe should perform the play, but in a new translation which he will produce without changes, because Shakespeare's original is a work of genius. Serlo, the manager of the troop, sees matters differently. Notably he sees a number of practical problems, the number of players available is restricted and the public is not used to plays of this kind. Significantly, Wilhelm comes around to Serlo's way of thinking: he makes some adaptations and the play is performed. In other words, the practical necessities of circumstance mean that he is compelled to produce a version that meets a specific purpose.

The eighteenth-century German reception of Shakespeare is one of the all-time great stories of translation and reception; and though it might seem far removed from everyday concerns, in fact Wilhelm's actions as a translator, tailoring his text to meet particular cultural and pragmatic constraints, are commonplaces of professional translation. Indeed, often 'translation' involves changes which may not seem like translation at all—eliding or reducing the message, or adding new material—and which offer a useful starting point for our consideration of translation as purposeful writing.

The following example is from a mail-order catalogue, published in both German and English. Both are in A4 format, and both are printed in the same font and size of type. But the English catalogue is less than half the length of the German one: many items are omitted altogether, and many others (though not all) are given less text than in the German original. In this example, the ST and the TT are both printed under a photograph of the item; the photograph is the same size in both, but the TT is only allotted a column of 27 mm of text, as against the 44 mm of the ST. The texts are presented below in parallel and with the same column width for ease of comparison.

ST	TT
Pfeifen von Hudson & Company. Das versilberte Original: **METROPOLITAN PFEIFE** Wahrscheinlich die berühmteste Pfeife der 5 Welt, denn die englische Hudson & Co. ('world renowned whistles') liefert sie seit 1873 an Scotland Yard. Sie wirkt mit ihrer Lautstärke von 115 dB aus der Nähe weitaus erschütternder, als jemand ahnen 10 kann, der sie bisher nur aus dem Kino kennt. Ob ihr Betrieb in London als Amtsanmaßung geahndet wird, entzieht sich unserer Kenntnis. Massives Messing, versilbert, Länge 6,5 cm. Bestell-Nr. **5539** **€ 15,00** (Manufactum 2003a: 356)	**THE ORIGINAL SILVERPLATED METROPOLITAN WHISTLE** Probably the most famous whistle in the world, because since 1873 Hudson & Co. has been supplying them to Scotland Yard. At 115 decibels, its sound is terrifying indeed. Solid brass, silver-plated. Length 6.5 cm. Order no. **5539 590** **£9.50** (Manufactum 2003b: 159)

The translation process here involves **reduction**. Primarily, this reduction is made necessary by the formal restrictions imposed on the translator, i.e. the permitted length of the text. But two of the translator's omissions are not: for an English-speaking audience, the explicit references to the company's Englishness and an evocative reference to London are less relevant. These are choices which are pragmatically or culturally governed, particularly by marketing considerations in this case.

More often, perhaps, than reduction, translation involves **expansion**, in the form of explanation or clarification (exegesis). Exegetic translation is often used in professional translation—literary and specialised—for cultural reasons. In the following example from a tourist brochure, the translator translates some of the names for clarity (e.g. 'the Nahe Valley'), but also includes the ST names (e.g. '*Naheland*') because the tourist is likely to see them on road signs and on maps:

ST	TT
Im Süden wird der Hunsrück eingerahmt von dem Flüsschen Nahe und dem Naheland. Gleich drei Heilbäder bieten Körper und Geist 5 Entspannung bei mineralhaltiger Erde, salzhaltiger Luft oder heilendem Wasser. Entlang der deutschen Edelsteinstraße rund um Idar-Oberstein werden Edelsteine geschliffen und zu 10 Kunstwerken veredelt. Von hier aus führt die Reise weiter ins romantische Rheintal, zwischen Bingen und Koblenz, ins Tal der Loreley [. . .].	In the south of the area the Hunsrück is framed by the small river Nahe and the Nahe Valley—Naheland. Three spas can provide relaxation for both body and spirit with their mineral rich earth, salty air and healing waters. Along the German gemstone trail—Edelsteinstraße—in and around Idar-Oberstein precious stones are cut and turned into works of art. From here the journey continues to the romantic Rhine valley—Rheintal— between Bingen and Koblenz, in the Loreley Valley [. . .].

Another cultural issue is that of reference or allusion, which may also require some kind of expansion. An allusion that is transparent to source-language readers might be opaque to TT readers without exegetic translation. Here is an example from Remarque's excoriating 1929 WW1 novel *Im Westen nichts Neues*. Himmelstoß is a blustering NCO. He encounters a group of soldiers he had humiliated when they were new recruits, and starts trying to bully them again. One of them, Tjaden, refuses to do as he is told: 'Tjaden erwidert gelassen und abschließend, ohne es zu wissen, mit dem bekanntesten Klassikerzitat. Gleichzeitig lüftet er seine Kehrseite' (Remarque 1955: 64). The allusion is to Goethe's *Götz von Berlichingen*, who rejects a call to surrender thus: 'Sag deinem Hauptmann [. . .], er kann mich im Arsch lecken' (Goethe 1985: 349). (Most editions since 1774 have dashes instead of the last three words, but such is their legendary status that German readers are well aware what they stand for.) The first published English TT is mystifying, and misleading: 'Tjaden replies, without knowing it, in the well-known classical phrase. At the same time, he ventilates his backside' (Remarque 1930: 94, trans. Wheen).

A later translation takes the exegetic approach: 'Tjaden gives an unworried and conclusive reply, quoting (although he doesn't know he's doing so) one of Goethe's best-known lines, the one about kissing a specific part of his anatomy. At the same time he sticks his backside up in the air' (Remarque 1994: 59, trans. Murdoch). This makes explicit much of what the ST leaves implicit, while preserving with its coyness something of the allusiveness of the ST. The cost is length and cumbersomeness, but at least the reader has a much better chance of understanding Tjaden's action.

Translators regularly make decisions about what to expand and what to reduce or even omit in their translations. However, these decisions may not always be consistent, as the following example from a document on social policy shows:

ST	TT
1990 etablierte sich die internationale Organisation 'Disabled People International' (DPI) in Deutschland unter der Bezeichnung Interessenvertretung 5 'Selbstbestimmt Leben' (ISL). (Stern 1996a: 9)	In 1990, the global organization Disabled People International (DPI) was set up in Germany as 'Interessenvertretung "Selbstbestimmt Leben" Deutschland' (ISL—i.e. Self-Determined Life). (Stern 1996b: 8)

On the one hand, the TT is exegetic, insofar as an English translation of the German '*Selbstbestimmt Leben*' is provided as an accompaniment to the transferred German phrase 'i.e. Self-Determined Life'; on the other hand, the TT neither translates nor explains '*Interessenvertretung*', even though this is also included in the acronym 'ISL'.

On occasion, a translator might employ a mixture of strategies in close proximity: there is no reason that the whole of a piece needs to be translated in the same way in order to shape the text for new readers. Take, for example, the following parallel German and English extracts from a bilingual in-flight magazine published by a German carrier (*Das Germanwings Magazin*, November 2014, published on behalf of Germanwings by Ink). The piece is publicising the world premiere of a play at a spectacular new riverside theatre in Hamburg:

ST	TT
Das Wunder von Bern im neuen Hamburger Theater **Ab 23. November** Mit der Uraufführung des Musicals *Das Wunder von Bern* eröffnet Stage Entertainment im November in Hamburg seinen Theaterneubau direkt an der Elbe . . .	**Das Wunder von Bern** **Stage Theater an der Elbe, Hamburg** **From 23 November** Stage Entertainment launches its new theatre on the banks of the river Elbe on 23 November with the world premiere of the musical *The Miracle of Bern* . . .

It is apparent that the titles of the German and English texts are different: the English heading shows the German name of the musical and also the full German name of the theatre, but fails to indicate that the theatre is new. The original German, on the other hand, omits the actual name of the theatre in the heading (and in fact throughout the whole article), just referring to the location of the performance '*im neuen Hamburger Theater*' and later repeating the information about it being new in the compound '*Theaterneubau*'. In the translation therefore, the information that the theatre is confined to the main body of the text, and the theatre's full name is added in the title. Perhaps the translator concluded that the German audience would know the name of the new theatre and it was therefore not necessary to include this, but that the international English-speaking audience was unlikely to know much about it at all, including its riverside location ('*an der Elbe*'). Other changes can be seen as a matter of taste, such as the formulation of the date of the performance: the German is precise in the title and vague in the first sentence, whereas the English is precise in both cases.

Elsewhere, the translator has little choice but to introduce expansions and reductions in order to deal with differences in the language systems. This is often inevitable, for example, when the translator has to convey a significant sociolinguistic distinction such as that between '*du*' and '*Sie*', as in this further example from *Im Westen nichts Neues*:

ST	TT
Himmelstoß wendet sich ihm zu: 'Das ist doch Tjaden, nicht?' Tjaden hebt den Kopf. 'Und weißt du, was du bist?' Himmelstoß ist verblüfft. 'Seit wann duzen wir uns denn? Wir haben doch nicht zusammen im Chausseegraben gelegen'. <div align="right">(Remarque 1955: 63)</div>	Himmelstoss turns to him. 'Tjaden, isn't it?' Tjaden lifts his head. 'And do you know what you are, chum?' Himmelstoss is taken aback. 'What do you mean, "chum"? I don't think we've ever drunk ourselves into the gutter together'. <div align="right">(Remarque 1994: 58–9, trans. Murdoch)</div>

The first 'chum' is an exegetic addition to 'you', an attempt to render the insubordinate familiarity of the '*du*'. It prepares the way for 'What do you mean, "chum"?', an exegetic translation which acts as a kind of **compensation** (more in Chapter 6) in view of the absence in the standard English linguistic system of an informal-formal second-person distinction. At the same time, however, 'chum' only gives the gist of '*du*', losing the specificity of second-person singular address.

Concluding remarks

Whatever the nature of the source material with which translators have to work, all translation tasks require knowledge of the subject matter (see Chapter 12 on research and resources) and of textual conventions (see Chapter 4 on genre), familiarity with the source language and source culture in general (see Chapter 5 on culture), and interpretive effort. But they also require knowledge of the nature and needs of the target public, familiarity with the target culture in general—and, above all, mastery of the target language. The next two chapters deal with two closely related key issues in translation: how close should my translation be? and what is meant by 'equivalence'?

Further reading

Bassnett, Susan 2007. 'Writing and translating', in Bassnett, S. and Bush, P. (eds) *The Translator as Writer*. London and New York: Continuum, pp. 173–83.
House, Juliane 2018. *Translation: The Basics*. London and New York: Routledge.
Newmark, Peter 1988. *A Textbook of Translation*. New York: Prentice Hall.
Palumbo, Giuseppe 2009. *Key Terms in Translation Studies*. London and New York: Continuum.
Shuttleworth, Mark and Cowie, Moira 1997. *Dictionary of Translation Studies*. Manchester: St. Jerome.

Practical 1

The first exercise below focuses on translating for a purpose, a topic to which we return in many places. The second assignment takes *intra*lingual rewriting as a starting point: you will be re-fashioning an English text for a different purpose and readership. The third exercise concerns translation in a constrained space, requiring a reduction in length for the target text. The last task asks you to consider whether a text needs to be culturally adjusted in any way for a new audience.

1.1 THINKING ABOUT TRANSLATING FOR A PURPOSE

Assignment

If you have had to translate in the language classroom, try to think back to your experiences; if not, just imagine you are a teacher setting a passage for translation. When you (or your imagined students) write a translation into your native language, what is it that determines the success of the translation (i.e. gets a good mark)? And when translating into the foreign language? How do these criteria change as you progress through university? Try to come up with a sheet of marking criteria and discuss in class: what are the characteristics of the best translations? The worst? What would cause a text to fail? The point of this exercise is to realise that writing a translation in the classroom in itself is a specific purpose, with (often uncodified) rules. To what extent do you anticipate that the criteria of success will be different in the workplace or in this course, as opposed to in the language class?

1.2 REWRITING A TEXT FOR A DIFFERENT PURPOSE AND AUDIENCE

Assignment

i   Identify the salient features of content and expression in the following ST, and say what you think its purpose is.

ii   Recast the ST in different words, adapting it for a specific purpose and a specific public (i.e. a specific readership or audience e.g. contemporary youth, rapping fans, older non-native speakers of English). Say precisely what the purpose and the public are. Treat the ST as if you were recasting the whole book of Exodus, of which it is a part. (As a rule, whenever you do a translation as part of this course, you should try to proceed as if you were translating the whole text from which the ST is taken.)

iii Comment on your overall approach and individual decisions you took in making the textual changes. (One way of doing this is to insert into your TT a note-number after each expression you intend to discuss, and then discuss the points in numerical order. Another possibility is to use the Endnote function in your word-processing program.)

Contextual information

The text is from the Authorized Version of the Bible, published in 1611. The best way of making sense of it is to read the rest of Exodus 14. The forces of Pharaoh, king of Egypt, are pursuing the children of Israel, led by Moses, who are seeking to escape slavery in Egypt. Seeing their pursuers, the people lose their nerve, and ask Moses why he has led them into this adventure.

ST

And the Lord said unto Moses, Wherefore criest thou unto me? speak unto the children of Israel, that they go forward:
   But lift thou up thy rod, and stretch out thine hand over the sea, and divide it: and the children of Israel shall go on dry ground through the midst of the sea. [. . .]
5   And the Egyptians shall know that I am the Lord, when I have gotten me honour upon Pharaoh, and upon his chariots, and upon his horsemen. [. . .]

ST

And Moses stretched out his hand over the sea; and the Lord caused the sea to go back by a strong east wind all that night, and made the sea dry land, and the waters were divided.

10   And the children of Israel went into the midst of the sea upon the dry ground: and the waters were a wall unto them on their right hand, and on their left.

And the Egyptians pursued, and went in after them to the midst of the sea, even all Pharaoh's horses, his chariots, and his horsemen.

And it came to pass, that in the morning watch the Lord looked unto the host of

15   the Egyptians through the pillar of fire and of the cloud, and troubled the host of the Egyptians,

And took off their chariot wheels, that they drave them heavily: so that the Egyptians said, Let us flee from the face of Israel; for the Lord fighteth for them against the Egyptians.

20   And the Lord said unto Moses, Stretch out thine hand over the sea, that the waters may come again upon the Egyptians, upon their chariots, and upon their horsemen.

And Moses stretched forth his hand over the sea, and the sea returned to his strength when the morning appeared; and the Egyptians fled against it; and the Lord overthrew the Egyptians in the midst of the sea.

(Exodus 14, v. 15–27)

1.3 TRANSLATING FOR A CONSTRAINED SPACE

Assignment

i   You have been commissioned to translate, in abridged form, the upmarket mail-order catalogue from which the following ST is taken. The TT is to take up three-quarters as many lines as the ST, so it should contain between 220 and 240 words (the ST only contains 236, but many of these are long compounds). Discuss the decisions that you have to take about your overall approach before starting detailed work on this ST.

ii   Produce a translation of the specified length.

iii   Discuss the main decisions of detail you took, concentrating on explaining your reductions, omissions and any exegetic elements that you introduced.

iv   Compare your TT with the published one, which will be made available to you by your tutor. Concentrate on the omissions and any exegetic elements.

Contextual information

The text introduces the long section on kitchen knives in the catalogue. The English catalogue is just as comprehensive, though more economical of space. Both repeatedly emphasise the superior quality of the knives offered.

ST

SCHNEIDWERKZEUG—FÜR DEN GUTEN SCHNITT

Küchenmesser—der Unterschied.
Bei Messern liegen Welten zwischen einem handwerklich gearbeiteten
Qualitätsprodukt und billiger Massenware.

5   Sie merken es—Schnitt für Schnitt.

Die Stähle:
schnitthart oder rostbeständig?
Zähe, Härte und Elastizität sind Eigenschaften, die nur als Möglichkeit im
(ursprünglich weichen) Eisen liegen und erst durch Schmelzen, 'Frischen',
10   'Puddeln' und die vielen anderen hüttentechnischen Prozeduren geweckt werden.
Hohe Härte und elastische Bruchfestigkeit sind die Kennzeichen eines guten
Messerstahls, und optimal vereinigt waren sie in den Werkzeugstählen mit relativ
hohem Kohlenstoffanteil. Dieser klassische Messerstahl ist allerdings nicht rostfrei,
und deshalb—wegen mangelnder Koexistenzfähigkeit mit der Spülmaschine also—
15   wurde er in den letzten Jahrzehnten von rostbeständigeren, aber weniger hoch
härtbaren Edelstählen aus der Messerproduktion fast vollständig verdrängt. Kenner
haben das immer bedauert.

Die Bearbeitung:
geschmiedet oder gewalzt.
20   Hochwertige Messer, bei denen es auf Langlebigkeit ankommt, werden geschmiedet,
also in jenem Verfahren der Metallverformung erzeugt, bei dem das Material unter
Hammerschlägen solange getaucht, gestreckt und verdichtet wird, bis es in Form und
innerem Gefüge optimal der späteren Funktion entspricht. Die Rohlinge für
einfachere Messer werden aus gewalztem Bandstahl gestanzt.

25   **Die Zurichtung: 'Haarscharf'**
bis zur Schrammenreinheit.
Ob geschmiedet oder gestanzt: Seine endgültige Qualität erhält ein Messer erst durch
die Zurichtung in der Schleiferei. Dort wird die 'Wate' (Schneide) aufgebaut, die
bei besten Messern in schlanken Schliffwinkeln bis zu 1/400 mm dünn wird, und
dort wird die Oberfläche bearbeitet, bis alle Schleifriefen für Hand und Auge
unerkennbar sind.

(Manufactum 2003a: 11)

1.4 TRANSLATING CULTURE-SPECIFIC ITEMS FOR
A NEW AUDIENCE

Assignment

i   You have been commissioned to translate the following short piece—a trial run
for a longer commission—from the tourism pages on the website of a locale in
North Rhine-Westphalia for an English-speaking audience. The ST is the opening gambit on the homepage. The potential readership for the TT includes visitors who are not native speakers of English. The ST consists of 68 words and sits
immediately underneath changing images of scenes from the local landscape,
including trees in blossom, lakes and walkers: the length of your translation (in
terms of space occupied) should not exceed that of the German original.

ii   Do some desk research looking at German tourism websites which have an English translation to see how cultural differences have been handled. You can also check out original English websites for similar areas to get a sense of the tone, the register and the general approach adopted.

iii   Produce a translation according to the client's requirements.

iv   Discuss the main decisions of detail you took, concentrating on explaining how you dealt with culturally specific items for a new audience e.g. did you expand or reduce these items?

v   Compare your TT with that of a fellow student:

   a   did you identify the same items as culturally specific? if not, why not?
   b   which items did you expand, how and why? how do your decisions compare to those of your partner?
   c   which items did you omit or reduce, how and why? how do your decisions compare to those of your partner?

vi   Your tutor will also be able to supply you with a proposal for the translation.

ST

WILLKOMMEN AM NIEDERRHEIN
'Tach auch'—im grünen Westen der Republik. Wir laden Sie ein: zum Rad fahren in flachem Gelände, Reiten im deutsch-niederländischen Grenzgebiet, Wandern auf Premiumwegen, Schlemmen in der 'Genussregion Niederrhein', zu ganz viel Kultur

5   an vielen Orten und noch mehr Natur in gleich zwei Naturparken. Aber auch zum Relaxen und Entspannen in unseren Beauty Spas und Wellness-Oasen.
Auf den Geschmack gekommen? Wir freuen uns auf Sie!

(Niederrhein Tourismus)

References

Primary

Goethe, J.W. von 1945/1960. *Goethes Werke*. Edited by Trunz, Erich. Hamburg: Wegner.
Goethe, J.W. von 1985. *Sämtliche Werke, Briefe, Tagebücher und Gespräche*. Frankfurt am Main: Deutscher Klassiker Verlag.
Manufactum 2003a. *Warenkatalog Nr. 16*. Waltrop: Manufactum.
Manufactum 2003b. *Catalogue No. 2*. London: Manufactum Ltd.
Niederrhein Tourismus n.d. *Willkommen am Niederrhein* [Online].
Remarque, Erich Maria 1930. *All Quiet on the Western Front*. Translated by Wheen, Arthur W. London: Putnam & Co.
Remarque, Erich Maria 1955. *Im Westen nichts Neues*. Berlin: Ullstein.
Remarque, Erich Maria 1994. *All Quiet on the Western Front*. Translated by Murdoch, Brian. London: Cape.
Stern, S. 1996a. *Die soziale Integration von Behinderten in Deutschland*. Bonn: Inter Nationes.
Stern, S. 1996b. *The Social Integration of People with Disabilities in Germany*. Bonn: Inter Nationes.

Secondary

Asimakoulas, Dimitris 2020. 'Rewriting', in Baker, M. and Saldanha, G. (eds) *Routledge Encyclopedia of Translation Studies*. 3rd edn. London and New York: Routledge, pp. 494-8.

Chesterman, Andrew 2000. *Memes of Translation*. Amsterdam and Philadelphia: John Benjamins.

2 Translation methods

Decisions about 'closeness'

In Chapter 1, we began our discussion by thinking about translation less as recoding the words of a text and more as a form of purposeful rewriting. In this chapter and the next we turn to two issues which have been the subject of discussion for millennia, namely: how close should a translation be? And what does it mean for a translation—whether of word, phrase or text—to be equivalent to the source? Through these discussions of 'closeness' and 'equivalence' we approach the relationships between the ST and TT from a number of different viewpoints, providing an overview, which subsequent chapters will then explore in more detail.

How 'close' should my translation be?

There are many possible answers to the question of how close your translation should be to the source text, depending on a number of factors. Translators make their decisions about the shape of the translation according to what, in their experience, is optimal in order to achieve their goal; indeed, a major part of learning to translate is in fact learning precisely to think about what those goals are and what factors influence your options. These factors include the genre (*Textsorte*) of the ST (business letter, poem, report, fire notice, short story, and so on), the function (*Texttyp*) of the ST (e.g. informative, operative/persuasive or expressive), the setting of the TT (where the translation is to be published or used in the target culture), the audience for the translation (who the primary readers are to be) (see Newmark 1988: 15, 13), and what the purpose of the translation is (e.g. is it for information purposes about the source culture or is it going to function as a quasi-original text in the target culture?) (see Risku 1999: 107–12; Martín de León 2020: 199–203). All these factors are part of what has been called the 'translation commission', the phrase itself being a not very transparent translation of the German *Übersetzungsauftrag*. Also known more helpfully as the 'translation brief', this is a set of instructions issued under ideal circumstances by the person who has commissioned the translation, detailing specifications for the considerations listed previously, all of which in some sense indicate the degree of 'closeness' the translator should be aiming for. However, we should note that many clients—or their intermediaries—do not understand the need to brief the translator ('just translate it'), and so it is part of the translator's job and expertise both to ask pertinent questions wherever possible, and to draw on experience and research to ensure their translation choices are informed.

In asking how close our translation should be, what we mean is how far our translation method—our overall approach to the translation brief—needs to favour or be oriented towards the target text, language and culture, or how far it should favour the source text, language and culture. In fact, this is not, or is seldom, an either/or question: rather we can think of our different translation options as existing on a sliding scale from word for word to literal to creative adaptation, moving from source-oriented to target-oriented. We discuss below some of the implications of these methods, beginning with the 'closest' translation of all, 'word-for-word' translation.

Methods of translation

ST-oriented methods

Word-for-word translation

'Close' translation is usually understood to mean 'close to the form of words in the ST'. In its most extreme form, it is sometimes called **interlinear** as well as **word-for-word translation** (see also Newmark 1988: 69); in this case, the TT does not follow the TL grammar, but has grammatical units corresponding as closely as possible to every grammatical unit of the ST without regard for the sense. Here is an example, a short extract from a furniture manufacturer's catalogue, to which we return below:

> *Das Sofa lässt sich mit wenigen Handgriffen in ein Bett verwandeln.*
> the sofa lets itself with few manipulations into a bed transform

Word-for-word translation is normally only used in Linguistics or language teaching; in the past it was used to gloss sacred texts, focusing on the 'difficult' words. One particular contemporary use, usually known as 'back translation', is conventionally employed by translation scholars to provide an insight into examples which are cited in languages other than that in which they are writing, since it cannot be assumed that all readers will be familiar with the languages used in the examples. Students writing essays on translation are also often asked to use back translation for their cited examples if the class deals with a range of languages. We should add, however, that even 'word-for-word' translation involves choices: in the previous sentence, *'verwandeln'* could easily have become 'change'.

Literal translation

Word for word can be distinguished from the more common **literal translation**, where the words or phrases are translated one-to-one but TL grammar is respected. A possible literal translation of our example is: 'The sofa can, with few manipulations, be transformed into a bed'. This translation involves a number of changes: (1) the reflexive verb '*lässt sich*' becomes the modal verb 'can'; (2) consequently, the infinitive '*verwandeln*' becomes the present passive infinitive 'be transformed', conveying the passive sense of '*lässt sich*' + infinitive (see Eisenberg 1986: 381); and (3) the position of the non-finite verb has changed, as English main clauses do not have the *Satzklammer* ('verbal bracket'), characteristic of German declarative main clauses (see Johnson 1998: 185–7, and Chapter 9): '*Das Sofa **lässt sich** mit wenigen Handgriffen in ein Bett **verwandeln***'.

Literal translation is on the whole much more likely to work effectively in closely related languages. Nevertheless, while German and English are genealogically close, sharing many lexical roots as members of the Germanic branch of the Indo-European language family, they are syntactically rather different and so you should be prepared to make a number of grammatical changes in your translations, particularly in relation to word order. This means that there will nearly always be a difference between a word-for-word and a literal translation between German and English. But then the purpose of these two methods of translation is also different. Whilst a word-for-word translation makes the structure and segmentation of the ST transparent, often for analytical purposes, a literal translation, formally or structurally much closer to the TL, can serve a different purpose.

A good example of how literal translation is used is in the translation of drama. So-called 'versions' of plays are created by well-known playwrights based on a close translation of an original commissioned for that purpose (see, for instance, Anderman 2009: 92–5). The nineteenth-century farce by Viennese writer Johann Nepomuk Nestroy—*Einen Jux will er sich machen*—was, for example, reworked by the English-language playwright Tom Stoppard on the basis of a literal translation as *On the Razzle* for the National Theatre in London. Unfortunately, the translator's indispensable contribution to 'versions' (or 'adaptations') is not always fully acknowledged.

TT-oriented methods

Translation methods such as close literal translation or interlinear translation are thus appropriate when foregrounding as much as possible of the ST's original linguistic form is a priority. Often, however, the particular form or phrasing of the original is less important than the text's communicative function. Returning to our sofa example, the literal translation can be understood, but it is not very 'natural', a criterion which is easier to sense than to define (see Rogers 1998 and Chapter 10 for more examples). Researching texts with similar design features in the TL is often helpful in establishing genre conventions and matters of tone or naturalness in keeping with the text's communicative function, in this case, as a sales text, predominantly persuasive. Other possibilities then suggest themselves for a translation:

With a few simple movements, the sofa can be converted into a bed.

This translation has the same morphological and syntactic changes or **shifts**, but adds a reordering of the information, foregrounding the ease with which the sofa can be converted; the terminology is also more suitable ('movements' and 'converted' instead of 'manipulations' and 'transformed'). This TT is more appropriate for a furniture sales catalogue in both structure and vocabulary, but a further possibility can still be imagined:

> It's quick and easy to convert the sofa into a bed.

The essential differences from the ST are still grammatical but with a different impact. Relative to the ST, (1) the sofa has its grammatical role switched from subject to object, implying a direct address to the reader ('[for you] to convert'); (2) a new, impersonal (or 'dummy') subject is introduced ('it'); (3) the adverbial phrase '*mit wenigen Handgriffen*' is turned into the complement of the new finite verb '[i]s' in an informal contracted form, positioning the interpretive phrase 'quick and easy' in a clause of its own, thereby giving it more weight; and (4) as a consequence, the English now comprises two clauses, a main clause and a non-finite subordinate clause, thereby changing the rhythm of the sentence. The text's purpose in both the ST and the TT is to sell convertible sofas, and the real selling point is now highlighted in a more prominent grammatical form, although both TT versions foreground how easy it is to perform the conversion. Four grammatical transpositions, then, but they are unexceptional and acceptable: this last translation is more reader-oriented and punchier, hence arguably better as a selling text than the alternative translations.

The translation brief might, however, change one of the ST features of the setting such as the medium of publication (e.g. ST in print, TT on the www), the time of publication (e.g. updating a ST for a more contemporary audience) or the audience itself. In the latter case, we can consider an even more radical translation of the sofa sentence, based on a translation brief which asks for a jokey tone:

> Take one sofa, press here, pull there—and hey presto, it's a bed!

This translation is addressed directly to the reader and achieves its humorous note by drawing on the features of completely different genres, namely, a recipe and a magic trick (an example of what is called 'intertextuality'). But that tone is also riskily achieved by details not found in the ST: 'press here, pull there' would be rash indeed unless the translator had actually checked the facts.

The closeness question and translation studies

If you feel that it is a naive question to ask 'how close should a translation be?', you should not, for many of the theories of translation in the twentieth century have addressed precisely that question. Some writers on translation take literal translation to be the basic approach, i.e. your starting point (see, for instance, Newmark 1988: 70). Others argue that the function of the target text within the target language and culture should be the focus of the translator's attention. The modern impetus for 'functionalist approaches' (see Nord 1997) came some 40 years ago, early in the development of translation as an academic discipline; the German scholar Katharina Reiß (1971, 1977/1989) proposed, for example, that the function of a text is crucial when evaluating the success of a translation, assuming that this remains the same for both the ST and the TT. Within the particular text typology which she adopted, she argued that when translating texts with an informative function, the content is the most important feature; in 'operative' texts (also 'persuasive'), the effectiveness of the appeal to the reader is dominant, whilst in 'expressive' texts, the form of the original is a crucial factor. These three types can be respectively exemplified by genres such as an encyclopaedia entry, an election leaflet seeking votes, and a novel. Reiß's ideas have since been developed, and in practice, these categories are more like 'ideal types', as many texts are complex constructs embodying and integrating many different features, as Reiß acknowledged.

The five exemplar translations discussed in this chapter illustrate how wide the choices which are available to you can be—even within a single sentence—and that the decisions you make are guided by a number of factors related to the translation such as its purpose and its audience.

Concluding remarks

To sum up, the decision on how 'close' to make your translation depends on a number of factors related to the translation brief which are hard to capture in binaries such as 'close' versus 'free'. Two main perspectives have been emphasised here. Firstly, the reason why the text is needed in the target culture, i.e. its purpose, can give a preliminary indication of whether a word-for-word (rare), a literal (in some circumstances) or a more creative translation solution is needed. Secondly, the dominant function of the text can guide you in terms of focus on content (informative), the reader's behaviour (operative/persuasive) or the author's voice (expressive). The next chapter will consider ways of analysing relative closeness in more detail, this time in terms of equivalence, the relationship between the source and target texts, languages and cultures.

Further reading

Baker, Mona and Saldhana, Gabriela (eds) 2020. *Routledge Encyclopedia of Translation Studies*. 3rd edn. London and New York: Routledge.

France, Peter (ed.) 2000. *The Oxford Guide to Literature in Translation*. New York: Oxford University Press.

Göpferich, Susanne 1999a. 'Text, Textsorte, Texttyp', in Snell-Hornby et al., pp. 61–4.

Kuhiwczak, Piotr and Littau, Karen (eds) 2007. *A Companion to Translation Studies*. Clevedon: Multilingual Matters.

Munday, Jeremy (ed.) 2009. *The Routledge Companion to Translation Studies*. New York and London: Routledge.

Munday, Jeremy 2016. *Introducing Translation Studies: Theories and Applications*. 4th edn. London and New York: Routledge.

Snell-Hornby, Mary, Hönig, Hans, Kußmaul, Paul and Schmitt, Peter A. (eds) 1999. *Handbuch Translation*. 2nd edn. Tübingen: Stauffenburg.

Practical 2

2.1 WHAT IS THE TRANSLATION FOR?

Assignment

Consider the following phrases, brief, but still potential texts. Suggest two translations for each, according to two different purposes: (a) for a non-German speaking linguist researching how notices are worded in a number of languages, including German and (b) for use on a notice to be situated on a newly painted fence and in someone's front garden, both as warnings.

i   Frisch gestrichen!
ii   Vorsicht! Bissiger Hund.

Did you need to research the answers to (b)? If so, how did you go about this?

2.2 COMPARISON: CLOSENESS AND TEXT FUNCTION

Assignment

i   How would you characterise the function of the ST and the TT extracts below? Or can you identify a mixture of functions? If so, which function do you think is dominant? Identify examples from each of the texts to support your case.
ii   Taking the published TT (printed below the ST) as a whole, how 'close' do you think it is to the ST? Explain your conclusions.
iii Where you think the TT can be improved? Give your own revised version and explain the revision.

Contextual information

The ST is from the first part an annual report (published in identical format in German and English) of the car manufacturer Audi. The second part of the report consists purely of the detailed financial statements and balance sheets, but the first part, elaborate in layout and illustration, combines publicity with information on the company's main activities and policies. The ST is taken from a section entitled '*Technik*', and concerns a new engine called the V8-TDI. The A8 is a model of car. '*Biturbo*' is explained in a glossary at the end of the report as follows: '*Der Zusatz "Biturbo" weist bei Audi V-Motoren darauf hin, dass zwei Abgasturbolader—einer je Zylinderbank—eingebaut sind*'.

Audi setzt weiteren Meilenstein in der Dieseltechnologie
Bulliges Drehmoment, hohe Leistung, Bestwerte in Beschleunigung und Durchzug:
Charakteristika eines Spitzensportlers.

5   Seit 1989 stellt Audi seine Vorreiterrolle bei der Entwicklung hoch effizienter und
leistungsfähiger TDI-Modelle immer wieder eindrucksvoll unter Beweis.

  Jüngstes herausragendes Beispiel ist der neu entwickelte 4,0-Liter-V8-TDI, der im
A8 zum Einsatz kommt. Er verleiht der leichtgewichtigen Luxuslimousine den
Charakter eines Spitzensportlers: Moderate Verbrauchswerte und hohe Laufkultur
machen den A8 4.0 TDI quattro auch zum idealen Langstreckenspezialisten.

10   **Der leistungsstärkste V8-Dieselmotor der Welt**
Mit dem neuen Modell vergrößert Audi das Angebot um eine weitere, sportliche
Variante. Der V8-TDI-Motor im Audi A8 ist mit 202 kW (275 PS) und 650
Newtonmeter Drehmoment der derzeit leistungs- und drehmomentstärkste V8-
Selbstzünder, der in einer Serienlimousine zu finden ist. Das maximale Drehmoment,

15 das zwischen 1.800 und 2.500 Umdrehungen pro Minute anliegt, verschafft dem
Fahrer in allen Geschwindigkeitsbereichen ein Durchzugserlebnis, das sich sonst nur
in Sportwagen erfahren lässt.

  Der 4,0-Liter-V8-TDI mit Biturbo-Aufladung und zwei Ladeluftkühlern ist ein
weiterer Vertreter der neuen V-Motorenfamilie von Audi, der bei den Benzinmotoren

20 bereits die 4,2-Liter-Aggregate im Audi S4 und Audi allroad quattro 4.2 angehören.
Wichtige Neuerung bei den V-Motoren: Anstelle eines Zahnriemens kommt ein
Kettenantrieb für Nockenwellen und Nebenaggregate zum Einsatz.

(Audi 2004a: 20)

Another landmark achievement in diesel technology for Audi
Substantial torque, high performance, and outstanding acceleration and pulling
power: all characteristics of a top athlete.

5   Audi has repeatedly restated its pioneering role in the development of ultra-
efficient, high performance TDI engines since as far back as 1989.

  The latest remarkable example is the new 4.0-litre V8 TDI, which is used in the
A8. It lends this lightweight luxury saloon the attributes of a top athlete. Moderate
fuel consumption and plentiful refinement also make the A8 4.0 TDI quattro the ideal
companion for long journeys.

10   **The most powerful V8 diesel engine in the world**
The new model represents the addition of a further sporty version to Audi's range.
The V8 TDI engine in the Audi A8 is currently the highest-powered, highest-torque
V8 diesel engine in any production saloon car, developing 202 kW (275 bhp) and
650 Newton-metres of torque. Its peak torque of 650 Newton-metres, which is

15 achieved from engine speeds of 1,800 to 2,500 rpm, offers a quality of traction across
the entire road-speed range that can otherwise only be experienced in sports cars.

  The 4.0-litre V8 TDI biturbo with two intercoolers is a further representative of
Audi's new family of V-engines, which already includes the 4.2-litre petrol versions
in the Audi S4 and Audi allroad quattro 4.2. One significant new feature of the V-

20 engines is that there is a chain drive for the camshafts and auxiliaries instead of a
toothed belt.

(Audi 2004b: 20)

References

Primary

Audi 2004a. *Geschäftsbericht 2003*. Ingolstadt: Audi AG.
Audi 2004b. *2003 Annual Report*. Ingolstadt: Audi AG.

Secondary

Anderman, Gunilla 2009. 'Drama translation', in Baker, M. and Saldanha, G. (eds) *Routledge Encyclopedia of Translation Studies*. 2nd edn. London and New York: Routledge, pp. 92–5.

Eisenberg, Peter 1986. *Grundriß der deutschen Grammatik*. Stuttgart: J.B. Metzlersche Verlagsbuchhandlung.

Johnson, Sally 1998. *Exploring the German Language*. London, New York, Sydney and Auckland: Arnold.

Martín de León, Celia 2020. 'Functionalism', in Baker, M. and Saldanha, G. (eds) *Routledge Encyclopedia of Translation Studies*. 3rd edn. London and New York: Routledge, pp. 199–203.

Newmark, Peter 1988. *A Textbook of Translation*. New York: Prentice Hall.

Nord, Christiane 1997. *Translating as a Purposeful Activity: Functionalist Approaches Explained*. Manchester: St. Jerome.

Reiß, Katharina 1971. *Möglichkeiten und Grenzen der Übersetzungskritik. Kategorien und Kriterien für eine sachgerechte Beurteilung von Übersetzungen*. München: Hueber.

Reiss, Katharina 1977/1989. 'Text types, translation types and translation assessment', in Chesterman, A. (ed.) *Readings in Translation Theory*. Helsinki: Oy Finn Lectura Ab, pp. 105–15 [Translated by Andrew Chesterman from Reiß, K. 1977. 'Texttypen, Übersetzungstypen und die Beurteilung von Übersetzungen', *Lebende Sprachen*, 22(3), pp. 97–100.].

Risku, Hanna 1999. 'Translatorisches handeln', in Snell-Hornby, M., Hönig, H., Kußmaul, P. and Schmitt, P. A. (eds) *Handbuch Translation*. 2nd edn. Tübingen: Stauffenburg, pp. 107–12.

Rogers, Margaret 1998. 'Naturalness and translation', *SYNAPS. Fagspråk, Kommunikasjon, Kulturkunnskap*, 2, pp. 9–31. Available at: http://hdl.handle.net/11250/2394654 (Accessed: 14 February 2018).

3   Equivalence and non-equivalence

Many of the issues concerning closeness of the TT to the ST which were discussed in the previous chapter can be related to the notion of equivalence. In some sense, asking how close your translation should be is another way of asking: what does it mean for a translation to be equivalent to the source text? In the first part of this chapter, we will look at some ways in which equivalence can be understood, and present one account of equivalence which introduces a number of issues that later chapters in the book will explore in more detail. We then consider some of the criticisms which have been levelled against a key concept in the development of Translation Studies, dynamic equivalence. In the third part of the chapter, we address some typical areas of non-equivalence and the challenges they set for translators.

The concept of equivalence

A preliminary and naive understanding of equivalence implies sameness, for example, of meaning if not of form. While we might intuitively speak of 'equivalent' words and phrases, or even texts, the relationship of sameness is not straightforward and the notion has been a contentious one in Translation Studies. We thus need to say what we mean, and what we do not mean, by 'equivalence' and 'equivalent'.

As we noted in Chapter 1, translation is a process which involves necessary change, because even closely related source and target languages and cultures are fundamentally different, and because the new communicative context may not exactly match that of the original; but translation is distinct from many other forms of writing in that it is defined by a necessary relationship—variable though that may be—to its source text. Clearly, in this sense, 'equivalence' does not mean 'sameness' in a simplistic sense of the term; rather the term 'equivalence' denotes the relationship between a ST and a TT—or parts of those texts—that can be understood as implying some kind of appropriate value to readers in a given context. For instance, in the sofa example (Chapter 2), each of the TT sentences illustrates varying degrees and types of equivalence, from formal to pragmatic; and each is in some sense a legitimate translation of '*Das Sofa lässt sich mit wenigen Handgriffen in ein Bett verwandeln*'.

Another way of putting this is to say that thinking about equivalence is a way of analysing the relationship between the source text and its possible translations. Dating from the late 1970s, Werner Koller's typology of equivalence is one of the first comprehensive accounts, and it remains one of the best known (Koller 2011). He distinguishes five types of equivalence, or what he calls 'frameworks' (*Bezugsrahmen der Übersetzungsäquivalenz*):

- **denotative**, relating to the world outside the text (material or immaterial)
- **connotative**, relating to the way in which words and phrases are used to achieve a particular effect
- **text-normative**, relating to the conventions established for particular genres
- **pragmatic**, relating to the supposed effect of the text on the readership
- **formal-aesthetic**, relating to the aesthetic form of the ST

Koller's 'framework' is a useful one because it provides a lens through which we can analyse aspects of the relationship between the ST and TT, but as with all models (of translation or anything else), some further issues need to be considered. We will discuss these in turn, starting with denotative equivalence, the focus here being on the word level.

Denotative equivalence

Perhaps the most obvious issues of equivalence turn around individual words—how to translate '*Gesamtkunstwerk*', or '*Tafelspitz*'. At the level of denotative equivalence, Koller categorises the different types of relationships between lexical items in languages into 'correspondence types'/*Entsprechungstypen* (2011: 230–43), for which a number of strategies—*Übersetzungsverfahren*—can be identified. Table 3.1 summarises Koller's typology, including possible translation strategies:

Table 3.1 Denotative equivalence: types of correspondence and translation strategies after Koller (2011: 231–43) (with some adaptations and examples added)

SL-TL correspondence type	Examples	Possible translation strategies
one-to-one	'control signal' > '*Stellgröße*'	• normally no difficulty except occasionally a choice of synonyms occurs e.g. 'car' > '*Auto*', '*Wagen*'
one-to-many, often meaning that there is no generic expression in the TL where there is in the SL, i.e. there is a lexical gap in the TL: e.g. '*Großvater*' (de)> '*morfar*', '*farfar*' (sv): Swedish has no generic term for 'grandfather'	'*Sicherheit*' > 'safety', 'security'	• ST or prior knowledge guides choice of specific expression • irrelevant in the TT • spell out all possibilities or find an alternative generic expression where possible

SL-TL correspondence type	Examples	Possible translation strategies
many-to-one: i.e. a distinction in the SL can be lost in the TL	*'ein Bekannter—eine Bekannte'* > 'an acquaintance'	• leave generic if distinction irrelevant • add a modifier e.g. 'male'/'female'
one-to-none i.e. there is a lexical gap in the TL, often related to cultural differences or different metaphorical expressions; some may become established in the TL, others may not	*'Bratwurst'* 'the grassroots of the nation' 'public relations' *'Berufsverbot'* *'Burberry'*	• transfer the ST word/expression to the TT as a loan word e.g. 'bratwurst' • loan translate (i.e. syllable by syllable) e.g. *'die Graswurzeln der Nation'* • use an available TL word/expression with a similar meaning e.g. *'Öffentlichkeitsarbeit'* • use an explanatory phrase e.g. 'exclusion from a civil service profession by government ruling' (*Collins*) • adapt i.e. find a cultural equivalent e.g. *'Lodenmantel'*
one-to-part i.e. the TT word/expression only partly overlaps in meaning with an SL word/expression i.e. the world is divided up in different ways in each language: SL word TL word	'Beamte' > 'civil servant' 'Hexe' > 'hag' (shared meaning includes old, ugly, woman without magical powers) 'witch' (shared meaning includes magical powers but also overlaps partly with the German *'Fee'*)	• use nearest equivalent where ST and TT meanings overlap e.g. 'civil servant' for a government official • add an in-text explanation or a footnote e.g. if the ST 'Beamte' refers to a teacher, or, substitute 'teacher' • choose the most appropriate equivalent for the context e.g. 'hag' or 'witch'

We return to some of these 'correspondence types'—with more examples—later in the chapter.

Connotative and pragmatic equivalence

Connotative equivalence goes beyond the purely denotative/referential to encompass the potential that a particular word or expression has to affect the recipient. So, for example, *'sterben'* (neutral), *'entschlafen'* (euphemistic) and *'ins Gras beißen'* (slang) (examples from Koller 2011: 243) are all possible translations of 'to die', but the effect is likely to be quite different in each case. An accumulation of several slang expressions would, for example, result in a text which could be either humorous or disrespectful, or perhaps both if black humour is the effect to be achieved. Errors in judging the connotative meaning of a word or expression—and hence also the overall tenor of a text—can lead to breakdowns in communication which can be just as serious as errors in denotation.

The notion that equivalence should encompass the effect on the reader has perhaps been most famously expounded by the Bible scholar Eugene Nida who proposed the concept of dynamic equivalence of effect (1964: 159), to which we return below, as the aim of translation. This also shares some characteristics with Koller's 'pragmatic equivalence'. One of the main questions here, according to Koller (2011: 252)—echoing our question in Chapter 2 of how close a translation should be—is how far the translator should go in meeting readers' anticipated needs without tipping over from what he calls *Textreproduktion* to *Textproduktion*, that is, moving from translation proper to writing a new text. For example, though not all scholars agree, the reworking of a ST for a different audience—*Textproduktion*—is excluded from what Koller understands to be a translation: he excludes, for example, a 'translation' of Defoe's *Robinson Crusoe* for children (many omissions) and a reworking of a specialist legal textbook for a popular audience (much simplification).

Text-normative equivalence

Koller's category of 'text-normative' equivalence (2011: 250–1) focuses attention on the need for the translator to look beyond the level of words or even sentences to the whole text when making decisions about equivalence. In Chapter 2, we considered some issues relating to genre, including its importance in the translation brief and the role of genre conventions in shaping translation decisions. Genres, dealt with in more detail in the following chapter, can be thought of as classes of texts which perform certain social functions expressed in recurring patterns of form. As cultures vary in their social structures and customs, so can genres.

These variations can affect features ranging from organisation (e.g. the order of text components in patents, see Göpferich 1999b) to tone (e.g. friendly or formal). Some scholars have suggested that in the genre of academic writing, for example, the style of writing in German can be characterised as 'author-oriented' and in English as 'predominantly co-operative, reader-oriented' (Kreutz and Harres 1997: 181). So certain adjustments—such as a simpler syntax, more signposts for the reader to indicate the structure of the paper and the direction of the argument, as well as changes to the method of citation—could be justified if a German sociologist, say, wanted an article translated into English for possible publication in an English-language learned journal. The TT would be equivalent to the ST in terms of meeting readers' expectations of genre conventions.

In trying to create a TT which is equivalent in terms of conventions, it is also wise for the translator to explore how typical the ST is of its genre: if a ST is judged to be, say, particularly subversive with respect to genre conventions for purposes of irony, then this would need to be reproduced in the TT. For example, the English comedian Russell Brand introduced humour into his resignation letter to the BBC after some risqué on-air repartee in a radio programme led to serious complaints. This deviation from the prototypical conventions of the genre would need to be reproduced in any TT for it to be considered 'equivalent' in tone, reflecting the identity of its author. What Brand did was to introduce an *un*conventional element of personal expression into the genre.

Formal-aesthetic equivalence

Koller's last equivalence type (2011: 255–69), concerns what he calls the aesthetic function of texts, the ways in which the ST author uses language to convey their meaning. Many authors develop an individual style, using rhyme, rhythm, metaphor, wordplay, syntax and words in a unique way, which can be important in translation, most obviously in the translation of canonical literary texts. These idiosyncrasies of style—often syntactically and lexically creative—can pose significant problems for translators. The compound adjective in the phrase '*stinkfreundliches Lächeln*', for example, poses a problem in its conflicting emotions: something unpleasant and something friendly, reflecting the fact that the character in question is in pain but apparently putting a brave face on things. There is no standard equivalent in English as this is an original phrase. The published translation—'super-friendly smile'—misses the irony in the author's innovative use of language (example from Kenny 2001: 171).

Issues of voice are much less likely to occur in non-literary texts. Even where they do, Koller argues that they are less constitutive of the relevant genre: in other words, he maintains that the content—the focus of the communication for *Sachtexte* (broadly speaking Reiß's informative text type)—can still be successfully conveyed, regardless of whether stylistic effects such as metaphors are retained or not.

Some issues with dynamic equivalence

Nida's concept of dynamic equivalence, ground-breaking in its day in terms of its focus on text reception rather than formal equivalence, stems from his activity as a translator of the Bible, a sacred text but one which he analyses as an operative text, i.e. a text which is reader-oriented and aims to affect or even change behaviour in some way. However, this rather appealing concept has a number of well-known problems, focusing in particular on the question of how we can possibly know what goes on in someone's head. More specifically, how can we know what the relationship between the ST message and source-culture receptors is. For that matter, is it plausible to speak of *the* relationship, as if there were only one: are there not as many relationships as there are receptors? And who is to know what such relationships can have been in the past? Indeed, these problems apply as much to the TT as to the ST: who can foresee the multiple relationships between the TT and its receptors, however well specified in the translation brief?

When making decisions about possible solutions to the reception problem, one suggestion is for the translator to assess what has been called the 'cognitive environment' (Gutt 2010) in which the utterance (spoken or written) features in order to understand the intention of the speaker/writer and the reaction of the hearer/reader. In translation, this cognitive environment may differ between the source and the target, meaning that inferences could be missed in the TT.

A good example is provided by an English version of a German newspaper article by the German novelist Ingo Schulze (12 January 2015) about a *Pegida* [*Patriotische Europäer gegen (die) Islamisierung des Abendlandes*] demonstration in Dresden (Schulze 2015a, 2015b). Noting the use of the slogan '*Wir sind das Volk! Wir sind das Volk!*', Schulze recalls its origin in the East German Monday demonstrations which preceded the fall of the Berlin Wall in November 1989 and the subsequent reunification of Germany in 1990. Whilst a literal translation ('We are the people!') is provided in the English version of Schulze's article, none of the political or historical background is made explicit for the English reader, who, in the absence of any personal knowledge of events in Germany at the end of the 1980s, is therefore operating in a different context, making it hard to draw relevant inferences. These might include the idea that the *Pegida* crowd was misappropriating the originally democratic slogan for less noble purposes, thereby also partially accounting for Schulze's reported discomfort with the use of the slogan. Thus, while the published translation is a close formal equivalent, as far as the communicative purpose of the text is concerned, it could be seen as pragmatically inadequate and therefore not equivalent. In order to simulate an equivalent cognitive environment, the translator could have chosen to **add** 'in October 1989, when crowds of protestors expressed their opposition to the East German regime and its claim to speak for "the people"'.

What both Schulze and the English translator do both assume, however, is that the educated readers of the *Süddeutsche Zeitung* and *The Guardian*, both 'quality' newspapers, will be familiar with the political concept of '*nützliche Idioten*'/'useful idiots'. The translation is therefore in this respect equivalent in its assumptions to those made by the ST author about readers' *general* political knowledge, arguably better justified than in the case of the uncontextualised replication, 'We are the people'.

In the rest of this chapter we examine some of the more problematic areas of equivalence between German and English, often discussed under the label of 'non-equivalence'.

Some problems of non-equivalence

Koller's inclusion of non-equivalence as a type of (denotative) equivalence (see also Baker 2011: 15–44) is odd in one way, but understandable in another, as translators *have* to find some kind of solution in the TT. As we have seen, many problems associated with non-equivalence are of a cultural nature involving features that are specific to the SL and the SC (source culture) but which are absent and/or unknown in the TL/TC (target culture)—Koller's one-to-none correspondence. In the rest of this chapter, we give a brief introduction to some problems of the equivalence concept, which will be explored in more detail later in the book.

Cultural issues

The translation of food or clothing terms ('material culture' after Newmark 1988: 97–8) presents very familiar difficulties, as do more serious issues such as the conceptualisation of illness. Neither the German ingredient '*Speck*' (a kind of pork belly fat) nor the Swabian soft egg noodles '*Spätzle*' exist in British cuisine, the 'kilt' is as specifically Celtic phenomenon as '*Dirndl*' is German or Austrian, and English speakers do not suffer from something called 'circulation disturbances' i.e. '*Kreislaufstörungen*'. The medical example illustrates well how conceptualisations of a universal physical phenomenon—here, the human body—can be culturally filtered.

The food examples can show us how different solutions might be preferred according to, say, the genre of the text. If the ST were a recipe in which '*Speck*' was an important ingredient, some kind of **substitution** might be needed, as '*Speck*' is not readily available outside the German-speaking area; research indicates that 'fatty bacon', 'pancetta' or 'lardons' are possibilities. If the source text is firmly rooted in the source culture, however, say a description of Swabian cuisine for a tourist brochure, then the translator could opt for a descriptive phrase to **add** to the **transfer** into the TT of the German term '*Spätzle*'. This kind of textual intervention is known as a '**couplet**', where two translation strategies are combined: in this case, a loan word ('*Spätzle*') plus an explanation in the text ('a kind of soft egg noodle', or 'Swabian soft egg noodles').

Also falling within a broad cultural remit, other common problems of non-equivalence are posed by administrative and organisational terms, for which there may or may not be an established equivalent. Take, for example, the political term '*Innenministerium*'; this has an established translation of 'Ministry of the Interior' (or '**recognised equivalent**' after Newmark). However, it may also be translated in a target *text* with an **addition** as the 'German Ministry of the Interior' if it is judged necessary to remind the reader which country is in question. Beyond such established equivalents, there may also be a case for a **cultural equivalent** such as the 'Home Office' or even 'the German equivalent to the Home Office'. Or perhaps a **couplet** combining two of these possibilities in some texts e.g. **transfer** + **cultural equivalent**: 'the *Innenminsterium*, the German equivalent of the Home Office'. We return to cultural issues in Chapter 5.

In all these cases, the translator has to choose a translation strategy which is optimal for the new *text*, its readership and the purpose of the translation. It is important to remember that the translator's job does not end with a dictionary consultation or Koller's correspondence types: the solution has to be crafted in a specific way according to the context of the translation, as translators have done since the time of Cicero. It is the translator's job to find *textual* solutions, for which the dictionary, glossary, termbase, and so on are often only a good starting point.

Issues of form and content

As we shall see throughout this course, it is the translator's job to work with a range of possible strategies which, in their view, make the TT fit for its purpose. In some cases, however, strategies such as **transfer**, **addition** or **substitution** may not be appropriate or readily available if dealing with a case of non-equivalence. A few very simple examples, at the primitive level of the sounds, rhythm and literal meaning of individual words, will illustrate this. Here, we are more likely to resort to another translation strategy, namely, **compensation**.

The translation of poetry presents one of the biggest challenges for translators as formal patterns (e.g. rhyme, metre, alliteration, assonance) vie with meaning for the translator's attention. Consider, for example, the following extract from a children's poem by Josef Guggenmos: '*War ein Ries' bei mir zu Gast,/Sieben Meter maß er fast*'. A possible translation which aims (not entirely successfully) to reproduce the metre and the rhyme whilst retaining the narrative message is as follows: 'A giant came to visit me,/Twenty feet, so tall was he'. The change from metric to imperial measurements is not entirely motivated by cultural considerations: 'twenty feet' scans better than 'seven metres'. Precision is unimportant here: whether the giant is seven metres or twenty feet tall makes little difference. In fact, the precise equivalent—22 feet 11.6 inches—would be more than odd in this text, although crucial in another, such as the length of a piece of equipment which has to be fitted into a given space. So again, we have different criteria when judging what is 'equivalent'.

Concluding remarks

Intuitively, equivalence is at the heart of translation. But as we have seen in this chapter, there are many good reasons to challenge the implication of 'sameness' and to nuance the concept in many different ways. To some extent, the scope of 'equivalence' as a concept depends on your view of the scope of 'translation', whether all-embracing—including adaptations, (software) localisation and audio-description (intermodal translation)—or more traditional—focusing on a written text, the meaning and form of which closely guides the production of a text in another language. But whatever your view, equivalence will turn out to be a relative concept which depends on a number of factors, including the text type (function) and the text genre, as well as the purpose of the translation as set out in the translation brief. It is these factors that will help to shape your decisions about which translation strategies to apply when creating your new target text.

Further reading

Bellos, David 2012. *Is That a Fish in Your Ear? The Amazing Adventure of Translation*. London: Penguin [what is 'translation'? pp. 322–7].

Boase-Beier, Jean 2020. 'Poetry', in Baker, M. and Saldanha, G. (eds) *Routledge Encyclopedia of Translation Studies*. 3rd edn. London and New York: Routledge, pp. 410–414.

Hatim, Basil and Munday, Jeremy 2004. *Translation. An Advanced Resource Book*. London and New York: Routledge [what is 'translation'? pp. 3–9; form and content, pp. 10–1; cognitive issues, pp. 57–64; dynamic equivalence and the receptor of the message, pp. 253–61].

Munday, Jeremy 2016. *Introducing Translation Studies: Theories and Applications.* 4th edn. London and New York: Routledge [Chapter 8.1 Translation as re-writing].

Newmark, Peter P. 1988. *A Textbook of Translation.* Hemel Hempstead: Prentice-Hall [functional/cultural equivalence, pp. 82–3; translation of political and administrative terms, pp. 99–102; translation of measurements, pp. 217–8].

Schmitt, Peter A. 1999a. 'Maßeinheiten', in Snell-Hornby, M., Hönig, H., Kußmaul, P. and Schmitt, P. A. (eds) *Handbuch Translation.* 2nd edn. Tübingen: Stauffenburg, pp. 298–300.

Practical 3

3.1 EVALUATING TRANSLATION STRATEGIES IN TERMS OF EQUIVALENCE

Assignment

Here is a ST for comparison with two published TTs. The exercise focuses on the notion of equivalence in terms of the two different versions.

i   Read through the ST and list potential equivalence problems, bearing in mind Koller's five types of equivalence.

ii Choose one or two equivalence types and identify one or two problems of each type, analysing how your chosen problems have been solved in each of the TTs: can you identify (a) which translation strategy has been used in each case; (b) a rationale for any differences? And (c) did you identify any 'problems' which turned out not to be; or (d) find any features of the TTs which indicate that you failed to anticipate a particular problem?

iii Consider whether you could improve on the solutions to any of the problems identified in (i). State your new solution together with your reasons for it in terms of equivalence.

Contextual information

The ST is from Erich Maria Remarque's *Im Westen nichts Neues* (first published 1929), perhaps the best-known of all Great War novels. A group of comrades who, as new recruits, had been bullied by *Unteroffizier* Himmelstoß (a postman in civilian life), encounter him at the front. One of them, Tjaden, insolently refuses to obey an order given by Himmelstoß, who storms off to report the matter to his superiors. Tjaden goes off into a hut so as to keep out of trouble. The others fall to reminiscing about their schooldays and wonder what, if anything, they learned at school. After a few minutes, Himmelstoß returns with a fat *Feldwebel*.

Wir erheben uns. Der Spieß schnauft: 'Wo ist Tjaden?'
Natürlich weiß es keiner. Himmelstoß glitzert uns böse an. 'Bestimmt wißt ihr es.
Wollt es bloß nicht sagen. Raus mit der Sprache'.
Der Spieß sieht sich suchend um; Tjaden ist nirgendwo zu erblicken. Er versucht
5   es andersherum. 'In zehn Minuten soll Tjaden sich auf Schreibstube melden'.
Damit zieht er davon, Himmelstoß in seinem Kielwasser.
'Ich habe das Gefühl, daß mir beim nächsten Schanzen eine Drahtrolle auf die
Beine von Himmelstoß fallen wird', vermutet Kropp.
'Wir werden an ihm noch viel Spaß haben', lacht Müller.
10   Das ist unser Ehrgeiz: einem Briefträger die Meinung stoßen.
Ich gehe in die Baracke und sage Tjaden Bescheid, damit er verschwindet.
Dann wechseln wir unsern Platz und lagern uns wieder, um Karten zu spielen.
Denn das können wir: Kartenspielen, fluchen und Krieg führen. Nicht viel für zwanzig
Jahre—zuviel für zwanzig Jahre.
15   Nach einer halben Stunde ist Himmelstoß erneut bei uns. Niemand beachtet
ihn. Er fragt nach Tjaden. Wir zucken die Achseln. 'Ihr solltet ihn doch suchen',
beharrt er.
'Wieso ihr?' erkundigt sich Kropp.
'Na, ihr hier—'
20   'Ich möchte Sie bitten, uns nicht zu duzen', sagt Kropp wie ein Oberst.
Himmelstoß fällt aus den Wolken. 'Wer duzt euch denn?'
'Sie!'
'Ich?'
'Ja'.
25   Es arbeitet in ihm. Er schielt Kropp mißtrauisch an, weil er keine Ahnung hat,
was der meint. Immerhin traut er sich in diesem Punkte nicht ganz und kommt uns
entgegen. 'Habt ihr ihn nicht gefunden?'
Kropp legt sich ins Gras und sagt: 'Waren Sie schon mal hier draußen?' 'Das geht
Sie gar nichts an', bestimmt Himmelstoß. 'Ich verlange Antwort'.
30   'Gemacht', erwidert Kropp und erhebt sich. 'Sehen Sie mal dorthin, wo die
kleinen Wolken stehen. Das sind die Geschosse der Flaks. Da waren wir gestern. Fünf
Tote, acht Verwundete. Dabei war es eigentlich ein Spaß. Wenn Sie nächstens mit
rausgehen, werden die Mannschaften, bevor sie sterben, erst vor Sie hintreten, die
Knochen zusammenreißen und zackig fragen: Bitte wegtreten zu dürfen! Bitte
35   abkratzen zu dürfen! Auf Leute wie Sie haben wir hier gerade gewartet'.
Er setzt sich wieder, und Himmelstoß verschwindet wie ein Komet.

                                        (Remarque 1955: 68–9)

TT (i)

We get up.
'Where's Tjaden?' the sergeant puffs.
No one knows, of course. Himmelstoss glowers at us wrathfully. 'You know very
well. You won't say, that's the fact of the matter. Out with it!'
5   Fatty looks round enquiringly; but Tjaden is not to be seen. He tries another way.
'Tjaden will report at the Orderly Room in ten minutes'.
Then he steams off with Himmelstoss in his wake.
'I have a feeling that next time we go up wiring I'll be letting a bundle of wire fall

on Himmelstoss's leg,' hints Kropp.

10   'We'll have quite a lot of jokes with him,' laughs Müller.—

That is our sole ambition: to knock the conceit out of a postman.—

I go into the hut and put Tjaden wise. He disappears.

Then we change our possy and lie down again to play cards. We know how to do that: to play cards, to swear, and to fight. Not much for twenty years;—and yet too

15   much for twenty years.

Half an hour later Himmelstoss is back again. Nobody pays any attention to him. He asks for Tjaden. We shrug our shoulders.

'Then you'd better find him,' he persists. 'Haven't you been to look for him?'

Kropp lies back on the grass and says: 'Have you ever been out here before?'

20   'That's none of your business,' retorts Himmelstoss. 'I expect an answer'.

'Very good,' says Kropp, getting up. 'See up there where those little white clouds are. Those are anti-aircraft. We were over there yesterday. Five dead and eight wounded. And that's a mere nothing. Next time, when you go up with us, before they die the fellows will come up to you, click their heels, and ask stiffly: "Please may I

25   go? Please may I hop it? We've been waiting here a long time for someone like you."'

He sits down again and Himmelstoss disappears like a comet.

(Remarque 1930: 100–2, trans. Wheen)

We stand up. The sergeant major puffs, 'Where's Tjaden?'

None of us knows, of course. Himmelstoss glares angrily at us. 'Of course you know, you lot. You just don't want to tell us. Come on, out with it'.

The CSM looks all round him, but Tjaden is nowhere to be seen. He tries a

5   different tack. 'Tjaden is to present himself at the orderly room in ten minutes'.

With that he clears off, with Himmelstoss in his wake.

'I've got a feeling that a roll of barbed-wire is going to fall on Himmelstoss's legs when we're on wiring fatigues again,' reckons Kropp.

'We'll get a good bit of fun out of him yet,' laughs Müller.

10   That's the extent of our ambition now: taking a postman down a peg or two . . .

I go off to the hut to warn Tjaden, so that he can disappear.

We shift along a bit, then lie down again to play cards. Because that is what we are good at: playing cards, swearing and making war. Not much for twenty years— too much for twenty years.

15   Half an hour later, Himmelstoss is back. Nobody takes any notice of him. He asks where Tjaden is. We shrug our shoulders. 'You lot were supposed to look for him'.

'What do you mean "you lot"?' asks Kropp.

'Well, you lot here—'

20   'I should like to request, Corporal Himmelstoss, that you address us in an appropriate military fashion,' says Kropp, sounding like a colonel.

Himmelstoss is thunderstruck. 'Who's addressing you any other way?'

'You, Corporal Himmelstoss, sir'.

'Me?'

25   'Yes'.

(*Continued*)

(Continued)

TT (ii)

It is getting to him. He looks suspiciously at Kropp because he hasn't any idea of what he is talking about. At all events, he loses confidence and backs down. 'Didn't you lot find him?'

30 Kropp lies back in the grass and says, 'Have you ever been out here before, Corporal Himmelstoss, sir?'

'That is quite irrelevant, Private Kropp,' says Himmelstoss, 'and I demand an answer'.

'Right,' says Kropp and gets up. 'Have a look over there, Corporal, sir, where the little white clouds are. That's the flak going for the aircraft. That's where we were

35 yesterday. Five dead, eight wounded. And that was actually an easy one. So the next time we go up the line, Corporal, sir, the platoons will parade in front of you before they die, click their heels and request in proper military fashion "Permission to fall out, sir! Permission to fall down dead, sir!" People like you are all we need out here, Corporal, sir'.

He sits down again and Himmelstoss shoots off like a rocket.

(Remarque 1994: 63–5, trans. Murdoch)

3.2 EQUIVALENCE, GENRE AND CULTURE

Assignment

There follows a link to a recipe for *Apfelkuchen mit Streuseln*, published online. The translation brief is to produce an English-language version for an online collection of recipes for German-style cakes and pastries.

i Work in pairs or small groups to produce an English translation, bearing in mind the following points.

ii How much freedom do you have in this translation compared to that in the translation of a novel such as *Im Westen nichts Neues*? And how would you account for any differences in the degrees of freedom?

iii Identify what you anticipate to be the main equivalence problems in the ST. Are these lexical or syntactic? Are they to do with genre conventions?

iv List what you think might be an appropriate translation strategy for each problem identified.

v Compare your draft translation with that of another group. Discuss any differences, explaining the reasons for your translation decisions.

ST

Apfelkuchen mit Streuseln (available at www.chefkoch.de/rezepte/220403135333 8061/Apfelkuchen-mit-Streuseln.html)

References

Primary

Remarque, Erich Maria 1930. *All Quiet on the Western Front*. Translated by Wheen, Arthur W. London: Putnam & Co.

Remarque, Erich Maria 1955. *Im Westen nichts Neues*. Berlin: Ullstein.
Remarque, Erich Maria 1994. *All Quiet on the Western Front*. Translated by Murdoch, Brian. London: Vintage.
Schulze, Ingo 2015a. 'Pegida-Demonstration in Dresden: Die nützlichen Idioten', *Süddeutsche Zeitung*, 27 January.
Schulze, Ingo 2015b. 'Pegida: Germany's useful idiots', *The Guardian*, 1 February. Translated by Derbyshire, Katy.

Secondary

Baker, Mona 2011. *In Other Words*. 2nd edn. London: Routledge.
Göpferich, Susanne 1999b. 'Patentschriften', in Snell-Hornby, M., Hönig, H., Kußmaul, P. and Schmitt, P. A. (eds) *Handbuch Translation*. 2nd edn. Tübingen: Stauffenburg, pp. 222–5.
Gutt, Ernst-August 2010. *Translation and Relevance: Cognition and Context*. 2nd edn. London and New York: Routledge.
Kenny, Dorothy 2001. *Lexis and Creativity in Translation: A Corpus-Based Study*. Manchester: St. Jerome.
Koller, Werner (unter Mitarbeit von Kjetl Berg Henjum) 2011. *Einführung in die Übersetzungswissenschaft*. 8th edn. Tübingen: Narr Francke Attempto.
Kreutz, Heinz and Harres, Annette 1997. 'Some observations on the distribution and function of hedging in German and English academic writing', in Duszak, A. (ed.) *Culture and Styles of Academic Discourse*. Trends in Linguistics. Vol. 104. Berlin: de Gruyter, pp. 181–202.
Nida, Eugene A. 1964. *Toward a Science of Translating*. Leiden: Brill.

Lexical and related sources

Collins German Dictionary 1999. 4th edn. Glasgow: Collins.

Section B

Some key issues

In this second section of the course, we start by picking up on two themes which emerged in the examples from Section A, namely the importance of genre and the pervasiveness of culture in shaping translation decisions.

Chapter 4 covers a topic on which much has been written in Translation Studies, especially since the 1980s, namely textual genre. One way of classifying texts as communicative entities is to group them according to their social purpose, usually well recognised in the general population e.g. a short story, or within a more specialised discourse community e.g. a technical data sheet. In describing the features of genres, the focus is on 'conventions' rather than 'rules', indicating that each genre is likely to be realised in practice by some prototypical texts and some more peripheral examples with degrees of variation within and between each language/culture. The approach we take in this chapter—of necessity, selective—is a functional one. Three case studies are presented and analysed from a translation perspective, each with a primary but not exclusive rhetorical function.

In moving on to cultural issues in Chapter 5, we aim to show that dealing with cultural differences is important in non-literary as well as in literary translation. Two overall approaches are presented, namely 'exoticism' and 'cultural transplantation', showing how particular strategies—calque (loan translation), cultural borrowing, cultural equivalent—can contribute to what could also be called the chosen 'global strategy' or approach. Once again, it is argued that 'pure' types are rarely found in practice and that the translator's expertise lies in judging which strategy is appropriate given the chosen overall approach, sometimes belying the dichotomies which we work with as models.

The third chapter in this section, Chapter 6, deals with one particular strategy, compensation. It has a whole chapter to itself as it is rather open-ended and therefore often under-represented in course books. When faced with a challenging problem for which no standard solution is immediately apparent e.g. wordplay or an absence of correspondence in forms of address, the translator has to be both analytical (what is the translation problem?) and imaginative (how do I fill the gap?). What distinguishes the use of a particular strategy as 'compensation'—still selected from the available 'toolbox'—is that the solution can be applied at a location in the translation which is not necessarily the 'same' as the location of the problem item in the source text. The strategy might also result in a different kind of mechanism in the translation, so a humorous wordplay may be replaced by an alternative humorous device. The examples discussed are taken from both literary and specialised texts, although compensation tends to be most often discussed in the context of the former, being perceived as a way of solving problems of stylistic effect or emotional force.

4 Textual genre and translation issues

In the previous two chapters on closeness and equivalence, the notion of genre (*Textsorte*) has cropped up in many different ways. In the current chapter we will be taking a more systematic look at genre as a crucial feature of both the source and the target text. In brief, you do not approach the translation of a safety notice in the same way as you approach the translation of a short story.

In Chapter 3, we offered a provisional explanation of genres as classes of texts which perform certain social functions expressed in recurring patterns of form. We noted that as cultures vary in their social structures and customs, so can genres. Understanding genre is important because it can help us to make generalisations as a basis for our decisions when understanding or producing texts.

The concept of genre covers the traditionally identified forms of literary expression (e.g. poem, novel, short story, *Novelle*), as well as texts bearing what Baker calls 'institutionalized labels' such as 'journal article', 'science textbook', 'newspaper editorial' or 'travel brochure' (Baker 2011: 123). We can also include texts beyond the 'professional', the 'academic', the 'literary' and the 'institutional' to embrace new genres such as those which have emerged from social media (e.g. tweets) and online communication (e.g. emails). One well-known definition of genres in professional contexts is:

> a recognizable communicative event characterized by a set of communicative purpose(s) and mutually understood by the members of the professional or academic community in which it regularly occurs. Most often it is highly structured and conventionalized with constraints on allowable contributions in terms of their intent, positioning and functional value.
>
> (Bhatia 1993: 13).

Like other cultural conventions and indeed like language itself, genres evolve, new ones emerge, and old ones can lose importance, though certain genres are less susceptible to change than others. For example, legal genres such as contracts and agreements—which have worked for many years and have their basis in an established profession—are unlikely to undergo any change without serious consideration, as this could lead to unanticipated loopholes. Most STs can be said prototypically to share *some* of their properties with other texts of the same genre (e.g. length, layout, degree of creativity or formulaicity), and, significantly, STs are perceived by an SL audience as being what they are on account of such genre-defining properties and the text's relation to other genres.

In order to assess the nature and function of the ST and to judge the relative typicality of a specific ST, the translator must have some sort of overview of genres in the source culture, be familiar with their characteristics and, where appropriate, how they are developing, as well as making themselves familiar with target-culture genres. It is not difficult to see, for instance, that the linguistic conventions typically used to give commands in instructions for use in German (infinitive) and English (imperative) can be different: '*Verpackungsmaterial ordnungsgemäß entsorgen*'/'Dispose of packaging material correctly' (example from Parianou and Kelandrias 2007: 528). Paying due attention to the nature and function of the TT helps the translator to create a text with the relevant features, from layout to phrasing. In some cases, the translator is aiming to create a text in the TL as if it had been written in that language, e.g. instructions for use, product packaging, safety information. In other cases, however, the conventions of the ST play a much stronger role. It is the translator's job to judge what is appropriate.

Classifying genres

There are many suggestions for how genres can be classified. An earlier edition of this course suggested five broad categories, both thematically and functionally based: extralinguistic (of the world), philosophical (the world of ideas), religious (the world of belief), persuasive (purposeful) and literary (imaginative). The UK translation scholar Peter Newmark has distinguished between literary and non-literary texts, the former dealing with the 'world of the imagination' concerned with 'persons', the latter with the 'world of facts', concerned with 'objects' (2004). Koller (2011: 278) makes a similar distinction between *Fiktivtexte* and *Sachtexte*, in other words, between texts that 'reflect one person's unique thought' and texts that 'reflect the extralinguistic world', according to Mossop (1998: 235). This is, of course, an obvious distinction to draw, but it is not without its problems. Newmark himself blurs the binary in an expedient way by introducing an interim class of texts 'between literary and non-literary texts'; as examples, he cites genres such as the essay and the autobiography as well as specific academic subject fields, broadly in the Social Sciences (2004: 10). But subject matter cannot in itself be the sole criterion for describing genres, because the same subject matter can figure in very different genres, e.g. 'sport' can feature in an academic journal (sports science article), a newspaper (report of a match) or in a magazine (advertisement for a sports-related product). We should also add that science texts can be highly creative and metaphorical such as the Danish physicist Nils Bohr's conception of the atom, which was inspired by the orbit of planets around the sun.

All this shows that attempts to assign clear-cut categories to the artefact, text, created by human beings for other human beings, quickly encounters difficulties, as does any model of human behaviour. The well-known translation scholar Mary Snell-Hornby suggested 30 years ago that language '[i]n its concrete realization [...]

cannot be reduced to a system of static and clear-cut categories' (1988: 31). Instead, she proposed a system of 'blurred edges and overlappings' (*ibid.*) in what she called the 'basic text types'—here, broad categories of genre—consisting of: Bible—Stage/Film—Lyric Poetry—Modern Literature—Newspaper/General information texts—Advertising Literature—Legal Literature—Economic Literature—Medicine—Science/Tech. (1988: 32). As examples of the blurring between 'types', Snell-Hornby cites the occurrence of 'technical terms' in non-science texts and the use of 'prototypically literary devices such as word-play and alliteration in "general" newspaper texts and advertising' (1988: 31–2).

The translator needs to be aware—and follow this through with ST analysis, as well as TL research—that not only may there be differences between the genre's conventions of the SL and the TL, there may also be differences *within* the same genre: we can recall the example of the expressive resignation letter from Chapter 3, in one sense an informative text but one with a highly personalised style. Another example—this time in the operative genre of recipes—is provided by the different 'voices' of best-selling authors Jamie Oliver and Delia Smith, the former cheeky and irreverent, the latter didactic; so for Jamie, wine is 'sloshed', for Delia, it is 'poured', for instance (Tanner 2012). Whether such differences are carried over in translation may well depend on the prevailing conventions of acceptability in the target culture in the relevant genre. Breaking new ground is also, of course, a possibility.

Differences *between* genres in the same language should be more obvious, but some can be rather elusive. For example, intralingual differences in cohesive conventions have been identified in English academic texts and business news stories: the frequency of conjuncts such as 'yet', 'therefore', 'finally', 'to conclude' is much higher in the former than in the latter (Morrow 1989). Thus, underuse or overuse of certain features can, in a way which is not immediately apparent, lead to a text which sounds inauthentic. Charting differences in frequency distributions is usually the preserve of the researcher rather than the practising translator, but developing an awareness of possible differences of this kind can help to sharpen the translator's analytical eye.

A modest proposal

Where do all these overlappings and different classifications leave the poor translator who is trying to sort out which class of texts the ST belongs to and what features to observe in the TT in order to guide their research and to shape their translation decisions? As a starting point, we suggest firstly that it is useful to recall Reiß's distinction between function (*Texttyp*) and genre (*Textsorte*), as a way of grouping text forms which does not rely on subject classifications. However, we cannot necessarily map genres and functions in any neat way: genres can function internally in a number of ways: persuading, informing, entertaining etc. and functions are conceptually broad categories which encompass many genres. In what follows, in order to illustrate for translation purposes how certain genres function, we consider texts as falling into two broad categories: on the one hand, texts whose *primary* function and use is governed by the presentation of information; on the other, texts whose *primary* function is to engage the reader, to entertain or to move. We might call these categories 'factual' and 'aesthetic' respectively, the two of course having significant overlap in terms of means but being fundamentally distinguished by the reader's expectation about their relationship to the empirical world. As always, broad definitions and models can only take us so far. We present three case studies, two belong broadly to the category of factual texts one to the category of aesthetic texts. This way of presenting genre has the advantage of revealing some shared characteristics between texts which are often masked by more detailed categorisations. We will also note how hybridity of function is exhibited in many genres: the world of 'real' texts is not an 'ideal' one.

We conclude the chapter with a brief discussion of an increasingly important characteristic of text which features in many literary and specialised genres, namely, multimodality.

CASE STUDY 1:   Encyclopaedia entries

Purely factual texts—content-focused according to Reiß (see Chapter 2)—of a pure or 'ideal' kind are very hard to find: even scholarly texts present and interpret data in particular ways, despite the apparently neutral conventions of academic writing. For our present purposes, we have chosen texts which might be considered as close to an objective, informative form of writing as possible: entries from an encyclopaedia of Linguistics, for which a German (original) and an English version are available (Bußmann 1990, Bussmann 1996). However, even here, despite the apparently objective nature of the exercise, the Preface to the translated English text acknowledges terminological problems in English reflecting methodological differences between linguists: 'The task of "translating" became, therefore, not a linear word-for-word rendering of German linguistic concepts into English, but rather an adaptation' (Bussmann 1996: vii)—an interesting comment since 'adaptation' is more commonly associated with literary translation, such as the recasting of an adult text for children.

The entry in the German ST chosen for comment here is *Lehnübersetzung*; in the English version, the comparable entry is 'loan translation', a strategy to fill a lexical gap in the TT (see Chapter 3, Table 3.1). In the entry as shown here, the single arrow in the German entries signifies a cross-reference to another entry; the double arrow in the English performs the same function (remember to check for variation in such conventions e.g. in a publisher's style sheet):

| **Lehnübersetzung.** Vorgang und Ergebnis einer genauen Glied-für-Glied Übersetzung eines fremdsprachlichen Ausdrucks in die eigene Sprache: *Dampfmaschine* für engl. *steam engine*, *Montag* für latein. *dies lunae, Geistesgegenwart* für frz. *présence d'esprit.* Zur Übersicht über den Lehnwortschatz im Dt. →Entlehnung (Übersicht). | **Loan translation** 1 In the narrower sense: the process and result of a one-to-one translation of the elements of a foreign expression into a word in one's own language: Eng. *Monday* for Lat. *dies lunae,* Eng. *accomplished fact* for Fr. *fait accompli.* 2 In a broader sense: (a) a loose translation of the foreign concept into one's own language, e.g. Ger. *Wolkenkratzer* (lit. 'cloud scratcher') for Engl. *Skyscraper,* or (b) an adoption of the foreign concept into one's own language, e.g. *brotherhood* for Lat. *fraternitas.* (⇒ *also* **borrowed meaning, borrowing, calque, loan word**). |

It is immediately apparent here that the English version is longer and structured differently from the German original (macrostructure), as well as containing different examples. The English 'loan translation' entry distinguishes between what it calls a 'narrower' and a 'broader' sense, a distinction not made in the German entry for '*Lehnübersetzung*'. But why? The reason is simple. Only the first sense of the English entry is strictly speaking a '*Lehnübersetzung*'; the second sense—a looser concept—is a '*Lehnübertragung*', dealt with in a separate entry in the German edition of the encyclopaedia: German linguists have established finer distinctions than linguists dealing with English for related phenomena. So even for apparently factual data, interpretations can vary. Trying to map equivalents therefore poses problems similar to those encountered when mapping culturally specific phenomena, but this is made explicit in the structuring of an encyclopaedia.

Returning to the first part of the English entry, from a microstructural perspective we can see that it corresponds closely to the German entry—both are highly nominal, both use italics for words in other languages. Differences can, however, be noted in three areas:

* the examples, as they need to show loans which have come into *that* particular language: a change in content
* the abbreviations (engl./Eng.; frz./Fr.): a matter of convention
* the addition of the introductory phrases 'In the narrower/broader sense:' in the two-part English entry to reflect the change in macrostructure

Translators might well have to make such adjustments to the content, as well genre conventions, when moving between languages and are advised to consult accordingly, in this case with the editor/s of the

English version. Cross-references to other entries would also need to be checked, especially as the linguistic world is mapped differently in the relevant German- and English-speaking discourse communities.

CASE STUDY 2:   *Gebrauchsanleitung* (Instructions for use)

Genres such as instruction manuals, laws and regulations, propaganda leaflets, menus and sales promotion letters have an operative/persuasive function, aiming to make listeners or readers behave in prescribed or suggested ways in relation to the world around them. Some have an option about future behaviour such as advertisements and recipes, and some do not, such as contracts or treaties (see Hatim and Mason 1990: 156–8). The linguistic and rhetorical conventions characteristic of the many genres with an operative function vary considerably: here we focus on a typical set of instructions for using a domestic device.

The following German ST and English TT are extracts from the '*Gebrauchsanleitung*' (operating instructions) for an appliance variously called a '*Fußbad*', '*Fußwanne*', '*Fußsprudel-Bad*' ('foot bath', 'foot spa', 'spa') (Bosch 2009). Interestingly, there is no consistent equivalent in the English translation for these apparent synonyms; so, for example, '*Fußbad*' and '*Fußwanne*' are both translated as 'foot bath', but 'foot spa' and 'spa' are on occasion used to translate '*Gerät*' (otherwise 'appliance'). Each language version in the multilingual documentation is organised in two columns per A4 page, the various languages appearing consecutively i.e. German, then English, then French and so on. We have displayed the texts in parallel below in order to facilitate comparisons between the German and the English:

Anwendung	**Application**
Allgemein	**General**
Durch die sanften Schwingungen und das sprudelnde Wasser können Muskeln gelockert und müde Füße erfrischt werden.	The gentle oscillations and the bubbling water relax muscles and reinvigorate tired feet.
Mit den beigelegten Aufsätzen kann man die Füße pflegen und massieren.	The attachments supplied pamper and massage the feet.
Eine Anwendung sollte nicht länger als 10 Minuten dauern.	A session should not last longer than 10 minutes.

Das Fußbad kann mit oder ohne Wasser benutzt werden.	The foot bath can be used with or without water.
Während der Benutzung sitzen und keinesfalls mit den Füßen im Gerät aufstehen!	**Sit down during use, and under no circumstances stand up with your feet in the spa!**
Das Gerät ist nicht für eine Belastung mit vollem Körpergewicht ausgelegt.	The appliance is not designed to take the full weight of the user.

The layout of any text is important for a number of reasons. In the present case, the column format—as also in newspapers and some magazines—affects the length of paragraphs in particular: the lines are shorter and the number of lines per paragraph is restricted, presumably to allow for easier reading and navigation through the text. The TT correctly follows the ST in this layout. Rather oddly for our expectations of instructions for use in German, the use of modals ('*können*', '*sollen*') is more evident than the more conventional use of the infinitive ('*sitzen*', '*aufstehen*'). However, the infinitive structure *is* used in the penultimate sentence of our extract, where, through its contrasting form, it draws attention to this sentence as a safety warning, reinforced further by the bold font and the preceding greater line spacing. The variation in verb forms can therefore be understood as functional rather than deviant.

While the choice of punctuation in the TT could be questioned—exclamation marks are not required with commands in English—the pace of the ST is well maintained by the change from modals to imperative in the TT. The final sentence offers a reinforcing explanation for the warning. In addition to the modal structures used in the first four sentences, the choice of certain words (notably adjectives and verbs) is also designed to emphasise the wisdom of the purchase in terms of its restorative qualities: '*sanft*', '*sprudelnd*', '*erfrischt*', '*pflegen*' ('gentle', 'bubbling', 'reinvigorate', 'pamper'). This rather lyrical feature is contrasted with a later section, namely the '*Garantiebedingungen*'.

Consumer-related quasi-legal issues often feature in 'Operating instructions'. The following information on the product's guarantee is the last item in each language section:

Garantiebedingungen	**Guarantee**
Für dieses Gerät gelten die von unserer jeweils zuständigen Landesvertretung herausgegebenen Garantiebedingungen, in dem das Gerät gekauft wurde. Sie können die Garantiebedingungen jederzeit	The guarantee conditions for this appliance are as defined by our representative in the country in which it is sold. Details regarding these conditions can be obtained

über Ihren Fachhändler, bei dem Sie das
Gerät gekauft haben oder direkt bei
unserer Landesvertretung anfordern. Die
Garantiebedingungen für Deutschland und
die Adressen finden Sie auf den letzten vier
Seiten dieses Heftes.
Darüber hinaus sind die Garantiebedingungen
auch im Internet unter der benannten
Webadresse hinterlegt. Für die
Inanspruchnahme von Garantieleistungen
ist in jedem Fall die Vorlage des
Kaufbeleges erforderlich.
Änderungen vorbehalten.

from the dealer from whom
the appliance was purchased.
The bill of sale or receipt must
be produced when making any
claim under the terms of this
guarantee.
Changes reserved.

It is immediately apparent that the English TT omits that part of the German ST (highlighted) which is concerned specifically with the conditions of the *German* guarantee. Such omissions or generic amendments are a regular feature of multilingual documentation accompanying internationally marketed products as the cultural setting (including legal conditions) of the text changes.

The vocabulary in this section is specialised ('*Landesvertretung*', '*Garantiebedingungen*', '*Inanspruchnahme*'), and shows no sign of the more colourful vocabulary of the earlier section: the foot bath is always referred to as '*Gerät*' in the ST and 'appliance' in the TT. The TT makes appropriate syntactic changes, such as the shift from the extended attribute phrase in the first ST sentence to a predicative phrase, and avoids the direct address to the reader of the ST ('*Sie können . . .*') by using a passive construction, the more usual form for a guarantee in English. The categorical adverbials '*jederzeit*' and '*in jedem Fall*' are also dropped in the TT. The final phrase '*Änderungen vorbehalten*' translated as 'Changes reserved' is the only slip, as the conventional English phrase is 'Subject to change without notice'.

CASE STUDY 3:   A *Dinggedicht* in sonnet form

Many texts have some form of aesthetic function, or appeal to the emotions in some way, whether that is a stylised editorial, an impassioned letter, or more narrowly defined literary texts as we will discuss here. For our example, we take the poem '*Blaue Hortensie*' from Rainer Marie Rilke's

Neue Gedichte (first published in 1907). The text and its translation presented here are given as they appeared in a 2011 edition by Susan Ranson and Marielle Sutherland, with the German text and the translation on facing pages (Rilke 2011: 68–9), presented here sequentially:

Blaue Hortensie

So wie das letzte Grün in Farbentiegeln
sind diese Blätter, trocken, stumpf und rauh,
hinter den Blütendolden, die ein Blau
nicht auf sich tragen, nur von ferne spiegeln.

Sie spiegeln es verweint und ungenau,
als wollten sie es wiederum verlieren,
und wie in alten blauen Briefpapieren
ist Gelb in ihnen, Violett und Grau;

Verwaschnes wie an einer Kinderschürze,
Nichtmehrgetragnes, dem nichts mehr geschieht:
wie fühlt man eines kleinen Lebens Kürze.

Doch plötzlich scheint das Blau sich zu verneuen
in einer von den Dolden, und man sieht
ein rührend Blaues sich vor Grünem freuen.

Blue Hydrangea

Dull and rough these leaves, like vestiges
of green paint left in a jar, grown
dry under flowers whose blue is not their own
but tint reflected from the distances.

They mirror it through stains of tears, blurred,
as though they wished it could be lost from them,
and have the look of old, blue letters, dimmed
to violet, and yellow-tinged, and greyed;

washed out like a child's pinafore,
like things no longer worn, kept for no use,
and as affecting as a life soon over.

Then with a start the blue seems new again
within one umbel, and before your eyes
a touching blue gladdens beside the green.

Like the most famous poem in the *Neue Gedichte* collection 'Der Pan-
ther', 'Blaue Hortensie' can be considered a *Dinggedicht*. This is an
instructive genre for our purposes, because it is defined in contrast to
more obviously subjective, lyrical forms—a *Dinggedicht* usually is a
poem which seeks to present a distanced, objective presentation of an
object in the real world—but is simultaneously defined as a modern variant of a classical poetic genre, the epigram, or *Bildgedicht*, that is the
poetic description of a work of art (Best 1972: 57). This *Dinggedicht* is
also a sonnet. The sonnet represents strictness of form, though there is
variation in rhyme scheme, and cultural variation in metre. The German
sonnet is in Petrarchan form, 14 lines of five iambic feet (containing five
stressed syllables) typically rhyming abba, abba, or less strictly, abba,
cddc, and then the sestet (the last six lines) rhyming cdc, cdc, or cdc,
efe (as here). In English there are also two native variations, the Shake-
spearean and the Spenserian, both slightly different from the Petrarchan: where a Petrarchan sonnet usually has a significant turning point
between the two quatrains and the two tercets, the English forms contain
a final couplet, the last two lines concentrating or summarising the poem
(Greene, Cushman and Cavanagh 2012, entry 'sonnet'). Rilke's poem
here in fact has the important caesura at the end of the first tercet, the
final tercet initiating change: '*Doch plötzlich . . .*'.

If we consider the English translation of Rilke's poem from a formal
perspective first, we note some discrepancies: where in Rilke's poem
rhyme is a clear structural marker, this is much less pronounced in the
English text, where there are mostly only impure rhymes or assonances
(vesti*ges*/distan*ces*, the*m*/di*mm*ed, pinaf*ore*/*over*); similarly while the
German text is more or less regular, with five iambic feet (i.e. five alter-
nate unstressed and then stressed syllables), the English translation is
less regular, with several lines notably deviating from this pattern ('of
green paint left in a jar, grown'; 'washed out like a child's pinafore').
Enjambment also plays a greater role in the English poem. In short, the
English text favours preserving the imagery of the poem over meeting
formal constraints, a procedure that is not at all uncommon in the translation of poetry, and which has perhaps greater legitimacy here in this
reflection on the colour of a flower, and within the context of a volume of
translations which appear alongside the original texts, and may thus be
used by readers as a way into the German original.

Conversely, the English text appears to signal its distinctly poetic nature to the reader syntactically and lexically: the poem's beginning in English is more marked, with the omission of the copula verb 'to be' and the inversion of subject ('these leaves') and predicative complement ('dull and rough'). The lexis is more differentiated and often of a higher and more literary register (*'letzt'* > 'vestiges'; *'freuen'* > 'gladden'; *'Dolde'* > 'flower', 'umbel'). In fact, the strategy of focusing on the imagery of the poem tends to lead to an expansiveness in the English images, and a greater presence of nouns, at least in the first stanzas which set the tone of the poem (*'letzt'* > 'vestiges'; ø > 'tint'; *'verweint'* > 'through stains of tears'); one might conclude that the English poem exaggerates *das Dingliche* in this *Dinggedicht*. This is perhaps most noticeable in the word 'umbel', which may strike many English readers as unfamiliar, certainly it is more specifically botanical than the German *'Dolde'*. This is a good example of a translator having to deal with relatively specialist vocabulary in a literary text: here the first strategy is a generalising translation (*'hinter den Blüten-dolden'* > 'under flowers'), the second, once the idea of the text has progressed, is more specific (*'Dolden'* > 'umbel') (more on this in Chapter 7).

In sum, this poem by Rilke is a good example of (a) how broad statements about literary genres need to be treated with caution (the idea that literature is detached form the world, or the idea that they are 'expressions' in a direct sense); (b) how genres always exist and function within constellations of other genres which evolve over time and (c) that genres are not to be thought of as empty vessels into which a text fits, but often have a significant role in determining what the text says.

Not least, as with other categories of genre, the translator needs to balance general observations about the category (this is literature), with detailed knowledge about the function of the specific genre (here, a German *Dinggedicht* in sonnet form from around 1900), and analysis of the text as it both fulfils and deviates from the norms of that genre: this poem is in fact principally about abstractions, the blue quality of the flower and about time.

Multimodal texts

Comic strips, graphic novels, TV adverts and websites are all examples of genres which are 'multimodal' texts, consisting of at least two 'modes' of communication: language, image and/or sound. Multimodal texts can be 'static' or 'dynamic'. As is the case for monomodal verbal texts, multimodal texts can have different functions and embrace a wide range of genres. An increasing number and range of multimodal texts are now being translated.

As an example of a static multimodal text, a cartoon-type format designed to give instructions to a multilingual audience can be found later in Chapter 13 (Consumer-oriented texts). Graphic novels such as *Der Boxer: die wahre Geschichte des Hertzko Haft* (2012) by Reinhard Kleist, produced in English as *The Boxer: The True Story of Holocaust Survivor Harry Haft* (2014) by the London-based publisher SelfMadeHero, fall into the category of functionally expressive or 'aesthetic' genres. And printed encyclopaedias— as a very established type of informative text—are hard to imagine without illustrations, maps and photographs, although as we have seen (Case Study 1), translation might involve changes to content for broadly cultural reasons.

Whether a particular text appears in print or digital form can depend on the genre. Many texts such as academic publications, novels and product information can appear in different media, i.e. in print and/or online, tending increasingly to appear online. The sole medium for other texts, such as SMSs (or 'texts'), or emails is digital; both can incorporate non-verbal signs, of which emoticons or more recently, Emojis, are an increasingly familiar feature. Whether such pictograms are universal—and therefore whether they need to be 'translated' or can simply be transferred—is a moot point (for a discussion, see Arndt 2016).

Moving on to dynamic multimodal texts, these also include many genres, such as feature films, TV documentaries and vlogs. Again, in some cases the medium may vary, so films can be viewed at the cinema, on TV, online or on mobile devices. The most familiar translation activities relating to dynamic texts (broadly, 'audio-visual translation' or 'AVT') are foreign-language subtitling and dubbing, although the field is growing fast in terms of game localisation, a huge commercial market, as well as media accessibility as legally required (e.g. subtitling for the deaf and hard-of-hearing and audio-description for the visually impaired). Functionally, dynamic genres also range across the text functions discussed here: for example, feature films can be characterised as principally expressive/aesthetic, safety videos as operative/persuasive and informative (often translated with a new voiceover rather than subtitles), and online lectures such as the TED series, as broadly informative, with an element of persuasive rhetoric.

In a single chapter, we do not have enough space to go into any more detail on multimodal texts. Instead, we refer you to the list of texts for Further Reading below.

Conclusion

Genre is a crucial factor influencing translation decisions in terms of content, (macro)structure, vocabulary choice, linguistic conventions and layout. And as the case studies in this chapter have shown, genres are rarely if ever of a 'pure' text type. For the translator, decisions are therefore often not straightforward: not only do genres conventionally vary in form and tone between linguacultures, they also vary within each linguaculture for a variety of reasons, including the existence of established subgenres, developments resulting from technological change, and the appearance of new genres to fill emerging social needs. Existing genres may also undergo change as writing practices evolve, and also as social conventions shift. Take, for example, the commissioning of retranslations of works from the literary canon by publishers.

In practice, most translators specialise, and part of that specialism includes building up a knowledge of genre conventions. Nevertheless, a good awareness of how genres function in certain ways and an ability to analyse texts in terms of genre will help you to produce translations that are fit for purpose.

Further reading

Becker, Sabina, Hummel, Christine and Sander, Gabriele 2006. *Grundkurs Literaturwissenschaft*. Stuttgart: Reclam, pp. 75–217 [A useful introduction to genre issues for students of literature.].

Bernal-Merino, Miguel Á. 2015. *Translation and Localisation in Video Games: Making Entertainment Software Global*. New York and London: Routledge.

Bhatia, Vijay K. 1993. *Analysing Genre: Language Use in Professional Settings*. London: Longman [Not specifically written from a translation perspective, this short book contains useful overviews on genres in business, legal and academic settings.].

Díaz Cintas, Jorge, Orero, Pilar and Remael, Aline (eds) 2006. Audiovisual Translation [Special Issue]. *JoSTrans*, Issue 06/July 2006 [Online]. Available at: www.jostrans.org/issue06/issue06_toc.php (Accessed: 12 February 2018).

Díaz Cintas, Jorge and Remael, Aline 2007. *Audiovisual Translation: Subtitling*. Manchester: St. Jerome.

Fawcett, Peter 1997. *Translation and Language: Linguistic Theories Explained*. Manchester: St Jerome. Chapter 9 'Text functions', pp. 101–15 [A brief discussion of text types and text functions.].

Munday, Jeremy 2016. *Introducing Translation Studies: Theories and Applications*. 4th edn. London and New York: Routledge. Chapter 5 'Functional theories of translation', pp. 113–40 [An introduction to approaches that prioritise text function and text type.].

O'Sullivan, Carol and Jeffcote, Caterina 2013. 'Translating multimodalities' [Special Issue]. *JoSTrans*, Issue 20/July 2013 [Online]. Available at: www.jostrans.org/issue20/issue20_toc.php (Accessed: 14 February 2018).

Perez-Gonzalez, Luis 2015. *Audiovisual Translation Theories, Methods and Issues*. London and New York: Routledge.

Snell-Hornby, Mary 1988. *Translation Studies: An Integrated Approach*. Amsterdam and Philadelphia: John Benjamins.

Weimar, Klaus et al. (eds) 2007. *Reallexikon der deutschen Literaturwissenschaft*. Berlin: De Gruyter, I, entries 'Gattung', 'Gattungsgeschichte' and 'Gattungstheorie', pp. 651–4, 655–8, 658–61 [Though a reference work, rather more advanced, contains very useful bibliographies.].

Zanettin, Federico 2020. 'Comics, Manga and graphic novels', in Baker, M. and Saldanha, G. (eds) *Routledge Encyclopedia of Translation Studies*. 3rd edn. London and New York: Routledge, pp. 75–9.

Practical 4

4.1 COMPARATIVE ANALYSIS

Assignment

i   Your task is to compare two texts (see websites shown below) created in German and in English for a very similar purpose, namely to get elected as mayor of a large city. The aim is to develop your awareness of web genre conventions in this context for German and English.

ii How would you characterise the function of each text, i.e. what is the dominant text type?

iii In comparing the two texts, the following formal features are of interest:

   a   Layout
   b   Use of images (relation to verbal text)
   c   Use of typeface/font
   d   Sentence and paragraph length
   e   Complexity of sentence structure (how many clauses? type of clause? elliptical structures?)
   f   Choice of vocabulary (formal/informal? general/specialised? neutral/emotive?)
   g   Use of headings
   h   Use of personal pronouns

iv What do you think the collective effect is of the features analysed in (iii), for example, in terms of achieving the purpose of each text?

v   How would you characterise the main points of similarity and difference between the two texts?

Contextual information

The texts chosen here for analysis are political declarations by candidates wishing to be elected as mayor of a capital city: Berlin (Michael Müller) and London (Sadiq Khan):

> https://michael-mueller-agh.de/
> https://sadiq.london/standing-up-for-london/
> (Your tutor can supply copies if necessary)

Both candidates represent parties on the centre left (SPD and Labour) and both were successful in their previous campaigns. These texts are what are often called 'parallel' texts i.e. a text is identified in the target culture with similar design features and function to those of the ST. They can be useful in providing guidance on translation decisions when the brief is to produce a TT which is a 'covert' translation (often anonymous texts). This would clearly not apply to the texts discussed here as the particular character of each candidate needs to be given voice.

Unternehmens zu ermitteln. Dazu werden die Renditeansprüche der Aktionäre und die Zinsen auf das Fremdkapital bestimmt und gewichtet. Die Kosten des
20 Eigenkapitals ermitteln wir auf Basis des Marktwertes der BASF-Aktien.
Eine Prämie über die Kapitalkosten können wir sowohl durch eine Verbesserung des EBIT als auch durch eine optimale Nutzung des eingesetzten Kapitals erzielen. Die Kennzahl unterstützt damit unsere Bemühungen zur Verbesserung der Kostenstrukturen, zum profitablen Wachstum und einer noch größeren Disziplin
25 beim Kapitaleinsatz.
Verankerung des Wertmanagements in den Zielvereinbarungen
Konsequenterweise nutzen wir den Wertschaffungsindikator EBIT nach Kapitalkosten auch als Basis der erfolgsabhängigen Managementvergütung. Der Vorstand gibt im Rahmen der operativen Planung diese Zielgröße für die gesamte
30 BASF-Gruppe sowie daraus abgeleitet für die einzelnen Unternehmensbereiche und Geschäftseinheiten vor. Die Zielerreichung bestimmt dabei entscheidend die variable Vergütung.
Für unsere Mitarbeiter, zum Beispiel in Produktion, Marketing, Vertrieb und Supply-Chain-Management, haben wir darüber hinaus ein Kennzahlensystem
35 entwickelt, das es ihnen ermöglicht, ihren persönlichen Beitrag zur Wertsteigerung zu erkennen und dementsprechend zu handeln. Durch ein verbessertes Wertmanagement wird unternehmerisches Denken auf allen Ebenen der BASF gefördert.

(BASF 2004a: 19)

4.4 TRANSLATION: *NOVELLE*

Assignment

i   You have been commissioned to produce a new translation of *Katz und Maus* (originally published in 1961), the novella by Günter Grass from which the following ST extract is taken. Discuss the overall approach that you decide to adopt before starting your detailed translation, justifying your decision in terms of the textual genre and its function.

ii Translate the ST extract into English.

iii Explain the main decisions of detail you took.

iv Compare your TT with the published one (Grass 1966, trans. Manheim), which will be made available to you by your tutor. Which features do you think are important here?

v   Having compared your version with Manheim's, do you think an adaptation/ update of the published translation might have achieved a better outcome? Discuss your reasons.

Contextual information

The narrator is a pupil at a boys' secondary school in Danzig during the Second World War. A former pupil of the school, now a U-boat captain, has come to give a talk about his war experiences. Pupils from the top two classes of the local girls' school have also been invited to the talk. The submariner wears a medal at his throat, which is actually more often referred to as '*das Ding am Hals*' than as an '*Orden*'. The '*Sprechmund*', insisted on (six mentions) as the narrator sets the scene, appears to be an authorial alienating device drawing attention to the artificiality of the language that is put into the mouth of the '*Kapitänleutnant*'. '*Wabos*' are '*Wasserbomben*'.

ST

Es füllte jener Kapitänleutnant mit dem hochgestochenen Ding am Hals seinen Vortrag, obgleich er zweihundertfünfzigtausend Bruttoregistertonnen, einen leichten Kreuzer der Despatch-Klasse, einen großen Zerstörer der Tribal-Klasse angebohrt hatte, weniger mit detaillierten Erfolgsmeldungen als mit wortreichen
5   Naturbeschreibungen, auch bemühte er kühne Vergleiche, sagte: '. . . blendend weiß schäumt auf die Hecksee, folgt, eine kostbar wallende Spitzenschleppe, dem Boot, das gleich einer festlich geschmückten Braut, übersprüht von Gischtschleiern, der todbringenden Hochzeit entgegenzieht'.
Es gab nicht nur bei den Mädchen mit Zöpfen Gekicher; aber ein nächster
10   Vergleich wischte die Braut wieder aus: 'Solch ein Unterseeboot ist wie ein Walfisch mit Buckel, dessen Bugsee dem vielfach gezwirbelten Bart eines Husaren gleicht'.
[. . .]
Peinlich wurde es, wenn er Sonnenuntergänge auszupinseln begann: 'Und bevor die atlantische Nacht wie ein aus Raben gezaubertes Tuch über uns kommt, stufen
15   sich Farben, wie wir sie nie zu Hause, ein Orange geht auf, fleischig und widernatürlich, dann duftig schwerelos, an den Rändern kostbar, wie auf den Bildern Alter Meister, dazwischen zartgefiedertes Gewölk; welch ein fremdartiges Geleucht über der blutvoll rollenden See!'
Er ließ also mit steifem Ding am Hals eine Farbenorgel dröhnen und säuseln, kam
20   vom wäßrigen Blau über kaltglasiertes Zitronengelb zum bräunlichen Purpur. Mohn ging bei ihm am Himmel auf. Dazwischen Wölkchen, zuerst silbrig, dann liefen sie an: 'So mögen Vögel und Engel verbluten!' sagte er wörtlich mit seinem Sprechmund, und ließ aus dem gewagt beschriebenen Naturereignis plötzlich und aus bukolischen Wölkchen ein Flugboot, Typ 'Sunderland', mit Kurs auf das Boot
25   brummen, eröffnete, nachdem das Flugboot nichts hatte ausrichten können, mit gleichem Sprechmund aber ohne Vergleiche, den zweiten Teil des Vortrages, knapp trocken nebensächlich: 'Sitze auf Sehrohrsattel. Angriff gefahren. Kühlschiff wahrscheinlich: sinkt übers Heck. Boot in den Keller auf hundertzehn. Zerstörer kommt auf in hundertsiebzig Bootspeilung, Backbord zehn, neuer Kurs
30   hundertzwanzig, hundertzwanzig Grad liegen an, Schraubengeräusch wandert aus, geht wieder an, hundertachtzig Grad gehen durch, Wabos: sechs sieben acht elf: Licht bleibt aus, endlich Notbeleuchtung und nacheinander Klarmeldung der Stationen. Zerstörer hat gestoppt. Letzte Peilung hundertsechzig, Backbord zehn. Neuer Kurs fünfundvierzig Grad . . .'
35   Leider folgten dieser wirklich spannenden Einlage sogleich weitere Naturbeschreibungen, wie: 'Der atlantische Winter', oder: 'Meeresleuchten auf dem Mittelmeer', auch ein Stimmungsbild: 'Weihnachten auf dem U-Boot' mit dem obligaten zum Christbaum verwandelten Besen. Zum Schluß dichtete er die ins Mystische gehobene Rückkehr nach erfolgreicher Feindfahrt mit Odysseus und allem
40   Drum und Dran: 'Die ersten Möwen künden den Hafen an'.

(Grass 1995: 78–80)

References

Primary

BASF Aktiengesellschaft 2004a. *Finanzbericht 2003*. Ludwigshafen: BASF.

BASF Aktiengesellschaft 2004b. *Financial Report 2003*. Ludwigshafen: BASF.

Bosch 2009. *Gebrauchsanleitung: Fußbad PMF 2232*. Extracts from 'Anwendung (Allgemein)'/'Application (General)' and 'Garantiebedingungen'/'Guarantee' [Online]. Available at: www.bosch-home.com/de/supportdetail/product/PMF2232/01#/Tabs=section-manuals/ (Accessed: 15 February 2018).

Grass, Günter 1966. *Cat and Mouse*. Translated by Manheim, Ralph. Harmondsworth: Penguin.

Grass, Günter 1995. *Katz und Maus*. Munich: DTV.

Kleist, Reinhard 2012. *Der Boxer: die wahre Geschichte des Hertzko Haft*. Hamburg: Carlsen.

Kleist, Reinhard 2014. *The Boxer: The True Story of Holocaust Survivor Harry Haft*. Translated by Waaler, Michael. London: SelfMadeHero.

Rilke, Rainer Maria 2011. *Selected Poems with Parallel German Text*. Translated by Ranson, Susan and Sutherland, Marielle. Oxford: Oxford University Press.

Secondary

Arndt, Tamara 2016. 'Emoji als universelle Sprache? Eine technische und terminologische Betrachtung'. *Fachzeitschrift für Terminologie*, 2(16), pp. 5–10. Available online at http://dttev.org/images/edition/ausgaben/edition-2016-2-e-version.pdf (accessed 13 February 2017).

Baker, Mona 2011. *In Other Words*. 2nd edn. London: Routledge.

Best, Otto F. 1972. *Handbuch literarischer Fachbegriffe: Definitionen und Beispiele*. Frankfurt am Main: Fischer.

Bhatia, Vijay K. 1993. *Analysing Genre: Language Use in Professional Settings*. London and New York: Longman.

Greene, Roland, Cushman, Stephen and Cavanagh, Clare (eds) 2012. *The Princeton Encyclopedia of Poetry and Poetics*. 4th edn. Princeton, NJ: Princeton University Press.

Hatim, Basil and Mason, Ian 1990. *Discourse and the Translator*. London and New York: Longman.

Koller, Werner (unter Mitarbeit von Kjetl Berg Henjum) 2011. *Einführung in die Übersetzungswissenschaft*. 8th edn. Tübingen: Narr Francke Attempto.

Morrow, Phillip R. 1989. 'Conjunct use in business news stories and academic journal articles: A comparative study', *English for Specific Purposes*, 8(3), pp. 239–54.

Mossop, Brian 1998. 'What is a translating translator doing?' *Target*, 10(2), pp. 231–66.

Newmark, Peter 2004. 'Non-literary in the light of literary translation', *JoSTrans*, Issue 01/ January 2004, pp. 8–13 [Online]. Available at: www.jostrans.org/issue01/art_newmark.php (Accessed: 8 March 2018).

Parianou, Anastasia and Kelandrias, Panayotis 2007. 'Instructions for use and their translation in a global age', in Ahmad, K. and Rogers, M. (eds) *Evidence-Based LSP: Translation, Text and Terminology*. Bern: Peter Lang, pp. 525–40.

Snell-Hornby, Mary 1988. *Translation Studies: An Integrated Approach*. Amsterdam and Philadelphia: John Benjamins.

Tanner, Nick 2012. *Jamie in German: The Translation of Jamie Oliver's Cookbooks into German*. Unpublished MA Dissertation, University of Surrey.

Lexical and related sources

Bußmann, Hadumod 1990. *Lexikon der Sprachwissenschaft*. 2nd edn. Stuttgart: Alfred Kröner.

Bussmann, Hadumod 1996. *Routledge Dictionary of Language and Linguistics*. Edited and translated by Trauth, Gregory P. and Kazzazi, Kerstin. London: Routledge.

5 Cultural issues in translation

In his famous, and famously vitriolic, defence of his own translation of the New Testament, the *Sendbrief vom Dolmetschen* (1530), Martin Luther argued that a translator should not look to the words of the Latin text for an appropriate translation, but rather to the users of German, and the users of his text, in short to the language as it functions within a community of speakers. Indeed, for him, *übersetzen* is *verdeutdschen*:

> Da der Engel Mariam grůsset uñ spricht/Gegrůsset seistu Maria vol gnaden/ der Herr mit dir. Wolan/so ists bisher schlecht den Lateinischen buchstaben nach verdeudschet/Sage mir aber/ob solchs auch gut deudsch sey? Wo redet der deudsch man also/du bist vol gnaden? Und welcher Deudscher verstehet/ was gesagt sey/vol gnaden? Er mus denken an ein fas vol bier/odder beutel vol geldes/Darůmb hab ichs verdeudscht/du holdselige /damit doch ein Deudscher/deste mehr hin zu kann denckē / was der Engel meinet mit seinem grus. Aber hie wŏllen die Papisten toll werden uber mich/das ich den Engelischen grus verderbet habe/Wie wol ich dennoch damit nicht das beste deudsch habe troffen. Und hette ich das beste deutsch hie sollen nehmen/und den grus also verdeudschen/Gott grůsse dich du liebe Maria (denn so viel wil der Engel sagen/und so wůrde er gered haben/wenn er hette wŏllen sie deutsch grůssen) Ich halt sie solten sich wol selbst erhenckt haben fur grosser andacht/du der lieben Maria/das ich den grus so zu nichte gemacht hette.
>
> (Luther 1965, Text B, 19)

Luther's argument here is in part an argument about literalness and idiomatic expression ('*voll*' collocates with beer, but not grace), but really, he posits the translation of this greeting as a cultural translation problem. Luther argues that the angel's words (highlighted) are culturally determined because if the angel had been greeting in German he would have acted differently. Luther rejects a literal translation as fundamentally unrecognisable as a greeting to a German, but also points out that he has taken a middle path, having chosen not to replace the angel's greeting entirely with a German one, but rather to have written something which is at least comprehensible to a German native speaker. It is this focus on the forms and pragmatics of language as governed by and informing the lives of its speakers that makes this a cultural issue, and it is cultural issues in translation which will be the focus of this chapter.

As you are working through this book, you will come across 'cultural issues' many times. We have already discussed problems of equivalence that can arise because of cultural differences in Chapter 3, for example. By cultural issues, what we mean are those kinds of translation problems which occur because there is a relationship between the source language and the source culture which does not have a direct parallel in the target language and culture. By culture we do not mean simply references to national traditions or cultural life in the sense of the arts, although of course these do pose problems and many of the most obvious cultural issues in translation are of this kind; rather we mean culture in a broad sense, encompassing a community's institutions, habits, traditions and ways of seeing the world. 'Cultural' issues in translation then can be everything from dealing with translating terms with literary and cultural resonance in a narrow sense, to institutional terms, to problems that are harder to identify, such as industry regulations, modes of address, or genre norms. Hence, 'cultural transposition' is the term we have chosen to designate a range of strategies translators use to overcome these sorts of problems. Let it be said, however, that most translation will involve cultural transposition of some kind, to the extent that most translation can be thought of as intercultural mediation.

Translation methods and strategies for dealing with cultural issues can be said to exist on a scale between 'domestication' and 'foreignisation' as in our Luther example. The extent to which a translation should be 'domesticating' and thus the kinds of strategies that will be used when dealing with cultural issues is one of the principal questions in Translation Studies and depends on a range of factors, notably on whether the translation will primarily serve to point the reader to the source text (such as in a bilingual edition of a story) or whether it will function independently (in the case of say, a set of instructions for operating a printer). In this chapter, we will for the most part be discussing short examples rather than whole texts, but the strategies may also be used to analyse the translation of whole texts.

Types of cultural issues

Our first example is from a booklet on the architectural history of Lübeck's *Rathaus*:

> Zum erstenmal wird ein Rathaus der 1158/59 von *Heinrich dem Löwen* an der jetzigen Stelle neu gegründeten Stadt kurz vor 1225 im Zusammenhang mit dem Hinweis auf die dort ausgeübte Rechtsfindung genannt. 1250, wenig später, ist schon von einem 'alten Rathaus' die Rede [. . .]. Über das Aussehen dieses ersten Rathauses ist nichts bekannt. Wegen seiner späteren Nutzung für die Weißgerber, die im Erdgeschoß ihre Verkaufsstände hatten, kann vermutet werden, dass das damals als 'Lohhus' bezeichnete Gebäude unten als offene Halle ausgebildet war.
>
> (Wilde 2014: 1)

The first problem, apart from the word '*Rathaus*' itself, is the proper noun '*Heinrich dem Löwen*'. The issue is not so much that an English version does not exist, it does, but rather that for an English-speaking reader the reference to 'Henry the Lion' may not be transparent. Here a short gloss, an exegetic **addition** may be appropriate. The second, more obviously 'cultural' problem is the word '*Lohhus*', which here probably means 'tanners' building', but with a dialect form, '-*hus*'. In this case the term is transparent enough for the German reader that it has simply been integrated into the standard German to give some local colour: the translator may here opt to preserve the original term (a **cultural borrowing** or **loan word**) but offer a translation too, at the first mention, i.e. a **couplet**. The final issue, which is more difficult to spot, is the term '*Weißgerber*'. '*Gerber*' means 'tanner', but '*Weiß-*' or '*Mineralgerber*' means a tanner who produced high-quality white leather products in the Middle Ages (in contrast to a '*Lohgerber*'!). While '*Weißgerber*' is common enough in German (as a name and in street names), English has no such neat and identifiable term. Here the best solution is a **generalisation** ('tanner'), because the tanners are incidental: what matters is the inference that the town hall must have been an open building because it was used by tanners as a place to set up stalls. This example also shows that a problem can at once be seen as linguistic (here a problem of denotative equivalence) or cultural (the fact that Germans are specific in the way they use these terms).

Our second example is this time an intralingual translation of sorts: a modern German translation of a Middle High German text (from *circa* 1200), the famous *Nibelungenlied*, which recounts the life of Siegfried, his murder and Kriemhild's vengeance. Below is a standard version of the text, here the beginning of *âventiure* 2, or 'chapter 2', with a well-known modern translation by Helmut Brackert:

Dô wuochs in Niderlanden   eins edelen küneges kint,
des vater der hiez Sigemunt,   sîn muoter Sigelind,
in einer rîchen bürge,   wîten wol bekant,
nidene bî dem Rîne: diu was ze Santen genant.

Sîvrit was geheizen   der snelle degen guot.
er versuochte vil der rîche   durch ellenhaften muot.
durch sînes lîbes sterke   er reit in menegiu lant.
hey was er sneller degene   sît zen Burgonden vant!

Es wuchs in den Niederlanden, in einer weithin berühmten, mächtigen Burg, die am Niederrhein lag und Xanten hieß, der Sohn eines edlen Königs heran, dessen Vater Siegmund und dessen Mutter Sieglind hießen.

Siegfried hieß der tapfere, treffliche Held. Er durchstreifte viele Reiche, um sich kämpferisch zu erproben. Um seine Kraft zu beweisen, ritt er in zahllose Länder. Wie viele tapfere Helden sah er später erst bei den Burgunden!

(*Nibelungenlied* 1970: 10–1)

Leaving aside syntactic changes, perhaps the most obvious change made here is the shift from verse to prose (albeit matching the stanza breaks). On the one hand, this is clearly an approach determined by the function of Brackert's text which, while being written so that it can be read on its own, primarily serves to guide the reader through the Middle High German narrative. On the other, the choice is culturally determined: while the primary mode of narrative was verse in the Middle Ages, the primary narrative mode today is prose. Other twentieth-century translations of historical literature have also rewritten verse into prose, perhaps most famously E.V. Rieu's 1946 translation of the *Odyssey*.

Another, unobtrusive but significant translation decision involves proper nouns which are modernised: *Siegmund, Sieglind, Siegfried, Xanten*, and similarly '*nidene bî dem Rîne*' which becomes '*am Niederrhein*'. With *Santen > Xanten*, the translation strategy is simply modernised spelling. With *Sîfrit>Siegfried* (a modern reconstruction, see Ehrismann 1987: 112), we have an example of using TL standard equivalents. Note: the translator here changes the name of the principal character in the story to accommodate what the TL reader expects (Siegfried is famous, *am Niederrhein* helps place the story in a setting the reader can identify concretely).

Rather more interesting are the words which still have similar forms in modern German, but which had a different cultural resonance in the courts of twelfth-century feudal Germany. '*Degen*' (cognate of English 'thane') notably still appears in modern German dictionaries. A major dictionary from around the same era of Brackert's translation gives '*Ritter*' as the first synonym for '*Degen*', followed by '*Gefolgsmann*', followed by '*Held*', which is Brackert's translation (Wahrig 1980). '*Ritter*' (knight) would be a problematic translation here, however, because the values of chivalry which are associated with that word are historical developments which the early forms of the *Nibelungenlied* predate (see Ehrismann 1987: 30–2). Older terms such as '*degen*', '*recke*' and '*helt*' appear alongside the more modish '*ritter*' ('*Ritter*') in the *Nibelungenlied*, because it is an old epic rewritten for a twelfth-century, Christian, courtly audience (see: Ehrismann 1987: 99–100). Brackert's translation is sensitive to the historical and cultural specificity of these terms and preserves the distinction in the text, rather than conflating the terms. Similarly, '*versuochen*' has a particular meaning here, in that Siegfried has proved his courage and strength and is thus able (later in the *âventiure*) to be dubbed a knight; here Brackert clarifies, replacing the following prepositional phrase with a verb phrase ('*um sich kämpferisch zu erproben*').

These examples show the range of issues that the cultural embeddedness of texts raises: problems to do with dialect, historical or cultural references, norms relating to the use of terms for trades, occupations, but also the kinds of subtler background which can easily go unnoticed, and here gave specific meaning to relatively common nouns and verbs. In short there is a difference between what Koller calls '*offene und verdeckte kulturspezifische Elemente*' (Koller 2011: 169). Indeed, although many of the examples we discuss in this chapter are lexical, the translator will usually need to address the cultural embeddedness of a text at all levels of language: in the lexis, syntax, text structure and pragmatics (Stolze 2009).

In all of these cases, it is the background knowledge and expectation that the reader/user in the source-text situation brings to the text which is crucial, which is why being aware of cultural issues, and the solving of cultural problems in translation often involves experience and research.

Forms of cultural transposition

Luther, in his *Sendbrief vom Dolmetschen* describes how, when faced with the translation of the angel Gabriel's greeting, he could have chosen a literal translation, but that would have posed cultural problems because a German would not recognise the communicative function of the phrase. He could also have chosen '*Gott grüße dich*', but instead chose a middle route which would be unnatural to a German reader but where the communicative function at least was clear. In short, he could choose between producing a 'domesticating' translation, which adapts the ST to meet TL cultural norms (how Germans greet each other), meeting the TT reader's horizon of expectations, or he could have chosen to produce a 'foreignising' translation, which maintains forms of the SL culture present in the ST at that particular time. As with other problems in translation then, approaches to cultural issues in translations can be seen as existing on a scale from the SL culture (foreignising) to the TL culture (domesticating), with two extremes, **exoticism** and **cultural transplantation**.

Two broad approaches: exoticism and cultural transplantation

A TT marked by **exoticism** is one which consistently uses cultural, lexical and grammatical features imported from the ST with minimal adaptation, thereby constantly signalling the exotic source culture and its cultural strangeness. This may be one of the TT's chief attractions, as in certain translations from Arabic (e.g. Nicholson 1987), but the TT will have an impact on the TL public quite unlike any that the ST could have had on an SL public, for whom the text is not exotic. At the other end of the scale is **cultural transplantation**, whose extreme forms are more like adaptations than translations—the wholesale rewriting of the ST in a target-culture setting. One example would be a 2005 Dundee production of *The Visit*, in which the Swiss Anytown of Dürrenmatt's *Der Besuch der alten Dame* (1956), with its long-haul trains that no longer stop, was transposed to a Scottish airport town where the last fragments of hope 'departed with the last Ryanair flight'.

Sometimes, the decision whether to operate cultural transplantation is taken out of the translator's hands by the TL publisher or even the target-culture censor. Despite their relatively high status and secure working environment, translators working in East Germany had to meet other ideological demands (Thomson-Wohlgemuth 2003). In such extreme cases, the decision is not the translator's to make, though this does raise issues around the ethics of translation and what Christiane Nord has called the translator's 'loyalty' towards their 'partners in translational interaction', i.e. their moral obligation not to deceive (Nord 1997: 125).

Cultural transplantation is sometimes used by literary translators where a ST contains a lot of dialect. Derek Bowman's translation of Theodor Fontane's Berlin novel *Irrungen Wirrungen* (1887) gave pseudo-cockney accents to working-class characters to evoke the urban setting of a capital city, for example (Bance and Chambers 1995: 300). Cultural transplantation (changing ST content and replacing it with TL culture-specific content) may appear radical when thinking about a novel, but for an informative text which is to function within the TL system this can often be essential. In a translation of a German text about steel, a text could be considered marked by exoticism if it did not signal to the reader or somehow deal with the fact that the national standards surrounding the composition of 'alloy steel' and '*legierter Stahl*' are different in the UK and Germany, although the terms are given as equivalents in authoritative dictionaries (Schmitt 1986); if, however, the translator adapted the text so that it consistently fitted the cultural (in this case legal and standard industry) practices without reference to German, then it could be considered cultural transplantation. In specialised texts, however, the translator's choice, e.g. in a structural engineer's specification for building regulation purposes, has potential safety implications.

Three strategies: calque, cultural borrowing, cultural equivalent

While cultural issues govern a translator's overall approach, within the same text, different problems may require different solutions (Ramière 2006). Below we discuss three strategies **calque, cultural borrowing,** and **cultural equivalent** (previously mentioned in Chapter 3 generally as 'loan translation', 'transfer' from SL, and 'cultural borrowing' (as below), and discussed here in greater depth).

Calque

A more reduced form of exoticism is a calque. A calque is a form of a linguistically close translation consisting of either an expression or word (lexical calque) or a structure (structural calque) which brings out the foreign in the TT (as a deliberate strategy) or which can be regarded as 'translationese', as in the following unidiomatic translation of a well-known proverb: '*Morgenstund hat Gold im Mund*' > 'Morning hour has gold in the mouth'. Unless the person requesting the translation of proverbs specifically wants to know how they work in the SL, the translator clearly has to use a conventional equivalent ('The early bird catches the worm'/'Early to bed and early to rise makes a man healthy, wealthy and wise'). While it is clear that calquing proverbs is likely to result in an unidiomatic rendering, lexical calquing (i.e. loan translation) can be a useful technique for filling lexical gaps in the TL e.g. '*Schrittmacher*' for 'pace maker' (see Chapter 3, Koller's 'one-to-none' denotative equivalence). Literary texts where proverbs play a significant role can be problematical: for example, in translating Theodor Fontane's novels, translators have to adopt a range of strategies, using equivalent TL expressions where available, and recreating proverbs where they are absent in the TL (Kirby 1995).

Cultural borrowing/couplet

Another alternative introducing an element of foreignness is to transfer a ST expression verbatim into the TT. This is termed **cultural borrowing** or **transfer** (see again Koller's 'one-to-none' denotative equivalence in Chapter 3). But cultural borrowing is different from calque, because it does not involve translation of the SL expression into TL forms. Translators often turn to cultural borrowing when it is impossible to find a suitable indigenous TL expression. '*Weltanschauung*' is an example: first attested in English in 1868, it is defined in the *Concise Oxford English Dictionary* as 'a particular philosophy or view of life; a conception of the world'. Cultural borrowing is frequent in texts on history or legal, social or political matters, in references to institutions or concepts which have no clear counterpart in the TL. As noted when we were discussing equivalence in Chapter 3, the simplest solution if we judge the borrowing to be opaque to the intended readers is often a **couplet**. We can recall that this involves inserting into the TT an explanation or gloss—sometimes described as a '**functional equivalent**'—of terms like '*Bundesrat*', '*Bund*', '*Länder*' or '*Bafög*' the first time they occur. Thereafter the SL term can be used as a loan word in the TT.

However, caution needs to be exercised in dealing with SL words that have become TL loan words, and vice versa. A good example is '*Lebensraum*', which is used in a much wider range of situations in German than in English. In English, having entered the language during the 1930s when the Nazis were using it as part of their expansionist rhetoric, it specifically denotes 'territory claimed by a nation or state as being necessary to its growth or survival'. Both the literal meaning and the connotations are now inescapable when the term is used in English. The same connotations are of course present in German too—but to what extent they are active depends on the context. The difference is that English knows only the one sense, whereas in German, despite historical memories still uppermost for some, the term '*Lebensraum*' is used routinely in Biology and is also found in texts on Architecture and Town Planning. In such contexts it is a value-neutral term meaning 'habitat', 'living space', etc., and to translate it with the loan word 'lebensraum', rather than with a term appropriate to the discipline, would be a serious error. The translator therefore needs to use this strategy with care, based on sound cultural knowledge of both cultures.

Cultural equivalent

Cultural equivalents, as the examples in Chapter 3 have shown, include terms and concepts which are different in the two cultures but which are parallel in some way. Cultural shifts can involve adaptation or cultural transplantation: weights and measures, for example, may need to be adapted, as in educational marking systems e.g. 1,1 > grade 'A' (see also Chapter 13) or, in other cases, transferred, depending on the context. Indeed, educational terms, embedded as they are in different educational systems, can be deceptively difficult to deal with. For example, '*Abitur*' and 'A levels' are both school-leaving examinations taken around the age of 18 or 19, but are clearly different in their form and content. Functional and cultural equivalents differ in so far as the former are 'neutral' or 'culture-free' ('German secondary school-leaving certificate') whereas the latter are culture-specific ('A-levels') (Newmark 1988: 83, our examples). As a translation strategy, translating '*Abitur*' only with the UK cultural equivalent might be seen to imply that the candidate actually sat A-level examinations, which if the German ST is, for instance, the CV of someone educated at a *Gymnasium* is unlikely. The transfer of '*Abitur*' to the English translation of the CV might be accompanied by a gloss/functional equivalent, although this addition is unlikely in a novel. However, we can note a trend in contemporary literature for a glossary of culturally specific terms to be provided at the end of translated works such as novels, anticipating that some readers may not be familiar with the target culture.

With the concept of cultural equivalence we may also denote shifts at levels other than the lexical level. At a pragmatic level, in a new translation of Kafka's *Der Verschollene*, Ritchie Robertson abbreviates and generalises terms of address: '*Frau Oberköchin*' and '*Herr Oberportier*' become 'ma'am' and 'sir' (Kafka 2012: xxxi–xxxii). At a syntactic level, Stolze notes that whereas lists of 'that'-clauses are a defining feature of British and American court sentences, the equivalent (*dass*-clauses) is unusual in German ones (2009: 132), further illustrating (see also Chapter 4 on genre) that texts—not just individual expressions—are also subject to differences of convention between cultures. Here, it would be odd for the translator culturally to transplant English-language conventions to a text which is culturally set in the context of the German legal system. If the result sounds 'exotic' to a UK or US lawyer, then so be it: this clearly signals that the text is 'other' in its legal origins.

Functionalist approaches and intercultural communication

The general extent to which a translation *ought* to be 'domesticating' or 'foreignising' has been a topic of considerable discussion in Translation Studies. Lawrence Venuti has argued that translation culture in the West assimilates, essentially expunging difficult foreignness. Conversely Hans Vermeer, for example, has argued that the success of a translation is judged less by its similarity to the ST and more by its role as an act of 'purposeful transcultural activity' (Schäffner 2009: 115). In our view, thinking about whether a text is or should be domesticating or foreignising is a false dichotomy, and in many senses these seemingly contradictory discussions are really addressing different things: Venuti is arguably writing about the effect of translation on culture essentially with reference to literary translation; Reiß, Vermeer, and other functionalists arguably take non-literary texts as their starting point. But even then, different approaches are possible. Literary texts are published by named authors, which favours a ST orientation in order to represent the author's voice, but they can still be adapted and shifted to a target-culture setting (e.g. a BBC production of Ibsen's *Hedda Gabler* transposed to rural Ireland). Specialised texts are often anonymous, meaning that the voice issue is superseded by target-culture genre conventions (e.g. instructions for use), but they can also, depending on context and subject matter, be rooted in a source-culture context, as is the case for many education-related and legal texts.

In any case, a cultural adaptation which conveys the ideas and issues of a literary text such as a play could well be said to be just as 'foreignising' for the reader as a translation in which misunderstood exotic references impede understanding. Cultural sensitivity in relation to specialised texts involves judgements about the cultural embeddedness of the ST in its source culture, or the greater universality of, say, product information which has to cross international boundaries.

Christiane Nord reframes the 'exoticism/transplantation' distinction with a differentiation between textual functions: a documentary function (such as a translation of a German legal document: the German document is the document which is important, the English text aids the comprehension of that text) and texts with an instrumental function (texts which do not point the reader to a ST but function independently in the TL, such as a car manual). Although these are broad brushstrokes, the distinction is an important one, and a useful starting point for you as you begin these practicals and move through this book.

Concluding remarks

Getting better at translation involves getting better at thinking through the specificities of how to make your text 'work' fully. All translation involves cultural mediation; the strategies involved in that process and the 'visibility' of the translator, to use Venuti's term, depend on the function and ultimately the purpose of the translation, something which itself occurs within the limits of what a given culture sees as 'translation'. To come back to Luther's *Sendbrief*, translating a text often means not just looking to the words to offer a translation, but to the cultural context—often that means translating concepts, forms and habits, not 'just' *Buchstaben*. Translation not only deals with, but is determined by culture itself.

Further reading

Berman, Antoine 2012. 'Translation and the trials of the foreign', in Venuti, L. (ed.) *The Translation Studies Reader*. 3rd edn. London: Routledge, pp. 240–53 [Takes issue with 'ethnocentric' translation.].

JoSTrans (*Journal of Specialised Translation* online at www.jostrans.org/) [Contains a number of interesting short articles on intercultural issues in specialised translation.].

Koller, Werner (unter Mitarbeit von Kjetl Berg Henjum) 2011. *Einführung in die Übersetzungswissenschaft*. 8th edn. Tübingen: Narr Francke Attempto [*Kulturspezifik der Übersetzung*, pp. 163–70.].

Luther, Martin 2017. *Ein Sendbrief vom Dolmetschen: An Open Letter on Translating*. Translated by Jones, Howard. Oxford: Taylorian Institute [Contains a useful guide to reading the text, a translation and facsimile.].

Munday, Jeremy 2016. *Introducing Translation Studies: Theories and Applications*. 4th edn. London and New York: Routledge [Chapter 5, pp. 72–88; Chapter 8, pp. 126–43; Chapter 9, pp. 144–61.].

Nord, Christiane 2018. *Translating as a Purposeful Activity: Functionalist Approaches Explained*. 2nd edn. London and New York: Routledge [Esp. section on 'Translating as intercultural action' in Chapter 2.].

Rogers, Margaret 2015. *Specialised Translation: Shedding the Non-Literary Tag*. Basingstoke: Palgrave Macmillan [On specialised translation and culture, pp. 23–30.].

Snell-Hornby, Mary (ed.) 1986. *Übersetzungswissenschaft—eine Neuorientierung*. Tübingen: Francke [Now a little dated but contains several interesting contributions. See especially her introduction (pp. 9–29) and the excellent article by Peter A. Schmitt, 'Die "Eindeutigkeit" von Fachtexten: Bemerkungen zu einer Fiktion', pp. 253–82.].

Snell-Hornby, Mary, Hönig, Hans, Kußmaul, Paul and Schmitt, Peter A. (eds) 1999. *Handbuch Translation*. 2nd edn. Tübingen: Stauffenburg, pp. 112–5 [For an overview of intercultural communication and how it relates to translation.].

Vinay, J-P. and Darbelnet, J. 1958/1995. *Comparative Stylistics of French and English: A Methodology for Translation*. Amsterdam and Philadelphia: John Benjamins [Translated and edited by Sager, Juan and Hamel, Marie-Jo from Vinay, J-P. and Darbelnet, J. 1958. *Stylistique comparée du français et de l'anglais: Méthode de traduction*. Paris: Didier.].

Practical 5

5.1 TEXT FOR DISCUSSION: NOVEL

Contextual information

The following is an excerpt from the 2013 novel *Königsallee*, by Hans Pleschinski. The novel is set in the early 1950s. In this episode in the first half of the novel, Thomas Mann's daughter, Erika Mann, is performing a sketch she has planned to mark her famous father's eightieth birthday.

Assignment

i   Read the text and analyse the types of cultural issues it poses for the translator.
ii   Outline and justify your global and local strategies, offering sample translations to illustrate your points.

N.B. The character Anwar is Indonesian and has poor German.

ST

'Ich habe mir eine kleine imaginäre Radiostation ersonnen. Sie sendet regelmäßig: *Das Wort im Gebirge*. In Sketchen zwischen Herrn Roßgoderer und Frau Motzknödel kann ich mich austoben. Wartet . . .' [...] 'Für seinen Achtzigsten nächstes Jahr habe ich mir schon eine Huldigung ausgedacht, die ich vorführen werde'. Mit einem Räuspern war
5   Erika Mann in einer Rolle, deren Stammessprache Anwar als Klangmasse wahrnahm. 'Herr Roßgoderer', kündigte sie mit verstellter Männerstimme an: 'Ich fang jetzt an und erzähl a bissl was von den Werken, ned woa, von diesem Thomas Mann. Als der hat seinen ersten großen Bucherfolg g'habt mit am Roman namens 'Puddenbruch—Abfälle einer Familie'. Darauf Frau Motzknödel', fiel sie ins Falsett: 'Ja, ich weiß nicht, Herr

ST

---

10 Roßgoderer, wenn man sich denkt eigentlich, was so eine ganze Familie also für
Abfälle z'samm bringt, ned, da muß man schon so a Ding, a Einbildungskraft, gell, a
Phantasie mitbringen.—Roßgoderer', sank die Stimme: 'Fernerhin—ich hab' den
Sketch noch nicht ganz fertig—hat er dann, hat ein sehr nettes Mädchenbuch
geschrieben, Frau Motzknödel, des heißt: 'Lotte Kröger'. Also ein sehr hübsches Buch
15 soll's sein un hat ja auch einen schönen Erfolg eingebracht. Sodann ham wir zu
vermelden eine größere Erzählung, die auch einiges Aufsehen aufgewirbelt hat, die
heißt 'Der Tod in Weimar'. Ich persönlich, Sie, habe keine Ahnung, was in dem Ding
also da drinsteht, aber . . .' Aus dem Baß wechselte sie wieder ins Gepiepse von Frau
Motzknödel: 'Also ich hab g'hört, grad die Erzählung, 'Der Tod in Weimar', also das
20 sei also äußerst—Ding, ned—also schwül, schwül'. [. . .] 'Ja, verzeihen Sie, Frau
Motzgoderer, äh, Motzknödel, wollen Sie damit andeuten, daß unser Jubilar, der
Thomas Mann, der, also ein Ding g'schrieben hat, ein . . . ein perverses Buch. Sie:
Mein Gott, also ich mein, natürlich—es is' halt a Ding . . . es is' eben halt schwül, ned'.
(Pleschinski 2015: 133–5, slightly abridged)

5.2 TRANSLATION: TOURISM BROCHURE

Assignment

i   The ST below is from a brochure from the Husum tourist board. The board is
looking to produce a full English version of the brochure. At present there is
only limited information on the website.

ii Translate the text into English, paying special attention to the cultural issues
involved.

iii Comment on your overall approach and decisions of detail you had to make.
Which of the strategies outlined previously did you use at different stages,
and why?

Note: the first line stands on a page of its own at the beginning of the brochure.
The rest of the text is accompanied by pictures and is from a different page of the
brochure. The telephone number is printed at the bottom of the page.

ST

Moin Moin und herzlich Wilkommen!
Hattstedtermarsch—Wobbenbüll—Horstedt
Kleine nordfriesische Paradiese
Weite, Wasser, Wiesen
5 Weit geht der Blick gen Westen—von Wobbenbüll über das Wattenmeer zur Halbinsel
Nordstrand. Unendlich ist der Himmel der Hattstedtermarsch, denn Weite prägt die
Niederung des Flüsschens 'Arlau', das übrigens als 'Köm-Grenze' gilt. Fragen Sie die
Einheimischen danach. Direkt an 'die Marsch' grenzt der 'Beltringharder Koog'—ein
Wasserparadies für Naturfreunde. Mehr erfahren Sie im wohl kleinsten
10 Naturkundemuseum des Nordens, im Schöpfwerk Arlau-Schleuse.

ST

Auf der höher gelegenen Geest liegt Horstedt, einst wichtiger Standort am
Ochsenweg bei den Viehtrieben von Jütland nach Hamburg. Weite und Watt, Wasser
und Wiesen, Knicks und Klönschnack—hier, nördlich von Husum, präsentiert sich
Nordfriesland mit all seiner Schönheit, Plattdeutsch-Stunde inklusiv.
15 **Hoch zu Ross**
Ein alter Brauch an der schleswig-holsteinischen Westküste ist das Ringreiten. Hoch zu
Ross im Galopp mit einer Lanze bewaffnet, zielt der Reiter auf einen kleinen Ring, der
an einem 'Galgen' hängt. Wer die meisten Ringe sticht, wird zum König oder Königin
gewählt. Eine Tradition, die man in allen Orten der Husumer Bucht erleben kann.
20 **Schimmelreiter-Land**
So einzigartig ist diese Landschaft, dass sie auch als Schauplatz mehrerer Theodor
Storm-Werke und Verfilmungen diente, so für Storms wohl bekanntestes Werk 'Der
Schimmelreiter', der in der berühmten Novelle über Deiche dieser Landschaft ritt.
Baden und Wattwandern
25 Beim Radfahren, Wandern oder Reiten finden Sie hier die Ruhe und Erholung, die Sie
sich für die schönsten Tage im Jahr wünschen. Und für kleine Leute wird Urlaub auf
dem Land zu einer nordfriesischen Entdeckertour. Zum Baden geht's an den Seedeich
beim Lüttmoorsiel oder Holmer Siel. Oder zum Wattwandern zur Hallig
Nordstrandischmoor. Die Tourist Information Husum vermittelt Ihnen gern ein
30 gemütliches Urlaubsdomizil in dieser Gegend—im Hotel achter'n Diek, auf dem
Fereienhof oder . . .

Service-Telefon: 0 48 41 / 89 87 0

(Tourismus und Stadtmarketing 2015: 2, 38.)

References

Primary

Das Nibelungenlied 1970. *Mittelhochdeutscher Text und Übertragung*. Edited and trans-
lated by Brackert, Helmut. Frankfurt am Main: Fischer.
Dürrenmatt, Friedrich 1956. *Der Besuch der alten Dame*. Zürich: Verlag der Arche.
Kafka, Franz 2012. *The Man who Disappeared (America)*. Edited and translated by Rob-
ertson, Ritchie. Oxford: Oxford University Press.
Luther, Martin 1965. *Sendbrief vom Dolmetschen*. Edited by Bischoff, Karl. Tübingen:
Niemeyer.
Pleschinski, Hans 2013. *Königsallee: Roman*. Munich: Beck.
Tourismus und Stadtmarketing 2015. *Husumer Bucht 2016 Urlaubsmagazin: Stadt Husum
und Ferienregion Husumer Bucht*. Husum: Tourismus und Stadtmarketing.
Wilde, Lutz 2014. *Rathaus Lübeck*. Berlin and Munich: Deutscher Kunstverlag.

Secondary

Bance, Alan and Chambers, Helen 1995. 'Fontane translation workshop', in Bance, A.,
Chambers, H. and Jolles, C. (eds) *Theodor Fontane: The London Symposium*. Stuttgart:
Heinz, pp. 297–302.
Ehrismann, Otfrid 1987. *Nibelungenlied: Epoche—Werk—Wirkung*. Munich: Beck.

Kirby, Sara 1995. 'Three women and their proverbs: An analysis of usage and translations', in Bance, A., Chambers, H. and Jolles, C. (eds) *Theodor Fontane: The London Symposium*. Stuttgart: Heinz, pp. 111–36.

Koller, Werner (unter Mitarbeit von Kjetl Berg Henjum) 2011. *Einführung in die Übersetzungswissenschaft*. 8th edn. Tübingen: Narr Francke Attempto.

Newmark, Peter 1988. *A Textbook of Translation*. New York: Prentice Hall.

Nicholson, R.A. 1987. *Translations of Eastern Poetry and Prose*. London: Curzon Press; Atlantic Highlands, NJ: Humanities Press.

Nord, Christiane 1997. *Translating as a Purposeful Activity: Functionalist Approaches Explained*. Manchester: St. Jerome.

Ramière, Nathalie 2006. 'Reaching a foreign audience: Cultural transfers in audiovisual translation', *JoSTrans*, Issue 06/July 2006, pp. 152–66 [Online]. Available at: www.jostrans.org/issue06/art_ramiere.pdf (Accessed: 14 February 2018).

Schäffner, Christina 2009. 'Functionalist approaches', in Baker, M. and Saldanha, G. (eds) *Routledge Encyclopedia of Translation Studies*. 2nd edn. London and New York: Routledge, pp. 115–21.

Schmitt, Peter A. 1986. 'Die "Eindeutigkeit" von Fachtexten: Bemerkungen zu einer Fiktion', in Snell Hornby, M. (ed.) *Übersetzungswissenschaft—eine Neuorientierung*. Tübingen: Francke, pp. 252–82.

Stolze, Radegundis 2009. 'Dealing with cultural elements in technical texts for translation', *JoSTrans*, Issue 11/January 2009, pp. 124–42 [Online]. Available at: www.jostrans.org/issue11/art_stolze.pdf (Accessed: 14 February 2018).

Thomson-Wohlgemuth, Gabriela 2003. 'Children's literature and translation under the East German regime', *META*, 48(1–2), pp. 241–9 [Online]. Available at: www.erudit.org/en/journals/meta/2003-v48-n1-2-meta550/006971ar/ (Accessed: 14 February 2018).

Lexical and related sources

Wahrig, Gerhard 1980. *Deutsches Wörterbuch*. Gütersloh: Mosaik.

6   Compensation

In previous chapters, we have introduced a number of strategies for dealing with various translation problems in different contexts. In the current chapter we single out one of these strategies for particular attention, namely, **compensation**, a rather elusive and often poorly defined concept. In fact, one of the main problems for both theoretical and pedagogical purposes has been defining the scope of 'compensation' (Harvey 1995: 77). In her well-known coursebook on translation, Mona Baker even excludes compensation from any detailed consideration on grounds of space (2011: 86). One reason for dedicating a whole chapter to a single strategy is precisely that, i.e. the choices available to the translator are legion, open and often creative. A further reason, as noted over two decades ago, is that compensation has a particular importance for translation pedagogy as it is 'first and foremost a technique available to translators engaged in the *process* of transferring meanings and effects across linguistic boundaries' (Harvey 1995: 66, *emphasis in the original*). Compensation is a way of mitigating translation loss which can, according to Newmark's rather broad account (1988: 90), involve 'meaning, sound-effect, metaphor or pragmatic effect'. In order to solve a translation problem by compensation, the translator can draw on any number of specific translation strategies, as we shall see.

What distinguishes compensation from other translation options is, according to Harvey, its 'stylistic, text-specific function' (1995: 77). There are many definitions or explanations of compensation. Here are two:

> compensation is the making up for the loss in translation of stylistic effect in the source text by the use of the same or another stylistic effect in the target text, either in the same textual location as in the source text or in another place in the text.
>
> (Harvey 1998: 268)

> [compensation] means that one may omit or play down a feature such as idiomaticity at the point where it occurs in the source text and introduce it elsewhere in the target text. This strategy is not restricted to idiomaticity or fixed expressions and may be used to make up for any loss of meaning, emotional force or stylistic effect which may not be possible to reproduce at a given point in the target text.
>
> (Baker 2011: 86)

The principal difference between these definitions concerns the location of the item of compensation in the TT. Whilst Harvey explicitly includes a **substitution** in the same location e.g. a different pun or idiom, Baker and most other authors focus instead on a different location for the compensatory strategy. One of the problems with this is actually deciding what the 'same' location is, as we shall see from the architecture example below. Our working understanding is as follows: where translation loss is unavoidable, the potential impact of this loss is mitigated by recourse to a range of strategies, in the same, adjoining or more distant position, such that important ST effects are rendered approximately in the TT by means other than those used in the ST.

Compensation in practice

A good example of compensation was provided in Chapter 1, where it was shown how the absence of the formal/informal *du/Sie* distinction in English ('you') was compensated by the **addition** of informal vocabulary, i.e. 'chum'. In this example, two different devices—grammatical system and lexical choice—are used in different but contiguous positions in the same sentence with the *aim* of creating the same cheeky effect.

There follows below another example, this time from a non-literary text in which an architect sarcastically criticises the slabs projecting over the front doors and steps in housing designed by a rival architect: '*Da sie weder Entwässerung noch Gefälle haben, bleibt der Schnee auf ihnen vermutlich bis zum Wegtauen und Abtropfen—gerade auf die "geschützten" Treppen—liegen, die so aus dem Regen in die Traufe kommen dürften*' (Adler 1927: 387). While '*vom Regen in die Traufe (kommen)*' can usually be translated without significant loss by its standard equivalent, '(to jump) out of the frying pan into the fire', the translator has to think again here because of the double meaning of the phrase, both as idiom and in a non-figurative sense. If the TT is to convey the writer's barb with similar polemic force, it must do it with compensation. Here is one possibility: '[. . .] the meltwater runs off—straight onto the "sheltered" steps, upon which one may thus truly say it never rains but it pours'. The ST uses a popular idiom to tease the architect. The standard equivalent cannot be used because the literal interpretation of 'frying pans' and 'fire' have nothing to do with melting snow, and would produce a rather absurd translation. The TT compensates for the potential loss of the literal meaning by **substituting** a popular but different idiom in the same place to do the teasing. The image is different, but it is a similar kind of rhetorical ploy to that of the ST, and aims at a similar effect. While retaining a suitably damp imagery, the TL idiom nevertheless loses its own figurative meaning: its function is not actually to say that 'misfortunes never come singly', but to preserve a style and tone. This is in itself a loss but is mitigated in turn by the **addition** of the slightly facetious formulation 'upon which one may thus truly say' and the rather more general negative sense of the substituted idiom.

The location of the substituted idiom could be said to be the 'same' in the TT as in the ST, in so far as it appears in the relative clause at the end of the sentence, but it follows the embellishment which affirms the ironic tone. It is because of such problems in defining 'location' that we have adopted—with Harvey—a broader understanding of compensation which does not insist on compensation occurring in a 'different' place from the original ST feature.

It has been claimed that compensation is more of a concern in the translation of literary texts than of specialised i.e. non-literary ones. However, it is certainly not excluded from the latter, as our architecture example has shown (see also Byrne 2012: 128–9). Specialised texts are less likely to contain jokes or wordplay, but metaphors and other tropes feature prominently in some subject areas such as Economics (e.g. 'haircut'), Politics (e.g. 'spin') and even (Popular) Science (e.g. 'selfish gene'). Nevertheless, many specialised terms which are metaphorically based have standard equivalents which are available in dictionaries or term banks and so do not require compensation. But some highly reader-oriented persuasive texts such as advertisements and political speeches overlap in their creative and rhetorical features with literary texts and may therefore require some kind of compensation, as standard solutions are less likely. The examples which follow are taken from literary texts, but the principles which are illustrated are equally applicable to some non-literary genres.

Analysing cases of compensation

Several of our examples come from W.G. Sebald's *Austerlitz* (2001). This is because it is a well-known and unusually compelling text, embraces a familiar and morally urgent subject, and has been translated by a distinguished English translator, Anthea Bell (Sebald 2002). The lessons we draw from it are, however, potentially applicable to any ST, not just to Sebald's.

In *Austerlitz*, many foreign expressions are quoted verbatim, in Flemish, French, Czech, etc., without translation or explanation. In practically every case, the English translator has kept this feature. This strategy ensures that TL readers face the same kind of challenge to their sophistication as SL readers. However, a difference between SL and TL readers' experience does arise when the narrator singles out *German* expressions as especially significant. These sometimes pose serious problems. Most come late on, when Austerlitz tells the narrator about the notorious Theresienstadt ghetto set up by the Nazis as, in effect, an antechamber to the concentration camps. We shall take two examples from a long, ten-page sentence which, in its exhaustive and often grotesque detail, imitates the suffocating nightmare existence of the inmates. In this context, certain words are so emotionally loaded that it is vital for the TT's purpose that the reader be aware of their full force, as the ST reader is intended to be. Here is one (the reference is to temporary improvements designed to conceal the true nature of Theresienstadt from a Red Cross visitation in 1944):

ST	TT
[. . .] über tausend Rosenstöcke wurden gesetzt, eine Kriechlingskrippe und ein Kleinkinderhort mit Zierfriesen, Sandkästen, Planschbecken und 5 Karussellen ausgestattet, [. . .] (Sebald 2001: 343)	[. . .] over a thousand rose-bushes were planted, a children's nursery and crèche or *Kriechlingskrippe*, as it was termed, said Austerlitz, in one of those perverse formulations, were adorned with pretty fairy-tale friezes and equipped with sandpits, paddling pools and merry-go-rounds, [. . .] (Sebald 2002: 339–40, trans. Bell)

Almost inevitably, the TT is an exegetic translation. Like the ST reader, the TT reader will see the irony of setting up a crèche and a nursery in a transit camp on the road to extermination. But the ST expressions are more expressive than their TT counterparts. Comparing them is an instructive illustration of semantic translation loss, for which the translator has tried to compensate by at least one explanatory **addition**. 'Nursery' denotes a place providing day care for young children. '*Kleinkinderhort*' has a similar denotative meaning, but differs in its connotations by drawing attention to the littleness and vulnerability of the children through its explicit reference to '*Kleinkinder*' and the sense of '*Hort*' as a refuge. There is an even stronger contrast between 'crèche' and '*Kriechlingskrippe*'. 'Crèche', a loan word from French, denotes a place where very young children can be looked after. '*Kriechlingskrippe*' is more vivid: it explicitly mentions babies at the crawling stage, and '*Krippe*' still regularly denotes a manger or crib (cognate with '*Krippe*'): the allusion of 'Nativity scene' in '*Kriechlingskrippe*' is, however, absent in 'crèche'. Taken together, the two ST words are far more compelling than their TT counterparts, particularly in their connotations of vulnerability and Christ's Nativity. Of course, for a German-speaker, these connotations are predominantly latent. But in this context they are triggered by two things: partly by the very inappropriateness of this show of tenderheartedness in Theresienstadt, but largely also by the alliteration on /k/ in the key words, which marks them out and crystallises their layers of meaning into an overall emotive sense of 'littleness', 'weakness', 'protection' and (via the allusion to Nativity) 'generous love'. The contrast between the sham of care and the reality of Theresienstadt is made strident and painful, and arguably even blasphemous.

The TL words can have little of this effect. The TT compensates for this potentially significant loss in two ways. The first is a **transfer** or **cultural borrowing**, '*Kriechlingskrippe*', which suggests that the very language used by the authorities is in some way noteworthy. The second device is the emotive exegetic **addition** to the cultural borrowing: 'as it was termed, said Austerlitz, in one of those perverse formulations'. This confirms that there is something objectionable about the official term, and although it does make explicit some of the critical attitude that is implicit in the ST, it is too general to be clear: which perverse formulations? and what's perverse about them? Here, for discussion in class, are some possible alternatives:

'*Kriechlingskrippe*', as it was termed, said Austerlitz, in another of their barbarisms.

'*Kriechlingskrippe*', as they termed it, said Austerlitz, in another barbarous
   perversion of the language.
'*Kriechlingskrippe*', as it was termed, said Austerlitz, in one of their barbarous
   perversions of the language.
'*Kriechlingskrippe*', as they barbarously called it.
'*Kriechlingskrippe*', as they chose to call it, said Austerlitz.

These suggestions use a similar strategy to the published TT's, but make the target
of criticism more explicit. However, they introduce an explicit emotiveness that is
absent from the ST: a major feature in Austerlitz's account of Theresienstadt is his
relative dispassionateness—more eloquent than exclamations of outrage. In addition, the specific ST connotations are lost; the closest these alternatives come to
compensating for this is in a connotation of wickedness in 'perversion', and, especially, of uncivilised, primitive and murderous cruelty in 'barbarous/barbarism'.

The next example illustrates another typical approach to compensation for lost
ST connotations. Early in the ten-page sentence, Austerlitz lists some of the myr-
iad jobs that the ghetto inmates were compelled to do. There were 60,000 people,
he says, forced to work

---

in einer von der Abteilung für Außenwirtschaft zur Profitschöpfung eingerichteten
Manufakturen, in der Bandagistenwerkstatt, in der Taschnerei, in der
Galanteriewarenproduktion, in der Holzsohlen- und Rindsledergaloschenerzeugung,
auf dem Köhlereihof, bei der Herstellung von Unterhaltungsspielen wie Mühle,
5   Mensch ärgere dich nicht und Fang den Hut, beim Glimmerspalten, in der
Kaninchenhaarschererei, bei der Tintenstaubabfüllung, der Seidenraupenzucht der SS
oder in den zahlreichen Binnenwirtschaftsbetrieben, in der Kleiderkammer, den
Bezirksflickstuben, der Verschleißstelle, im Lumpenlager, bei der
Bucherfassungsgruppe, der Küchenbrigade, der Kartoffelschälerei, der
10   Knochenverwertung oder im Matratzenreferat, [etc.]

(Sebald 2001: 337)

The arbitrary diversity and sheer number of these activities mirrors the intim-
idating incomprehensibility of the whole lunatic enterprise. But the emotional
impact of this passage is more than the sum of its parts. For instance, the reference
to parlour games acquires grisly overtones in this context, which literal translation
cannot convey. Here is the published translation of the whole extract:

---

in one of the primitive factories set up, with a view to generating actual profit, by the
External Trade Section, assigned to the bandage-weaving workshop, to the handbag
and satchel assembly line, the production of horn buttons and other haberdashery
items, the manufacturing of wooden soles for footwear and of cowhide galoshes, to
5   the charcoal yard, the making of such games as Nine Men's Morris and Catch the Hat,
the splitting of mica, the shearing of rabbit fur, the bottling of ink dust, the silkworm-
breeding station run under the aegis of the SS or, alternatively, employed in one of the
operations serving the ghetto's internal economy, in the clothing store, for instance, in
one of the precinct mending and darning rooms, the shredding section, the rag depot,
10   the book reception and sorting unit, the kitchen brigade, the potato-peeling platoon,
the bone-crushing mill, the glue-boiling plant or the mattress department, [etc.]

(Sebald 2002: 333, trans. Bell)

The ST expressions that concern us here are the parlour games. '*Mühle*' is translated as 'Nine Men's Morris', and '*Fang den Hut*' as 'Catch the Hat', although these games are no longer well known. '*Mensch ärgere dich nicht*' is more of a problem. It is much the same game as 'Sorry', a children's variant of Ludo in which players take fiendish delight in thwarting one another and saying 'sorry' as they do so. Compared with 'Sorry', the German term has greater potential for exquisitely polite malicious glee. This is perhaps why '*Mensch ärgere dich nicht*' has been **omitted** from the translation. The loss is, however, very successfully compensated for, together with another loss incurred in the translation of '*Mühle*'.

Although nothing in the etymology of 'Nine Men's Morris' suggests it, the reference to a group of men and the collocation of 'men' with 'morris' is likely to prompt an association with Morris dancing, a form of entertainment, and Nine Men's Morris is a sociable game. In this context, there is a potential irony in these TL connotations that might partly compensate for the loss of those in '*Mensch ärgere dich nicht*'. Even so, '*Mühle*' here has gruesome overtones that Nine Men's Morris certainly lacks. It acquires these in two stages. Firstly, this context of unremitting labour will, for some readers, awaken the basic sense of '*Mühle*' as 'mill' or 'grindstone', and so perhaps also the association of '*Knochenmühle*', in its colloquial figurative sense of a place of unremitting toil (as in e.g. '*der Betrieb ist die reinste Knochenmühle*'). But then, a few lines later, almost comically slipped in between potato-peeling and the mattress department, comes '*Knochenverwertung*', the 'utilisation' or 'exploitation' of bones. For many readers, this will clinch the implication of '*Knochenmühle*' in its literal sense as well as its figurative one—especially as the text is addressed to a public all too aware that the Nazis did sometimes literally 'process' the bodies of their exterminated victims.

Acceptable translations of '*Knochenverwertung*' here would be 'bone-processing' or 'recycling bones'. But the ST word offers a good opportunity to compensate for the loss incurred in translating '*Mühle*' as 'Nine Men's Morris'. This is what the translator has done, turning the abstract '-*verwertung*' element into specific physical instances of utilisation or processing and explicitly mentioning a bone-works: 'the bone-crushing mill, the glue-boiling plant', a kind of **explicitation** strategy. The TT is certainly less economical than the ST, and goes into explicit, concrete detail where the ST is implicit, abstract and generic. Yet the translator's chosen solution triumphantly compensates for the loss incurred in the **omission** of '*Mensch ärgere dich nicht*' and in the innocent associations of 'Nine Men's Morris'.

The Theresienstadt examples mostly involve problems posed by connotations. But connotation is not the only thing that can necessitate compensation. Compensation often solves problems posed by grammatical structures. A common problem is the difference between SL and TL verb systems as in the following example involving the German subjunctive, taken from Bernhard Schlink's *Der Vorleser* (1997), translated as *The Reader* (2003) by the Scottish-American translator Carol Brown Janeway. Five women are on trial for an alleged war crime. One of them is Hanna, with whom the narrator, the law student Michael, has a complex relationship. Michael attends the proceedings. Eventually, the charges are read out:

> In der zweiten Woche wurde die Anklage verlesen. Die Verlesung dauerte eineinhalb
> Tage—eineinhalb Tage Konjunktiv. Die Angeklagte zu eins habe . . ., sie habe ferner
> . . ., weiter habe sie . . ., dadurch habe sie den Tatbestand des Paragraphen
> soundsoviel erfüllt, ferner habe sie diesen Tatbestand und jenen Tatbestand . . ., sie
> 5   habe auch rechtswidrig und schuldhaft gehandelt. Hanna war die Angeklagte zu vier.
>
> (Schlink 1997: 101)

There is an acute problem here. Michael comments on the special form of language used in the reading of the charges—'*eineinhalb Tage Konjunktiv*'—and gives six examples. This *Konjunktiv I* is used for certain limited special purposes, is formal, and is instantly recognised. The convention of using it for reported speech is nowhere more scrupulously observed than in reporting unproven allegations. Yet, although it is utterly conventional in this situation, Michael deliberately emphasises it, with the dash and repeated '*eineinhalb*'. The suggestion is that a day and a half of this stuff is highly tedious, and that the linguistic impersonality does not reflect the emotional reality of the position the defendants find themselves in.

For translating subjunctives, there are some recognised procedures. However, for '*eineinhalb Tage Konjunktiv*' the translator does have a choice: between a literal and a more creative solution. The former would be technically accurate, but would baffle most English readers as English uses means other than the subjunctive to signal reported speech. It would also not account for Michael's reaction. A contextually more imaginative translation could compensate for the loss by expressing Michael's reaction through other means. The first course is, however, taken in the published TT:

> In the second week, the indictment was read out. It took a day and a half to read—a
> day and a half in the subjunctive. The first defendant is alleged to have. . . .
> Furthermore she is alleged. . . . In addition, she is alleged. . . . Thus she comes under the
> necessary conditions of paragraph so-and-so, furthermore she is alleged to have
> 5   committed this and that act. . . . She is alleged to have acted illegally and culpably.
> Hanna was the fourth defendant.
>
> (Schlink 2003: 103, trans. Janeway)

The legal jargon and the repetition of 'is alleged' convey oppressive formality, so some of the ST effect is preserved. But can one compensate for the loss of Michael's attitude? To drop the term 'subjunctive' might be a pity, since there could be some TL readers who do understand its implications. One possibility, then, would be to embed the key word in an exegetic translation:

> During the second week the charges were read out. The reading took a day and a half.
> A day and a half of the stiff subjunctive verbs used for indictments: Prisoner no. 1 is
> alleged to have. . . . It is further alleged that she. . . . Subsequently, it is alleged, she. . . .
> In so doing, it is alleged, she committed a felony as defined in Subsection such and
> 5   such. . . . She is further alleged to have committed a felony in terms of Subsection this
> and Subsection that. . . . She is charged with having acted unlawfully and with malice
> aforethought. Hanna was Prisoner no. 4.

'Stiff subjunctive verbs' suggests there is something alien about the legal language, and the liberal injection of TL legal jargon gives a flavour of this. So, although an important ST effect is lost in the literal translation of '*Konjunktiv*' (assuming the TT reader has no relevant knowledge of German grammar), there is some compensation for that in the rest of the sentence. This solution has a serious drawback, however: it contains no subjunctives. A better exegetic rendering might therefore be to drop reference to the subjunctive and to compensate in a different way: 'The reading took a day and a half—one and a half days of the stuffy language used for indictments'. The switch to 'one and a half days' draws extra attention to the length of time, and so prepares the way for 'stuffy'. We preferred 'stuffy' to alternatives like 'stiff', 'starchy' or 'pompous' because it has stronger connotations of the stifling atmosphere of a boring courtroom. Once this atmosphere is set, the rest of the published TT can be used, because there is no longer any need for extra jargon.

Omitting the rather dry reference to the subjunctive and its associations is therefore a translation loss, but keeping it would arguably be a bigger one; a suitable **paraphrase** is substituted in order to compensate for this loss. However, it is important to note that this is the full extent of the compensation in this example. The use of 'is alleged' to render '*habe*' is not really a case of compensation. Certainly, 'she is alleged' is more redolent of the courtroom than 'she is said' or 'it is claimed that', but that is simply a matter of deciding on the correct conventional expression for the context.

Concluding remarks

The examples we have analysed illustrate three of the most common features of compensation. The first is that it generally (but not always) involves a change in place, the TT effect often occurring in a different textual position—relative to other features in the TT—from the corresponding item in the ST. Not all our examples clearly show this, but the '*Mühle*'/'*Mensch ärgere dich nicht*' compensation is a particularly good case of a distributed or 'displaced' (Harvey 1995: 72) solution.

Compensation usually also entails a change in 'economy', which has been characterised as 'compensation by merging' or 'compensation by splitting' (Hervey and Higgins 1992). In the first case, the TT feature will be shorter than the corresponding ST one. More often, though, ST features have to be spread over a relatively longer stretch of the TT, whether continuous or divided into parts. This is almost inevitable when there is any element of exegetic translation. This, too, is seen in all our examples.

Finally, it is useful, following Harvey (1995), to distinguish between the desired effect of the compensatory strategy in conveying irony, humour, a hidden threat, and the device or devices used to achieve it, ranging from phonic through lexical to grammatical. The ST and TT devices can be the same, e.g. an idiom aimed at a humorous effect in the ST may be replaced by a different idiom in the TT, but still an idiom, or different, e.g. the loss incurred through the absence of a grammatical feature may be compensated by the addition of a word with a particular semantic load, or, a ST rhyme or pun may have to be replaced with a different form of word-play. Compensation may also involve making explicit in the TT what is implicit in the ST, or vice versa. It may involve substituting abstract for concrete, or concrete for abstract. All these sorts of change may be confined to single words, but they more usually extend to whole phrases, sentences or even paragraphs. Sometimes, indeed, a whole text may be affected, as in Practical 6.2 below.

To conclude, the question of whether and how to compensate can never be considered in and for itself, in isolation from other crucial factors: context, style, genre, the function of the ST, the function of the TT, the TT's readership, etc. Compensation is needed whenever consideration of these factors confronts the transla-tor with a challenging compromise and is unlikely to be successful if inspiration is not allied with analysis. It is not a matter of putting any old fine-sounding phrase into a TT in case any weaknesses have crept in, but of countering a specific, clearly defined loss with a specific, clearly defined compensatory gain. So, before decid-ing on how to compensate for a translation loss, it is best to assess as precisely as possible what the loss is and why it matters both in its immediate context and in the TT as a whole. When all the possibilities have been reviewed, the decisive question is: 'Will the proposed compensation make the TT *more* fit for its purpose, or *less*?'

Further reading

Low, Peter 2016. *Translating Song: Lyrics and Texts*. London and New York: Routledge [see Practical 6.2].

Stolze, Radegundis 1999. *Die Fachübersetzung. Eine Einführung*. Tübingen: Gunter Narr [Section 7.3.2.2: Kompensatorische Übersetzungsverfahren, pp. 224–7; details many relevant and well-illustrated strategies.].

Thome, Gisela 2002. 'Methoden des Kompensierens in der literarischen Übersetzung', in Thome, G., Giehl, C. and Gerzymisch-Arbogast, H. (eds) *Kultur und Übersetzung. Methodologische Probleme des Kulturtransfers*. Tübingen: Narr, pp. 299–314.

Practical 6

6.1 TRANSLATION: COMPANY REPORT

Assignment

i   You are translating Part 1 of the Audi AG annual report from which Practical 2.2 was taken. (Some further details about the report are given there.) Discuss the decisions that you have to make before starting detailed translation of this ST extract, paying particular attention to the constraints imposed on your TT by the layout requirements explained in the contextual information.

ii   Translate the text into English.

iii   Discuss the main decisions of detail you took, paying special attention to cases where you used compensation.

iv   Compare your TT with the published one, which will be made available to you by your tutor.

Contextual information

The ST for this assignment is advertising copy carefully laid out to accompany the '*Technik*' chapter's photographs and informational text (see Practical 2.2). The car featured is the *A8 L 12-Zylinder*. The ST starts on a left-hand page, and then stretches across all six A4 pages of the chapter as a kind of continuously developing header; thus it is split into six fragments, one to a page, each marked off by suspension points before and after. Certain words are printed in larger type—one on each page except the first. On each of pages 19–23, the ST is printed in a single line across the page without undue stretching. Audi require the English-language edition of their company report to be laid out exactly like the German edition. The numbers we supply in square brackets are the page numbers of the original publication.

ST

[18] Er ist gewohnt, vorn . . .

[19] . . . mitzufahren. Vorwärtsdrang ist seine typische Eigenschaft. Stets und zu jeder Stunde . . .

[20] . . . Die Gewissheit, gut zu sein: Anspruch des Gewinners. Hochschalten in
5 den sechsten Gang . . .

[21] . . . Entschlossenheit heißt Format beweisen. Führen mit Stil und Klasse. Im Detail und mit Niveau . . .

[22] . . . Genau wie sein A8. Blinker links. Sanfte Beschleunigung. Sicher lenkt er auf die Überholspur . . .

10 [23] . . . Erfolg mit allen Sinnen genießen. Jeden Tag aufs Neue. Für heute ist er erst einmal am Ziel.

(Audi 2004a: 18–23)

6.2 TRANSLATION ANALYSIS: SONG

Assignment

Comparing the ST and TT printed here, examine the main cases where the translator seems to have used compensation to alleviate translation loss. Say why you think the compensation is successful or unsuccessful; if you think it could be improved, give your own translation, and explain why you think it is better. Include in your analysis cases where you think that significant translation loss is incurred without the translator apparently having tried to alleviate it with compensation; give your own translation of these cases, and explain why you think it is better. Keep in mind that the English version of the song will need to be performed to the same music as the original German. You can find versions of the song performed on YouTube, including by its author/composer, Wolf Biermann.

Contextual information

It will be useful to bear in mind that the ST is a song with a ballad-like rhythm which the translator imitates fairly closely. As a singer-songwriter in the GDR, Biermann's critical political songs made him a thorn in the flesh of the regime throughout the 1960s and 1970s. In 1976, while he was performing in the Federal Republic, he was stripped of his citizenship by the East German authorities. Although banned from the East German media, Biermann's critical, acid songs, proclaiming his own personal communism and his opposition to hypocrisy and degradation, continued to penetrate every corner of German culture. Kunststück is one of his lighter pieces, but it is characteristic in its blend of politics with celebration of a love of life and of the common man.

ST	TT
Wenn ich mal heiß bin	When I get hot, son
Wenn ich mal heiß bin	When I get hot, son
lang ich mir ne Wolke runter	I reach up and grab a cloud
und wring sie über mir aus.	and wring it out over me.
Kalte Dusche.	Ice-cold shower.
6 Kunststück.	Piece a cake.
Wenn ich mal kalt bin	When I get cold, son
Wenn ich mal kalt bin	When I get cold, son
lang ich mir die Sonne runter	I reach up and grab the sun
und steck sie mir ins Jackett.	and pop it under my coat.
Kleiner Ofen.	Little oven.
12 Kunststück.	Piece a cake.
Wenn ich bei ihr bin	When I'm with her, son
Wenn ich bei ihr bin	When I'm with her, son
schwimmen Wolken mit uns runter	clouds come floating down, son, with us
rollt die Sonne gleich mit.	and the sun comes down too.
Das ist Liebe.	That's love for you.
18 Kunststück.	Piece a cake.
Wenn ich mal müd bin	When I get tired, son
Wenn ich mal müd bin	When I get tired, son
lang ich mir den lieben Gott runter	I reach up and grab the dear Lord
und er singt mir was vor.	so he'll sing me a song.
Engel weinen.	Angels weeping.
24 Kunststück.	Piece a cake.
Wenn ich mal voll bin	When I get pissed, son
Wenn ich mal voll bin	When I get pissed, son
geh ich kurz zum Teufel runter	I nip down to see the devil
und spendier Stalin ein Bier	and buy old Stalin a beer.
Armer Alter	Poor old bugger.
30 Nebbich.	Nebbish.
Wenn ich mal tot bin	When I am dead, son
Wenn ich mal tot bin	When I am dead, son
werd ich Grenzer und bewache	I'll be keeping an eye on the border
die Grenz zwischen Himmel und Höll.	the border of heaven and hell.
Ausweis bitte!	Passports ready!
36 Kunststück.	Piece a cake.
(Biermann 1977: 70–2)	(Biermann 1977: 71–3, trans. Steve Gooch)

References

Primary

Adler, L. 1927. 'Siedlung in Berlin-Britz', *Wasmuths Hefte für Baukunst*, 11(10).
Audi 2004a. *Geschäftsbericht 2003*. Ingolstadt: Audi AG.
Biermann, Wolf 1977. 'Kunststück', in Gooch, Steve (trans) *Wolf Biermann: Poems and Ballads*. London: Pluto Press.
Schlink, B. 1997. *Der Vorleser*. Zürich: Diogenes.
Schlink, B. 2003. *The Reader*. Translated by Janeway, Carol Brown. London: Phoenix.
Sebald, W. G. 2001. *Austerlitz*. München: Hanser.
Sebald, W. G. 2002. *Austerlitz*. Translated by Bell, Anthea. London: Penguin.

Secondary

Baker, Mona 2011. *In Other Words*. 2nd edn. London: Routledge.
Byrne, Jody 2012. *Scientific and Technical Translation Explained: A Nuts and Bolts Guide for Beginners*. London and New York: Routledge.
Harvey, Keith 1995. 'A descriptive framework for compensation', *The Translator*, 1(1), pp. 65–86.
Harvey, Keith 1998. 'Compensation and the brief in a non-literary translation: Theoretical implications and pedagogical applications', *Target*, 10(2), pp. 267–90.
Hervey, Sándor and Higgins, Ian 1992. *Thinking Translation: A Course in Translation Method, French to English*. 2nd edn. London and New York: Routledge.
Newmark, Peter 1988. *A Textbook of Translation*. New York: Prentice Hall.

Section C

Formal properties of texts

So far in this book, much of our attention has been directed towards the translation as a product, thinking primarily about the translation as a piece of writing which will have to function adequately in the target language system and which meets the needs of a particular brief. In the following group of chapters we turn our attention back to the source text, in a sense, and ask how linguistic structures at many levels contribute to the construction of texts and how a deeper understanding of those structures can help us identify, account for and manage inevitable systemic differences that arise when moving between German and English.

We begin with an overview of lexical meaning (Chapter 7), the aspect of meaning with which students may feel they are most familiar. We then move on to the largest unit of meaning, the text (Chapter 8), a perspective which can help to contextualise many translation decisions and which students are less likely to have considered. The importance of information ordering—i.e. ordering beyond grammatical constraints—within the sentence is considered in Chapter 9, before we tackle words and phrases from a grammatical perspective (Chapter 10). The final chapter in this section deals with how the sounds of words can impact on written translation (Chapter 11).

7 Meaning and translation

Translation is centrally concerned with interpreting and (re)creating aspects of meaning in texts, often using a variety of sources ranging from other texts to codified collections such as dictionaries (see Chapter 12 on Research and resources). In monolingual dictionaries, lexicographers try to capture the meaning, or in most cases, the meanings, of words and expressions (whether general-purpose or specialised) using definitions and, less helpfully, synonyms. In bilingual dictionaries in print or online—often the first and favourite choice of student translators—definitions are rare and lists of undifferentiated equivalents common.

In this chapter we consider various relations of meaning, mainly between words and expressions, and show how even some apparently straightforward 'basic' meanings can be problematic. Building on the discussion of equivalence in Chapter 3, we suggest some ways of dealing with the translation issues which arise.

From basic denotative meaning to translation strategies

The central meaning of a word or expression is a matter of categories into which a language divides the totality of experience. This is usually called the 'denotative' aspect of meaning and is a characteristic of nouns. Thus, the basic meaning of the word 'umbrella' derives from the fact that there are similar objects exhibiting the same essential characteristics—and all sorts of other objects that are excluded from this category. There are many cases, however, where a particular class of objects can be designated by more than one linguistic expression, i.e. by **synonyms**, such as 'gamp', an archaic word for 'umbrella'. Denotative meaning (i.e. of nouns) can be broadly understood as the codified dictionary definition, which sets out the meaning potential for communicative use of actual word forms in texts—i.e. the act of referring—where particular nuances or selective aspects of the meaning are realised, 'activated' or foregrounded in context. This distinction (see Lyons 1977: 206–15) goes some way to accounting for the fact that the same ST word might be translated differently in different TTs.

For practical purposes, we shall take it that comparisons of denotative meaning can also be made between different languages. For example, in most contexts 'father' and '*Vater*' in the sense of male parent cover exactly the same range of essential characteristics, and are therefore **equivalent** in terms of the class of objects in the world which they denote in specific instances. Nevertheless, there are, as we have seen in Chapter 3, a range of possible types or degrees of 'equivalence' and translation strategies for dealing with these. In a sense, the only true formal 'equivalence' is the one-to-one type. We can recall the other types as one-to-many, many-to-one, one-to-part, or one-to-none.

One way of characterising the one-to-many and many-to-one types of denotative equivalence is to regard the translation strategy for the former as 'particularising' and for the latter as 'generalising'. For example, depending on situation or context, the English word 'exit' has to be translated either as '*Ausfahrt*' or as '*Ausgang*'. The English word is a kind of interlingual **hyperonym** i.e. it is wider and more general than either of the German ones. Translating from German to English, on the other hand, the converse is the case, i.e. '*Ausfahrt*' has to be translated as 'exit', with the discretion to modify the generic word to form the more specific **hyponym** 'motorway exit', if required by the context. A generalising translation is acceptable if the omitted specification is either unimportant or is implied in the TT context. Even items in the natural world can be classed differently in each language. The German terms '*Falter*' or '*Nachtfalter*', for example, are both subsumed under the more general 'moth', but with one major exception. When holes are gnawed in stored clothes, German requires the specific term '*Motte*', while English is still content with 'moth'.

Processes as well as objects can display the same many-to-one relationship. For example, German has two well-known standard terms for 'to eat': '*essen*', used of humans, and '*fressen*', of animals; this lexical lack of specificity in English is in most cases unlikely to cause any problems, unless an insult to a person is intended by the metaphorical use of '*fressen*' ('gorge' instead of 'eat' might work here or a compensatory **addition**, 'like a pig').

Moving on to partial equivalence (one-to-part), we can cite as an example the English word 'anticlimax'. According to *Collins* (in the English-German section) '*Enttäuschung*' is given as a translation of 'anticlimax'. Significantly, under '*Enttäuschung*' in the German-English section, the same dictionary does not give 'anticlimax', but only 'disappointment' (plus 'let-down' in a phrase). The fact is that there is no single German word that covers exactly the same semantic range as 'anticlimax'. In such cases, researching the use of both the SL and TL words in texts (online using a search engine) or in online dictionaries which include contextual examples (e.g. Leo or Linguee, Chapter 12) is recommended.

A generalising or particularising translation will only be *un*acceptable if the TL does offer a suitable alternative, or if omitting or adding the specification creates a clash with the overall context of the ST or TT. Compare the German text below—the first paragraph of a concise report—with the TT that accompanied it:

ST	TT
Die Ultraschallprüfung von Walzmaterial auf Inhomogenitäten ist ein wichtiges Anliegen der qualitätsüberwachenden und der stahlerzeugenden und verarbeitenden Betriebe der Stahlindustrie. (ECSC—HOESCH 1987a: 507)	The ultrasonic testing of rolled products is an important request for the quality assurance of steel producing and manufacturing factories of the steel industry. (ECSC—HOESCH 1987b: 507)

Conspicuous though the anomalous 'request' may appear to be, the unwary translator can be led into making the wrong choice if relying on a bilingual dictionary which simply lists possible equivalents. The *Collins English-German Dictionary*, for instance, lists: 'request; matter of concern' for '*Anliegen*' (1999); nor does the current monolingual *Duden Online Wörterbuch* help: '*Angelegenheit, die jemandem am Herzen liegt; Wunsch, Bitte*'. Carrying out a further back-check on 'request' would produce '*Ersuchen*', not '*Anliegen*', providing further evidence of the complex web of meanings both within and between languages which dictionaries fail to capture. A more accurate TT would be: 'Ultrasonic testing of rolled products is a major concern/priority for the quality assurance, production and manufacturing branches of the steel industry'. (The TT's silence with regard to '*Inhomogenitäten*' is probably not an error but a generalising translation in line with industry practice.)

In a second example, the issue is whether particularisation should be avoided altogether. A leaflet outlining 700 years of Düsseldorf church history for visitors required strict economy of language combined with readability. Faced with the ST's '*Schließung der meisten Klöster*', the translator has to choose between the fussy-sounding particularising translation 'monasteries and convents' and a vaguer generalising rendering such as 'religious houses'—preferring the latter on balance, given the genre.

Hard to categorise is another type of semantic German-English contrast which is subject to context. This is a case of English being more general than German. For example, the verbs '*liegen*' and '*stehen*' have their dictionary equivalents, their basic meanings being 'to lie' and 'to stand'. But they can also occur with the primary function of locating an object, as in '*Das Buch liegt auf dem Tisch*' and '*Die Vase steht auf dem Tisch*'. In English, the tendency in such cases is to use the verb 'to be' as a locating verb, a semantically weaker and less specific option: 'The book is on the table' and 'The vase is on the table'. What is semantically important for the German, i.e. whether the object concerned is horizontal ('*liegen*') or vertical ('*stehen*'), is irrelevant in the English. Using 'lie' or 'stand' is not ruled out, but would result in a semantically marked construction: for example, 'the vase was lying on the table' suggests an accident of some kind.

Of contexts, dictionaries and texts

From the previously-mentioned it should be clear that dictionaries are tools and resources, but imperfect ones. One reason we spent time over these examples was to draw attention to the potential translation pitfalls even in apparently straight-forward cases. Another was to encourage an attitude of constructive suspicion towards all dictionaries, monolingual as well as bilingual. Dictionaries and other lexical resources are indispensable in suggesting potential meanings, but caution is advised in terms of how the context influences the actual meanings in particular texts and formulations.

It is well known that monolingual dictionaries often disagree over basic mean-ings. With abstract terms in particular, an element of subjectivity is often involved, but the same applies to many concrete terms, such as 'dish' and 'bowl', 'pond' and 'pool'. Bilingual dictionaries, too, often suggest very different TL possibili-ties for given words or phrases. Thus, unlike the *Collins*, the *Oxford-Duden* gives for 'anticlimax' not '*Enttäuschung*' but two suggestions which—depending on how you define 'anticlimax' in the first place—are either one-to-many or a partial overlap in terms of equivalence: '*Abstieg*' and '*Abfall*'. There is less disagreement over technical terms; both these dictionaries give '*Antiklimax*' for 'anticlimax' in its specialised literary-rhetorical sense. Clearly, it is vital to remember that, except in the case of some highly specific technical terms, no dictionary can cover all the possibilities for translating a given word or expression, and even technical terms evolve in meaning and usage. What all this means in practice is that translators often need to check meanings in more than one source, including the Internet as a huge resource of usage in context, and with friends, colleagues and experts—but also that the final decision is the translator's own responsibility (see Chapter 12 on Research and resources).

Let us conclude this section with an example which clearly illustrates how familiar words can face translators with troublesome issues of basic meaning that are not easy to schematise. As an example, take the apparently transparent but potentially problematic term '*Arbeitsplatz*'. We start from a revision job (see Chapter 16) on an unsatisfactory draft TT of a text from the *Bundesverband der deutschen Industrie*, from which the following is an extract:

ST	TT
Denn intelligente Kommunikationssysteme [. . .] führen zu einem Umbau der internen und externen Organisationsstrukturen der Unternehmen und öffentlichen 5 Verwaltungen, durch den die Arbeitsplätze produktiver gestaltet werden.	Intelligent communication systems [. . .] change the internal and external organisational structures of enterprises and public administration that makes it possible to structure workplaces more productively.
(BDI 2004a: 56)	(unpublished draft TT)

The draft is both wordy and dense; consequently, the apparently straightfor-ward '*Arbeitsplätze*' might not attract immediate attention, although its collocate '*gestalten*' should alert the reviser to at least two possibilities: might the ST author have been referring to the restructuring or redesign of people's jobs, rather than of the places where they work? The collocation '*Arbeitsplätze schaffen*', for exam-ple, should be (but is not always) translated as 'create jobs'. A major bilingual specialist dictionary translates '*Arbeitsplatz umgestalten*' as 'to redesign a job'. But very commonly too '*Arbeitsplatz*' means literally the physical place where people work (whether 'workstation' or 'working environment' more generally). Online research for '*Arbeitsplätze gestalten*' reveals examples illustrating ergonomic issues, i.e. the literal sense of physical 'workplaces', as well as the more abstract 'jobs'. While these two senses—lexically distinguished in English—seem sharply demarcated in their *Duden* definition, that does not preclude the inclusion of both senses when the term is used in a text. In fact, it turns out that neither 'jobs' nor 'workplaces' is entirely adequate: for the record, the published TT included both terms.

Beyond denotative meaning

Denotative meaning is only one aspect of lexical meaning. Referential content can, and more often than not is, accompanied by various associative meanings such as emotional colouring, social and personal viewpoints, cultural assumptions and so on. Intertextual references or echoes are particularly effective reminders of the multilayered nature of texts because they specifically recall another reading or listening experience. Finding words to convey the echoes and overtones of words and expressions is often a crucial but challenging translation issue, as these meanings can be unstable.

Such overtones have been variously categorised and labelled: we can think of them as associations which, over and above the denotative meaning of a word or expression, form part of its overall meaning. Here we distinguish five major types of meaning beyond denotation (some of them adapted from Leech 1981).

The first type is **connotation**—probably the most general type—which is concerned with emotional associations of various kinds. This type of meaning is sometimes seen as more peripheral than the more stable, more context-dependent and less open-ended denotative meaning (see, for instance, the German alternative designation for *Konnotation: Nebenbedeutung*). However, an inappropriate choice of word for a particular context can lead to a serious breakdown in communication. Translators therefore have to tread carefully. For example, while '*Visage*' and '*Gesicht*' are denotatively equivalent to 'face', the former is clearly pejorative, the latter neutral. We refer you back to Chapter 3 for more examples.

The second type is **allusive meaning**, often implicit and created when an expression evokes a saying, quotation, object, person or event based on the author's assumption that the intended readers will share the requisite knowledge or experience. So referring to a particular male friend as '*ein wahrer Romeo*' would evoke the familiar image of a keen romancer of women—alluding to Shakespeare's famous play—without actually saying this.

Once spotted and understood, an appropriate TC allusive meaning should ideally be found, although in practice some form of **compensation** is often needed as allusions can be highly cultural and less well known than our Romeo example. A simple example can be found in an advertisement for a German electrical firm, where the text contains the slogan 'SEIN WISSEN IST IHR SANFTES

RUHEKISSEN', evidently based on an allusion to the proverbial saying '*Ein gutes Gewissen ist ein sanftes Ruhekissen*', indicating that: 'This firm is so conscientious and reliable that the customer's responsibility may be transferred to it without a qualm'. The German proverb seems to have no well-known counterpart in English; even if there were one, neatly weaving an allusion to it into an advertising slogan would tax the translator's ingenuity. The most practical approach here would probably be to use **compensation**. Here are two possibilities: 'SAFE HANDS MAKE LIGHT WORK', and 'RELAX! HE'S GOT A GOOD HEAD FOR LIGHTS!'

For the ST author, allusion is a useful shorthand. It may be casual and incidental; it may be humorous. In Martin Walser's *Ein fliehendes Pferd*, a bumptious small-boat sailor becalmed on a leaden day curses the *Bodensee* (Lake Constance) for its lack of challenge: '*Das sei vielleicht was für Opas, in deren Wipfeln Ruh ist*' (Walser 1978: 106). The allusion is to Goethe's famous lines '*Über allen Gipfeln/ ist Ruh,/In allen Wipfeln/Spürest du/Kaum einen Hauch*'—lines jumbled by Walser to underline the speaker's savage mood. A published translation has recourse to Cardinal Newman: 'It might be all right for old fogies for whom the fever of life is over' (Walser 1980: 76, trans. Vennewitz).

Another type of associated meaning is **attitudinal** (sometimes also called 'affective meaning'), the part of the overall meaning of an expression that consists of some personal or widespread *attitude to the referent*. This type of meaning is sometimes hard to distinguish from connotative meaning, as we may rely on the connotations conventionally associated with particular word choices in order to express our emotions. Leech calls this a 'parasitic' category (1981: 16). Attitudinal connotations can be important when related to people, but can also be used to refer to a system or practice or way of thinking. Take the following extract from a historical account of the Nazis' *Aktion T4* euthanasia programme:

> Die Angehörigen erhielten nach einem ausgeklügelten Geheimhaltungssystem gefälschte Todesnachrichten, die sogenannten 'Trostbriefe', die eine 'Erlösung' der Kranken von ihrem Leid suggerierten. Dennoch kam es innerhalb der Bevölkerung zu einer erheblichen Beunruhigung wegen der Krankenmorde.
>
> (Hohendorf et al.: unpublished)

The term '*ausgeklügelt*' might be rendered by any of the following: 'cleverly worked out', 'carefully devised', 'ingenious', 'sophisticated', 'crafty', 'cunning', etc. How do we go about choosing the best of them in terms of attitudinal meaning in this particular context where the well-chosen word signals calculated ruthlessness? The text as a whole has an underlying single line of argumentation, a restrained but critical account of the euthanasia programme. As also in instances of connotative meaning, context is crucial; the translator's responsibility is to mirror, as faithfully as possible, the attitudinal values implicit or expressed in the text as a whole. The tone of the Hohendorf article on the Nazi *T4* programme is predominantly factual and objective. The relatively restrained tone of the ST means the translator must not introduce explicitly strong attitudinal meanings, although there is no case for introducing the weak *positive* attitudes implicit in the first three options; and the last two, while not excessively pejorative are unsuitable, 'crafty' suggesting triviality and 'cunning' being potentially allusive ('a cunning plan'). 'Sophisticated' thus arguably represents the best option, in keeping with the cool tone.

The fourth type of associated meaning is **collocative meaning**, whereby a word acquires associations through its habitual co-occurrence with some other word; for translation, it is important to remember that we cannot assume the same collocational pattern in the SL and the TL. For instance, whilst 'traffic' and 'transport' might be considered synonyms by virtue of their occurrence as possible equivalents of '*Verkehr*', they are rarely, if ever, interchangeable. So '*öffentlicher Vekehr*' is 'public transport' (not 'public traffic') and '*starker Verkehr*' is 'heavy traffic' (not 'heavy transport') (*Duden Online Wörterbuch*). Collocative habit is not easy to predict or analyse: You can 'shut' or 'close' a door in a literal sense, but metaphorically only 'close' a chapter in your life, and where a German road-sign reads 'STRASSE GESPERRT', the translation will normally be 'ROAD CLOSED', not 'ROAD SHUT'. It is easy for the unwary translator to slip into translationese in such cases.

It often happens that an expression acquires a meaning over and above its denotative meaning by the fact that its form calls to mind the sense of a polyseme, i.e. a closely related word with the same form but a different sense, often metaphorically derived. This is usually called **reflected meaning**. An often-cited example compares the connotative difference between the synonyms 'Holy Spirit' and 'Holy Ghost' (see Leech 1981: 16). The semantic link between 'Holy Ghost' and 'ghost' in the sense of 'spook' or 'spectre' means that that particular reflected meaning is latent in the term 'Holy Ghost'; likewise, the 'spirit' element in 'Holy Spirit' may call to mind the use of 'spirit' to mean 'distilled liquor'. It needs to be emphasised, however, that reflected meanings, because they come from a different field, are normally *latent*—or dormant—associations, and are activated by context, as in the first line of the well-known hymn: 'Thine be the glory, risen, conquering Son'. Even without the context of traditional Easter symbolism, the reflected meaning of 'sun' latent in its homophone 'Son' is triggered by the word 'risen'. Homophone pairs are unlikely to be reproduced in the other language, and so **compensation** would be the most likely translation strategy.

While an awareness of the various types of associative meaning can be a potentially useful analytical tool for the translator, they are not always easy to distinguish in practice. In fact, the academic literature on lexical semantics presents many different categorisations. What is important when translating is to recognise that certain lexical choices have meanings beyond what they denote or refer to. Failing to recognise such a meaning in a ST—meant perhaps as an insult or as a sign of approval—and thereby misrepresenting the intention of the author in the TT can seriously damage the quality of a translation. Any translator therefore needs to read as widely as possible in both languages and to develop a broad and sound general knowledge, as well as good antennae in order to know when to research further. Codified resources such as dictionaries can help in this research, but seeing how words work in running text is equally, if not more important.

Concluding remarks

This chapter has dealt with the slippery issue of lexical meaning, focusing on the way in which words and expressions are used and translated. Some of the translation strategies discussed in earlier chapters—e.g. addition, compensation of various kinds—have been discussed here and will crop up again as you work your way through the practical assignments, as will the intralingual relations between senses such as synonymy, hyponymy, polysemy and so on. What we hope to have demonstrated is that words and expressions can be complex in the way they map meanings, not only between languages but also within languages. There is rarely, if ever, a straightforward one-to-one relation between meaning and form: put simply, one form can have several meanings (homonymy/polysemy) and one meaning can have several forms (synonymy). This can even be the case in the vocabularies of *Fachsprachen*. This, and the differences in the ways in which form-meaning relations map our understanding of the world—both abstract and material—in each language (types of 'equivalence'), are the norm, not the exception. Dictionaries can only capture some of this complexity, and as we have tried to show, should be treated as a starting point in your meaning research, not as the endpoint.

Further reading

Beaton, Kenneth Bruce 1996. *A Practical Dictionary of German Synonyms*. Oxford: Oxford University Press.
Durrell, Martin 2000. *Using German Synonyms*. Cambridge: Cambridge University Press.
Hatim, Basil and Munday, Jeremy 2004. *Translation: An Advanced Resource Book*. London and New York: Routledge [See Unit 5: The analysis of meaning—Introduction; Extension; Exploration.].
Leppihalme, Ritva 1997. *Culture Bumps: An Empirical Approach to the Translation of Allusions*. Clevedon: Multilingual Matters.

Practical 7

7.1 ONE-TO-MANY MEANINGS: THE CASE OF '*SICHERHEIT*'

Contextual information

The German word '*Sicherheit*' has three obvious possible translations in English: 'certainty', 'safety' and 'security'. We are concerned here with the 'safety'/'security' distinction: both are often included under a single sense in dictionary entries. See, for instance, the entry for '*Sicherheit*' in *Collins* (accessible through the online dictionary resource Reverso). German native speakers often have difficulty seeing any distinction—as there is only one word in German—but the two English words are not necessarily interchangeable: 'security services' and 'safety services' are rather different. Many organisations advise visitors or employees on various regulations accordingly: 'For your safety and security'.

Assignment

i   Compile a definition (in English) for each English word to show a German native speaker what it means (acknowledging your sources).
ii   Find appropriate examples (a phrase, a clause or a short sentence) to illustrate these meanings (acknowledging your sources).
iii   Find examples of how '*Sicherheit*' has been translated in texts (literary and/ or specialised) and to evaluate these translations.

In tackling your task, you may want to consult more German-English bilingual dictionaries, monolingual dictionaries in each language, as well as online text corpora or simply use a search engine to find texts—both German and English—in which the words are used.

Useful websites to start your research include the following (more detailed information can be found in Chapter 12; the URLs are included below in the References):

- British National Corpus
- COSMAS (Corpus Search, Management and Analysis System) at the Institut für deutsche Sprache*
- Leo
- Linguee
- Reverso
- Sketch Engine (looking up translations in a corpus of texts and their translations)**

  * You will need to register for COSMAS: see the overview page for more information at www.ids-mannheim.de/cosmas2/uebersicht.html
  ** You will need to register for Sketch Engine: a free 30-day trial is available at https://the.sketchengine.co.uk/register/trial

7.2 ANALYSING MEANING CHOICES: ART EXHIBITION LEAFLET

Assignment

i   Study the ST and published TT below and make a detailed analysis of examples which could be the result of the translation strategies outlined in this chapter to deal with various aspects of meaning. You are mainly concerned with lexical meaning but some structural issues affecting meaning are also evident.

ii   Where possible, give a revised TT that is a better translation, and explain your decisions.

Contextual information

The ST and accompanying TT come from a leaflet issued by the Bucerius Kunst Forum in Hamburg announcing an art exhibition that ran there from 6 April to 13 July 2003 under the title *Lucas Cranach. Glaube, Mythologie und Moderne*. The exhibition was one of a series entitled *Alte Meister der europäischen Kunst*.

ST	TT

Alte Meister der europäischen Kunst
 Mit einer Ausstellung zum 450. Todestag
 von Lucas Cranach d.Ä. wird dieser
 Zyklus fortgesetzt. Zu sehen sind etwa
 5 100 Gemälde, Druckgraphiken und
 Bücher des großen deutschen Malers.
 Ihnen sind Cranach-Paraphrasen von
 Künstlern des 20. Jahrhunderts
 gegenübergestellt, darunter Picasso,
 10 Kirchner und Giacometti. In den
 kommenden Jahren werden weitere
 erstrangige Leistungen alter europäischer
 Kunst präsentiert: frühe Ikonen aus
 Nowgorod, spanische Malerei des
 15 Barock und Wolkenbilder des 19.
 Jahrhunderts.
                                  (Bucerius 2003: 2)
	Old Masters of European Art
	 This cycle continues with an exhibition
	 commemorating the 450th anniversary of
	 Lucas Cranach the Elder's death. Around
	 100 paintings, prints and books of the
	 great German master are on exhibit.
	 These are compared with Cranach
	 interpretations of 20th century artists
	 including Picasso, Kirchner and
	 Giacometti. In the near future, additional
	 first-rate endeavors of old European art
	 will be on display including early
	 Novgorod icons, Spanish Baroque
	 paintings and cloud paintings from the
	 19th century.
	                                  (Bucerius 2003: 2)

7.3 TRANSLATION: LEXICAL MEANING IN A SPECIALISED TEXT

Assignment

i   For publication in the English-speaking world, you are translating the policy document from which the following ST extract is taken. Discuss any decisions that you have to take before starting detailed translation of this text, and outline and justify the method you adopt.

ii   Translate the text into English.

iii Discuss the main decisions of detail you took, concentrating on noteworthy issues relating to lexical choices from the point of view of any of the types of meaning discussed in this chapter. Did you find any of the translation strategies outlined in the chapter helpful?

iv   Compare your TT with the published translation, which will be made available to you by your tutor.

Contextual information

The ST comes from the telecommunications chapter (III.7) of *Für ein attraktives Deutschland. Freiheit wagen—Fesseln sprengen*, published in 2004 by the Bundesverband der Deutschen Industrie e.V. The document presented the German employers' comprehensive programme for national economic recovery. Subsection headings throughout have the same grammatical structure as the § 7.1 heading, i.e. injunctions using an infinitive verb. There is an obvious misprint in the ST. The published text mentioned in (iv) is an excerpt from the BDI's own English version, *For an Attractive Germany. Venturing Freedom—Casting Off Shackles*.

ST

7.1 Wettbewerb und Liberalisierungserfolge langfristig sichern
Der Mobilfunk ist das beste Beispiel dafür, dass sich leistungsfähige Informations- und Kommunikationssysteme am schnellsten auf wettbewerblich organisierten Märkten für Telekommunikations-Infrastruktur und bei einem wettbewerblich organisierten Angebot
5 entsprechender Dienste entwickeln. In diesem Bereich führt der bestehende Wettbewerb (vier Infrastrukturwettbewerber und über 10 Service-Provider) zu einer marktgeleiteten Preisbildung. Für die Wahrung dieses Wettbewerbs reicht die Ex-Post-Kontrolle des allgemeinen Wettbewerbsrecht aus, um auftretenden Missbräuchen zu begegnen. Die Regulierung auch nur eines einzigen Marktes im Mobilfunk hätte weitreichende Folgen
10 für die betroffenen Unternehmen und für die im Wettbewerb entstandene Marktstruktur. Denn zusätzlich zum dafür erforderlichen Aufbau neuer Kostenrechnungssysteme und der damit verbundenen Bürokratie würden erfolgreiche Geschäftsmodelle in Frage gestellt. Im Hinblick auf Bestrebungen nach einer Preisregulierung im Mobilfunk gilt die grundsätzliche Forderung, dass der deutsche Gesetzgeber gegenüber
15 Regulierungsbestrebungen seitens der Europäischen Union klar Position zugunsten einer am Subsidiaritätsprinzip orientierten Ausgestaltung von Regulierungseingriffen bezieht.

(BDI 2004a: 56)

7.4 LEXICAL MEANING IN THE TRANSLATION OF POETRY

Assignment

i   Taking the expressions printed in bold, categorise and discuss their meaning in the context, keeping in mind the types of lexical meaning discussed in this chapter.

ii Translate lines 2–10 into English and compare with the translation which your tutor will provide OR find a published version to critique.

iii How helpful did you find the translation strategies outlined in this chapter for this particular genre? Do—or should—other strategies apply in poetry because of the tensions between form and meaning?

Contextual information

Paul Celan is the pseudonym of Paul Antschel, who was born in 1920 in Czernowitz, Romania, and died in 1970. His homeland became part of the Soviet Union in 1940 and was then occupied by the Germans. His Jewish origins meant ghetto and forced labour for him and disappearance to concentration camps for his parents. 'Todesfuge' was said by Siegbert Prawer to confound those who would divorce modern art from actuality. Leonard Forster, in a 1971 edition, described 'Todesfuge' as probably the most famous poem written in German since 1945. Many would still agree.

ST

TODESFUGE

Schwarze Milch der Frühe wir trinken sie abends
wir trinken sie mittags und morgens wir trinken sie nachts
wir trinken und trinken
5   wir schaufeln ein Grab in den Lüften da liegt man nicht eng
Ein Mann wohnt im Haus der **spielt mit den Schlangen** der schreibt der schreibt wenn
es dunkelt **nach Deutschland dein goldenes Haar Margarete**
er schreibt es und tritt vor das Haus und es **blitzen** die **Sterne** er pfeift eine Rüden herbei
er **pfeift seine Juden hervor** läßt schaufeln ein Grab in der Erde
10   er befiehlt uns **spielt auf nun zum Tanz**

Schwarze Milch der Frühe wir trinken dich nachts
wir trinken dich morgens und mittags wir trinken dich abends
wir trinken und trinken
Ein Mann wohnt im Haus der spielt mit den Schlangen der schreibt
15   der schreibt wenn es dunkelt nach Deutschland dein goldenes Haar Margarete
Dein aschenes Haar Sulamith wir schaufeln ein Grab in den Lüften da liegt man nicht
    eng

Er ruft stecht tiefer ins Erdreich ihr einen ihr andern singet und spielt
er greift nach dem Eisen im Gurt er schwingts **seine Augen sind blau**
stecht tiefer die Spaten ihr einen ihr andern spielt weiter zum Tanz auf

20   Schwarze Milch der Frühe wir trinken dich nachts
wir trinken dich mittags und morgens wir trinken dich abends
wir trinken und trinken
ein Mann wohnt im Haus dein goldenes Haar Margarete
dein aschenes Haar Sulamith er spielt mit den Schlangen

25   Er ruft spielt süßer den Tod der Tod ist **ein Meister aus Deutschland**
er ruft streicht dunkler die Geigen dann steigt ihr als Rauch in die Luft
dann habt ihr ein Grab in den Wolken da liegt man nicht eng

Schwarze Milch der Frühe wir trinken dich nachts
wir trinken dich mittags der Tod ist ein Meister aus Deutschland
30   wir trinken dich abends und morgens wir trinken und trinken
der Tod ist ein Meister aus Deutschland sein Auge ist blau
er trifft dich mit bleierner Kugel er trifft dich genau
ein Mann wohnt im Haus dein goldenes Haar Margarete
er hetzt seine Rüden auf uns er schenkt uns ein Grab in der Luft
35   er spielt mit den Schlangen und träumet der Tod ist ein Meister aus Deutschland

dein goldenes Haar Margarete
dein aschenes Haar Sulamith

(Celan 2003: 65–6)

7.5 TRANSLATION: LEXICAL MEANING IN A
JOURNALISTIC TEXT

Assignment

i   You have been commissioned to translate a selection of articles from the
German press between 1990 and 2000 for inclusion in a textbook on politics during the period. The intention is to give the English-language reader
an idea of evolving reactions to the political scene as they were expressed
at the time. The articles are to be translated as if for a quality newspaper of
the relevant period. The ST here is taken from one of these articles. Discuss the decisions that you have to take about your overall approach before
starting detailed translation of this ST, and outline and justify the approach
you adopt.

ii   Using the headlines as contextual information, translate the text into English.
You can then compare and evaluate your translation using the target text version which will be provided by your tutor.

iii   Discuss the main decisions of detail you took with respect to lexical choice,
paying particular attention to the aspects of meaning which contribute to the
tone of the article and comparing your decisions to those in the proposed TT
version.

Contextual information

The ST is the first half of an article that appeared in the *Frankfurter Rundschau* on
11 September 1998. The *FR* is a middlebrow daily that describes itself, fairly, as an
'*unabhängige, linksliberale und überregionale Qualitätszeitung*'. The topic of the
article—right-wing parties targeting first-time voters—can therefore be expected
to be treated critically in tone and content. The *Republikaner* espoused a similar
anti-immigration ideology as today's *Alternative für Deutschland*, although by
the late 90s, their limited electoral success was waning. The *DVU* is the *Deutsche
Volksunion*; the *NPD* is the *Nationaldemokratische Partei Deutschlands*. Kurt
Tucholsky (1890–1935) was a man of multiple talents, a notable satirist and an
anti-militarist writer, a left-wing democrat who attacked not only the '*Dolchstoß*'
legend but also the inadequacies of Weimar liberalism. He left Germany for good
in 1924, disaffected with political developments. Once they were in power, the
Nazis quickly deprived him of his citizenship.

ST

Selbst linke Querdenker werden umgarnt
MIT WELCHEN METHODEN DIE RECHTSEXTREMEN PARTEIEN UM
ERSTWÄHLER BUHLEN
Sie sind gegen Atomkraft und für Umweltschutz; sie umgarnen 'sozial Engagierte'
5   und 'linke Querdenker'; sie liebäugeln mit Volksabstimmungen und beklagen die
Verrentung der Bonner Polit-Kaste. Wer? Die Grünen? Von wegen. In diesem
Wahlkampf geben sich Deutschlands Rechtsaußen jugendlich. Clever, finden
Politologen—und gefährlich.

ST

Das Blättchen ist hübsch anzusehen und liest sich flockig: 'Wir sollten mit
10 gutem Beispiel vorangehen und ökologische Politik als nationale Herausforderung
begreifen', empfiehlt blau auf weiß ein gewisser 'Martin'. 'Die Bonner Politik hat
aus Deutschland einen Rentnerstaat gemacht, in dem die Jungen nicht mehr viel zu
sagen haben', schreibt 'Michael'. Nebenan lächelt wohlgefällig eine Handvoll
Twens, selbst Kurt Tucholsky kommt zu Wort, und ganz hinten wird liebevoll
15 'unser Buvo' porträtiert. Dessen Name: Rolf Schlierer, 43 Jahre alt,
Bundesvorsitzender der rechtsextremen Republikaner.
'Sehr zufrieden', sagt Parteisprecher Klaus-Dieter Motzke, sei man mit der
ersten Ausgabe von *Junge Deutsche*, die im Mai an ebensolche verteilt wurde. Mit
einer Auflage von 200 000 Stück ist soeben der Nachfolger erschienen. Auch er
20 werde an Stellen verteilt, wo man Jugendliche eben so trifft—etwa 'in und vor
Schulen'. Es gelte, so Motzke zur *FR*, der Partei 'ein anderes Gesicht zu geben'.
Mit dem Wunsch stehen die Republikaner nicht alleine da. Spätestens seit der
Wahl in Sachsen-Anhalt, als fast jeder vierte junge Mann der DVU seine Stimme
gab, wittern die Rechtsextremen wieder Morgenluft. Anders als früher sind
25 folgerichtig nicht borniert Rentner und Ewiggestrige Adressaten der rechten
Lockrufe, sondern junge und Erstwähler. Und so tummeln sich NPD-Aktivisten
schon mal in Technotempeln, verzichtet die DVU wohlweislich auf NS-Symbolik
und postieren die Republikaner Jeans- und Sonnenbrillenträger unter kessen
Sprüchen wie 'Deutschland für alle—nee für uns'.

(Schindler 1998)

References

Primary

BDI (Bundesverband der deutschen Industrie) 2004a. *Für ein attraktives Deutschland*.
Berlin: Bundesverband der deutschen Industrie e.V.

Bucerius *c.*2003. *Bucerius Kunst Forum. Vorschau 2003/04*. Hamburg: Bucerius Kunst
Forum GmbH.

Celan, Paul 2003. *Der Sand aus den Urnen. Mohn und Gedächtnis*. Historisch-Kritische
Ausgabe, 2./3. Band, 1. Teil. Frankfurt am Main: Suhrkamp.

ECSC—HOESCH Hüttenwerke (BR Deutschland) 1987a. 'Ultraschallprüfung von Walz-
material unter Verwendung elektrodynamischer Wandler', in *Euroabstracts Section II*.
Vol. 13/8. Luxembourg: Commission of the European Communities.

ECSC—HOESCH Hüttenwerke (BR Deutschland) 1987b. 'Ultrasonic examination of
rolled products using electrodynamic transducers', in *Euroabstracts Section II*. Vol.
13/8. Luxembourg: Commission of the European Communities.

Hohendorf, G., Rotzoll, M., Richter, P., Eckart, W. and Mundt, C. 2003. 'The victims of
the national socialist "T4" euthanasia programme', *Futura*, 18(1), pp. 23–34 [Only published in English; German ST remains unpublished.].

Schindler, J. 1998. 'Selbst linke Querdenker werden umgarnt', *Frankfurter Rundschau*, 11
September.

Walser, M. 1978. *Ein fliehendes Pferd*. Frankfurt am Main: Suhrkamp.

Walser, M. 1980. *Runaway Horse*. Translated by Vennewitz, Leila. London: Martin
Secker & Warburg.

Secondary

Leech, Geoffrey 1981. *Semantics: The Study of Meaning.* 2nd edn. Harmondsworth: Penguin.
Lyons, John 1977. *Semantics.* Vol. 1. Cambridge: Cambridge University Press.

Lexical and related sources

British National Corpus n.d. Available at: www.natcorp.ox.ac.uk/; https://corpus.byu.edu/bnc/ (Accessed: 1 March 2018) [Provides access to 100m words of written and spoken English and to other corpora of English such as the extensive Brigham Young BYU/BNC corpus.].
Collins German Dictionary 1999. 4th edn. Glasgow: Collins.
Duden Online Wörterbuch n.d. Available at: www.duden.de/suchen/dudenonline (Accessed: 1 March 2018).
Institut für deutsche Sprache n.d. *COSMAS II.* Available at: www.ids-mannheim.de/cosmas2/ (Accessed: 2 March 2018) [Corpus of German texts; full online access to the collection can be obtained by registering at https://cosmas2.ids-mannheim.de/cosmas2-web/. Using the *Anmeldung* button, you will be asked to enter your details as well as a username [*Kennung*] and a password [*Kennwort*]. For background on *Projekt Korpusrecherchesystem* see http://www1.ids-mannheim.de/direktion/kl/projekte/recherchesystem.html.].
Leo n.d. Available at: www.leo.org/ (Accessed: 2 March 2018) [Provides a range of equivalents in bilingual lists with some information on subject field and the possibility of an interactive discussion list for queries.].
Linguee n.d. Available at: www.linguee.com/ (Accessed: 2 March 2018) [Provides parallel contextualised examples from existing translations.].
Reverso n.d. Available at: www.reverso.net (Accessed: 2 March 2018) [Provides parallel contextualised examples of equivalents.].
Sketch Engine n.d. Available at: www.sketchengine.co.uk/ (Accessed: 2 March 2018) [Includes ready-made text corpora in German and English at www.sketchengine.co.uk/documentation/tenten-corpora/ and text-analysis tools; see also www.sketchengine.co.uk/user-guide/user-manual/concordance-introduction/parallel-bilingual-concordance/.].

8   Text-related issues in translation

We began this book by underlining that translation is fundamentally about textual interpretation and production, a point we elaborated in Chapter 4 on genres, which looked at specific text forms. In this chapter we explore in more detail issues to do with the way in which texts are constructed, irrespective of genre, something which has been called 'textuality'. Consider the following excerpt from Theodor Fontane's *Unwiederbringlich* (1892), and the new translation by Helen Chambers and Hugh Rorrison (2010):

ST	TT
Das Zimmer war dasselbe, darin er, gleich am Tage nach seiner Ankunft, seine erste Audienz bei der Prinzessin gehabt hatte. Da hing noch das große Bild König Christians VIII. und gerade gegenüber das des verstorbenen Landgrafen, der Flor um den Rahmen noch grauer und verstaubter als damals. (Fontane 1962: IV/2/770)	The room was the one where he had had his first audience with the Princess after his arrival. The same large picture of King Christian VII still hung there, and directly opposite, the deceased Landgrave, the crêpe over the frame even greyer and dustier than before. (Fontane 2010: 194–5, trans. Chambers & Rorrison)

The most significant change in this translation is the replacement of the German '*König Christian VIII*'. with 'King Christian VII'. This is not a translation mistake. Rather the translators discovered an inconsistency in their ST. Near the beginning of the novel, the main character, Holk, sees a painting of King Christian VII of Denmark. Near the end, the narrator tells us that Holk sees the same picture, only this time we are told it is Christian VIII. The translators took the decision that this was an error, partly because the narrator refers back to the painting so explicitly, but partly because the figure in the painting is symbolically significant: Christian VII signifies the immorality and decadence of the Danish court; Holk has just committed adultery while at court, and is about to leave his wife to start what he (falsely) believes will be a new life. The painting functions thus as part of an ironic commentary on the delusions of the main character. In this instance then, the translators' problem here was not the individual words in question, which were straightforward ('*König Christian*

VIII'.), but rather the significance of those words within the text as a whole; and, more importantly, the translation decision was based primarily on their understanding of how the whole text worked as a structure of meaning—what *'Christian VIII'*. 'meant' was determined by both by the immediate context (the narrator's comments 'the same large picture') and knowledge of the text's deeper, associative structure.

In this chapter, then, we are concerned with exploring translation decisions informed by analysis of the ST at a textual level, that is at a level beyond the individual sentence. As we have seen in the previous example, that can involve a translation decision about a single noun phrase, but it can also involve shaping a whole sentence, or working on the whole text. This area of Translation Studies draws on a number of related branches of enquiry, namely text linguistics, discourse analysis, and functional grammar, but, importantly, is also related to critical analysis as it is more traditionally practised in literary and philological studies.

For most of the twentieth century, linguistic analysis was conducted at the sentence level. From the standpoint of text linguistics and discourse analysis which began to emerge in the 1960s but gained real ground in the 1970s and 1980s, this is inadequate, given that language use occurs in broader linguistic contexts. The premise of text linguistics and discourse analysis is that (a) a **text** as a larger unit influences the forms of individual sentences or utterances and that (b) a text is governed by underlying principles which can be analysed as an object of linguistic enquiry.

It goes perhaps without saying that literary and textual studies of a more traditional sort and text linguistics overlap, with the important difference that (a) text linguistics has sought to provide models for texts in general, while traditional scholarship has typically focused on literary texts and (b) text linguistics is often informed by an understanding of a text as or within an act of communication. It is, however, worth noting that the influential linguist Eugenio Coseriu takes literary texts as his point of departure because in his view, they are the most complex of all textual forms. We should underline that text linguistics and translation models based on text types develop together.

Patterns of textual structure and creation of textual meaning

It is a common enough experience when translating that we start sentence by sentence and then go back and adapt our initial draft because our understanding of the textual argument has evolved. As teachers of translation, it is also a common experience for us to read students' work in which individual word choices do not make sense in context. Here we are encountering textuality—that sense of collective and cumulative significance and relevance which is difficult to define but which differentiates a text from a series of unrelated sentences. The forms which texts take vary considerably, ranging from a single word (e.g. in a notice) to thousands of words (e.g. a novel) or even hundreds of thousands of words (e.g. an installation manual for highly complex nuclear plant) and many texts incorporate non-verbal content such as images and graphics (see Chapter 4 on multimodal texts).

What we seek to do in this chapter is improve our translation practice and our translation analysis by highlighting some of the ways texts work and how that is relevant for translation. Essentially, we are concerned with two distinct but inter-related issues: (a) the significance that the structure of a text has for meaning, both for the choice of individual words within sentences, but also textual meaning, i.e. the meaning created by a text as the sum of its parts; (b) textual structure as an object of translation in itself (i.e. not just the words of a text but the sense of the argument as an object of translation).

Let us begin our analysis of textual structure by introducing two concepts of central importance for text linguistics and which have been productively adopted by translation scholars: cohesion and textual coherence (Halliday and Hasan 1976; Neubert and Shreve 1992). **Cohesion** may be defined as the trans-parent linking of sentences (and larger sections of text), for example by explicit discourse connectors like 'then', 'so', 'however', subordinating conjunctions such as 'when' or 'because' and coreferential links such as personal pronouns and deictics such as 'this' or 'that'. These act as signposts pointing out the thread of discourse running through the text. To use Blum-Kulka's formulation, cohesion is 'an overt relationship holding between parts of the text expressed by language specific markers' (Blum-Kulka 1986/2004: 291). **Coherence** is a more difficult matter than cohesion, because, by definition, it is not explicitly marked in a text: it is a tacit, but discernible, thematic or emotional develop-ment running through the text. Coherence is what makes a series of utterances into a meaningful unit. If the translator fails to understand a central theme in the ST—as was the case for UK students translating a journalistic German text on the culturally unfamiliar concept of '*Kirchensteuer*'—the result is one of cogni-tive dissonance. In other words the TT makes no sense, even if it is linguistically fluent (see Rogers 2005).

It goes without saying that textual coherence is a relative concept and may assume many forms: a text's coherence may be the result of a progressing argu-ment (in a scientific paper) or a narrative (in a novel), but it may also be created by extended metaphor, or by the text's diction, its drawing on words belonging to similar or related semantic fields. Coherence denotes the underlying structure of the text, cohesion the marking of that structure; the concepts coherence and cohesion describe a range of textual features which can range from intersenten-tial relations (moving from one sentence to another) to charting the ways whole texts constitute coherent units, such as the symbolic patterns in *Unwiederbring-lich*. As we shall see in our first example below, the knowledge that the reader brings to the text is an important factor influencing degrees of coherence and in some cases, the interpretation of cohesive ties, particularly anaphora such as pronouns (see also the discussion of 'cognitive environment' in Chapter 3 on equivalence).

Before we go on to think about the specific translation issues that text-level analysis raises, let's consider two examples which demonstrate different tex-tual strategies of coherence and cohesion. The following two texts are the first paragraphs of introductions to German and Viennese Modernism, the first written for undergraduates, the second both for students and scholars:

I

Kaum ein Begriff ist derart diffus und umstritten wie '**die Moderne**'—einschließlich seiner Verwandten: die Modernen, das Moderne, modern, Modernismus, Modernität. Das hat verschiedene Gründe. Zum einen wird der Moderne-Begriff in den verschiedenen Disziplinen, so in Philosophie, Sozial-, Geschichts-, Kunst- und
5 Literaturwissenschaft, unterschiedlich definiert. Zum andern ist der Moderne-Begriff sowohl eine historische Kategorie zur Bezeichnung einer Epoche als auch eine systematische Kategorie zur Charakterisierung bestimmter Inhalte, Postulate, Ideologeme dessen, was als 'Moderne' erscheint oder sich als solche deklariert.
(Fähnders 2010: 1)

II

Was bedeutet eigentlich der Terminus *Wiener Moderne*? Hätte sich dieser Begriff nicht längst als allgemein üblicher Terminus in den Literatur- und Kulturwissenschaften eingebürgert, so geriete man angesichts dieser Frage unweigerlich in eine ähnliche Lage wie der bedauernswerte Lord Chandos des 'Wiener Modernen' Hugo von
5 Hofmannsthal, dem die 'mit schlafwandelnder Sicherheit' geäußerten Begriffe und Urteile seiner Umgebung plötzlich 'so unbeweisbar, so lügenhaft, so löcherig wie nur möglich' erschienen [. . .]. 'Löcherig' allemal ist die Bestimmung des Gegenstandes, den dieser Band behandelt.
(Lorenz 2007: 1)

Both of these examples are from academic publications, which we can expect to make clear arguments, but they work in different ways. The first is clearly more cohesively marked: it employs conjunctive ties (*'zum einen', 'zum andern'*); moreover, these conjunctive ties function as pairs, strengthening the text's sense of transparent progression (*'sowohl . . . als auch'*). Not least, the first example is notable for its repetition (*'Moderne-Begriff'* and *'Kategorie'*) and coreference, referring back or forward with a pronoun: 'Das *hat verschiedene Gründe*'. The second text, while it has comparable content, achieves its sense of coherence differently: here the looser sense of progression is in part the result of the more varied lexis, the use of related but different words (*'Terminus', 'Begriff', 'Urteil'*), but stems principally from the external reference: the second text not only refers back to itself rather more obliquely, its coherence is the product of an intertextual reference; it refers outside itself, quoting Hofmannsthal, drawing on the reader's presumed knowledge. While part of this difference is surely down to individual style, the first text is primarily aimed at students, the second is also written for researchers, so that the target readership plays a significant role in determining the textual strategies employed.

The next example shows how thinking about the way sentences relate to each other within the text as a larger structure of meaning is important even in texts with simple syntactic forms. In the following advertisement a colour photograph shows a wide field with a Renault Mégane superimposed, driving round the tight curves of an appropriately magnified Scalextric track. The headline text reads: '*Schon als Kinder wussten wir, dass nur die Straßenlage zählt*'. On the facing page, under the car name and in smaller print, the text continues:

> Wir wussten zwar nicht, was das bedeutet. Aber wir kannten den Effekt: Den meisten
> Spaß machen die Wagen, die förmlich an der Fahrbahn kleben. Und die schnell und
> zuverlässig jede Kurve nehmen. Mit dem neuen Renault Mégane können Sie diesen
> Effekt jetzt auf der Straße täglich erleben. Reservieren Sie noch heute Ihre Probefahrt
> 5   und überzeugen Sie sich vom Mégane-Effekt.

The colon after '*wir kannten den Effekt*' has a cohesive function, doing duty for either a relative clause (e.g. '*Effekt, der darin besteht, dass* . . . ') or a sentence break plus the explicit cohesion marker '*nämlich*'. It also marks for emphasis the short sentence with the advertisement's key message about road-holding. Then, with '*Und die schnell . . . Kurve nehmen*', a similar effect is achieved in a different way. Parallel relative clauses in German always bind conspicuously together because of the verb placing. And the message is brought home by the structural separation of this relative clause into a separate 'sentence': the punchy placement of a subordinate clause rather than a main clause between two full stops adds further emphasis to the message. The text's cohesion is achieved through **grammatical anaphora**, repeating grammatical structures, and repetition of individual words ('*Effekt*' binds the beginning and the end of the paragraph). The coherence of the text is the product of the image the advertisement draws on and the **ellipsis** which highlights and knits together the two relative clauses that contain the text's central message.

A 2003 Skoda advertisement features an unusually wide variety of cohesion types. Above a picture of the car, it has three separate headlines, of which the first is in two lines, as indicated, and prominent:

Edel und stark,
Hilfreich und gut.
Der Škoda Octavia COLLECTION, sportlich sparen, komfortabel fahren.
Škoda. Ganz schön clever.

The main text (omitting only the contact details) reads:

> **Einspruch!** Sportlichkeit und Komfort sind keine Gegensätze. Das Sondermodell
> Škoda Octavia COLLECTION ist der Kronzeuge. Die Beweislage ist bestechend, egal
> ob Combi oder Limousine: Xenonlicht, Climatronic, Bordcomputer, Alu-Felgen und
> vieles mehr. Sie sparen eine Menge Tagessätze, nämlich bis zu 1.700 Euro. Bleibt nur
> 5   noch eine Frage offen: welche Motorisierung? Dazu sollten Sie mit sich ins Gericht
> gehen, denn dieses Urteil müssen Sie selbst fällen. Im Namen des Gesetzes: Ganz schön
> clever. Sie haben ihn angefasst, jetzt müssen Sie ihn auch Probe fahren.
>
> (Škoda)

Here the main body of the text relies heavily on a binding metaphor, signaled by the insistent use of law-court terminology—'*Einspruch*', '*Kronzeuge*', '*Beweislage*', '*Tagessätze*', etc. The translation difficulty here, then, is less the result of grammatical transpositions, as in the Mégane example, and more the product of the different ranges of words and idioms available in German and English. Where in other contexts the verb phrase in the second sentence, '*mit jemandem ins Gericht gehen*' might be rendered metaphorically with 'give someone a talking to', here our translation choices are determined by the need to maintain the legal metaphor. The additional difficulty involves avoiding terms that are appropriately legal, but have negative connotations, such as 'sentence', and maybe even 'judgement'. In order to capture the legal metaphor in the English translation, any formal equivalence has to give way to tone and meaning. A translation might thus read, 'take time to consider the evidence, you're the judge in this case'. In other words, our translation choice at the level of individual words is determined primarily by their immediate function within the text as a structure of meaning.

From the previous examples it should be clear that there is a range of ways in which texts both function as coherent units and signal that coherence through cohesive markers. In the previous two examples, reproducing the patterns of cohesion presented a challenge, but both structurally (in the Mégane advertisement) and lexically (in the Skoda advertisement), using equivalent structures and vocabulary was usually achievable. The following descriptive passage from Heimito von Doderer's 1951 novel, *Die Strudlhofstiege* presents a more complex case:

Freilich, man wußte so halb und halb, worin man lebte, ganz beiläufig, aus dem Augenwinkel gesehen: in Umgebungen, die, an Schweigsamkeit nicht zu überbieten, sich dennoch unaufhörlich mit Übergewalt aussprachen. In den Schluchten und Rissen nah an den Wänden des Bergs, in diesen Wunden des Walds, die jeder Frühling wieder
5   mit dumpf trommelnden Wassermassen neu aufriß, lag jetzt, da sie sommerlich grün zum Teil wieder heilten, der verlassene und trockene feine Sand in den großen Becken zwischen glattgewaschenen Blöcken. Längst hatten Gebüsch und Geäst von beiden Seiten das leere Bachbett neuerlich überwölbt.

(Doderer 1995: 228)

The first challenge here stems from the **cataphoric** (forward-referring) '*worin*'— here word-for-word renderings (in which/the place in which) are more cumbrous than the more natural 'where', but choosing 'where' has obvious repercussions for the rest of the text that the repeated preposition '*in*' holds together. In the first sentence, the phrase '*in Umgebungen, die . . .*' clearly completes the announced '*worin*', and the two prepositional phrases that begin the next sentence, '*in den Schluchten . . .*' create a sense of continuity. Yet in fact the text 'flows' in the opposite direction in this second sentence—'*in den Schluchten*' does indeed recall the first sentence, but is grammatically independent of it, being the obligatory adverbial complement of the verb '*liegen*'. The syntactic complexity of this second sentence poses further problems: this sentence binds the extract's first sentence about violent surroundings and the following description of an empty brook because the appearance of the subject (*'der verlassene . . . Sand . . . Blöcken'*) is teasingly delayed until the end of the sentence; the sentence-initial pre-verbal slot is occupied by the two adverbial complements of *'lag'* (*'in den Schluchten'*, *'in diesen Wunden des Walds'*)—a word order which is typical in German—and each is expanded. This sentence will certainly need transposing in English. In translating this passage then, it is likely that the problematic cohesive structure afforded by the repeated preposition will need to be abandoned, and its effect created with other means. One solution for the first sentence might be to use a demonstrative: 'Obviously we had some idea of where we lived, seen out of the corner of the eye as it was and in passing—**these** were surroundings that expressed themselves always with great violence, despite their incomparable silence'.

Considering translation at a textual level thus prioritises the production of a TT which functions as a text and seeks to minimise or manage incoherence and shifts in cohesion which are the products of the translation process. Further, it considers the translation of the ST's 'textuality' as something which has to be translated, i.e. reproduced, as Albrecht Neubert and Gregory Shreve (1992: 93) have argued:

> Text-based translation attempts to re-establish in the target text a coherence which is functionally parallel to that of the source text. A translator cannot usually re-establish coherence using literal sentence-for-sentence renderings. L2 coherence must be recreated using the translator's own understanding of the coherence structure of the original to direct modifications in the L2 textual surface.

The phrase 'functionally parallel' is key here for, as we have seen, texts function in different ways in part according to their purpose, genre and text type: the density of a text, or its textuality, is a phenomenon which exists on a sliding scale, with literature or closely argued expert-to-expert specialised texts at one end and lists of independent items such as a parts list at the other, though other factors such as the time constraints on the ST production and its situation also play a significant role.

As for relations between larger units on the textual level (paragraphs, chapters, etc.), these are generally less problematic than intersentential relations. As usual, the translator must first ask what the function of such features is in the ST, and what the norms are for representing these functions in the particular TL genre: identifying so-called parallel texts i.e. original TL texts with the same design features, is helpful here. Commercial considerations may also come into play: for instance, a publisher may be afraid that a text full of long paragraphs or unusually short ones would not sell in the target culture. Or, if the division into paragraphs does have a thematic or emotive function, the translator should hesitate before significantly altering it. In some genres, however, there can be no question of the translator choosing whether or not to alter ST paragraphing: in texts having the force of law, for instance, the ST structure generally has to be observed, however inelegant or difficult this makes the text for a non-specialist. Or in advertisements, the placing of words or phrases as headings or straplines is the result of marketing and design expertise and is not usually changed.

Translating German cohesive markers

Let us now move on to examine one particular area in more detail, the translation of cohesive markers. It is in general more common in German than in English for texts to be explicitly structured with connectors (*'nun'*, *'also'*, *'zwar'*, *'nämlich'*, *'auch'*, *'so'* in the sense of *'zum Beispiel'*) that signpost the relationship between sentences. An English TT using explicit connectors to reproduce all those found in a German ST will often sound unidiomatic or pedantic. This also applies in cases where German obligatorily requires some kind of extension to the verb—often prepositional—which also anticipates a following clause, such as, ' . . . *die Deutschen denken ganz anders darüber: sie wollen* . . . '. Compare: ' . . . the Germans think quite differently about it: they want . . . ' with ' . . . the Germans think quite differently: they want . . . '.

Our first point is a general one: the translator can be drawn into translating too mechanically and repetitively. Even where ready equivalents are available, when it matters to have the TT flow naturally, it is a good thing to vary the formula occasionally by judicious restructuring of the sentence. Thus *'folglich'* (etc.) can often be rendered by e.g. 'This means that . . . ' or 'It follows that . . . '.

Our second point is that some frequently used German discourse connectors lack ready idiomatic equivalents in English, and may tempt the translator into unidiomatic TL usage. One commonly encountered example is *'zwar'*. Close in meaning to *'freilich'* and *'allerdings'* in the sense of 'admittedly', *'zwar'* routinely occurs as an advance partner of a *'jedoch'*, *'andererseits'* or commonly, *'aber'* to come: '*Groß waren die vier Hunde zwar nicht, dafür bellten sie aber sehr häufig'*. In this role, *'zwar'* more often than not would be too emphatic if rendered with 'admittedly' or 'indeed'. Compare: 'The four dogs were indeed not big, but they certainly barked frequently' and 'While the four dogs were not big, they certainly made up for it with their frequent barking'. Or, again, German *'so'* corresponds in literal meaning to the decidedly formal English 'thus' at the beginning of an illustrative sentence. Yet, more often than not, 'thus' is ruled out in many genres on grounds of register, and other variants ('in this manner' etc.) are often cumbrous, so that it may be more appropriate in the TL to leave the link implicit, or rephrase, as the translators of a set of instructions for an electric razor have done: '*So halten Sie Ihren Rasierer in Bestform'* becomes 'Keeping your shaver in top shape' (*Gebrauchsanweisung* Braun Series, 8; 12). A third example is *'vielmehr'*, used almost mechanically in many German texts to introduce a positive statement following a negative. The stock English equivalent, 'rather', is suitable in many cases—so often, in fact, that it tends to be written down uncritically in TTs where English actually requires a different connector, or none at all. Consider the following two sentences from an academic article about the French artist Boucher:

Das Ausbleiben kirchlicher Aufträge bedeutete also keineswegs, daß damit seine Karriere als religiöser Maler beendet gewesen wäre. Vielmehr entstanden in den fünfziger Jahren eine Reihe privater Andachtsbilder, die in der Pariser Kunstszene für Aufsehen sorgten.

(Schieder: unpublished)

To render '*vielmehr*' by 'rather' in this TT—whether initially or elsewhere—would yield a faintly but distinctly unidiomatic calque. The best TL connector here might be 'In fact . . . '. Yet the logical relation between the two sentences is still perfectly clear without any TL connector: '. . . did not by any means signify the end of his career as a religious painter. In the 1750s he went on to produce . . . '. Even in academic argument, then, it is not mandatory for connectors in German STs to be translated one-for-one in English.

The relatively more frequent provision of these connectors in German, at least in narrative and analytical genres, is also well illustrated by the phrase '*denn auch*'. Essentially it marks an expectable consequence of an action or event just reported. Unlike '*vielmehr*', it has never acquired a stock English translation. Close in function to the modal particle '*auch*', which stresses the reasons for something being the case or not being the case, '*denn auch*' is used quite freely in some older literary texts, in linking narrative. But it is also to be found in more modern and less discursive contexts such as the Schieder essay on French art history quoted earlier. Here is one of four occurrences in 16 pages:

ST	TT
Seine Illustrierung der Heilsgeschichte in Form pittoresker Graphiken schien dem Ort ihrer Publikation nicht angemessen— in den nachfolgenden Auflagen des 5 Breviariums tauchten sie denn auch nicht mehr auf. (Schieder: unpublished)	His presentation of the Christian story in the form of picturesque visual images seemed inappropriate to the place of their publication—and in later editions of the breviary they no longer appeared. (Schieder 2006)

The cause-and-effect implication here is clear in the TT without any indication more explicit than the dash plus 'and'. However, it is an indication of the elusiveness of '*denn auch*' in TL terms—in spite of its consistent *meaning*— that the four occurrences in the Boucher article find four different translations. In one case, the antecedent 'cause' consists of complex argument and a three-line quotation. The '*denn auch*', marking the upshot, therefore needs relatively explicit translation:

ST	TT
Die meisten von Bouchers alttestamentarischen Kabinettsbildern fanden denn auch den Weg in angesehene Privatsammlungen; [. . .] (Schieder: unpublished)	It was only natural, then, that most of Boucher's Old Testament cabinet pictures should find their way into notable private collections; [. . .] (Schieder 2006)

As these examples show, the translator's task with cohesive markers is not so much to render the individual term as to *read its function* and provide TL linking that is appropriate not only in terms of the argument (coherence) but also of the TL's linking conventions in the relevant genre and register.

Concluding remarks

Translation problems at the textual level can emerge when, as frequently occurs, literal translation would affect the textual function of the TT negatively. If you are new to translating, then very many of your first mistakes will have been the result of ignoring the immediate context of the words you were translating, or choosing the wrong register, or failing to use the overall argument of the text (i.e. its coherence) to help you understand an obscure sentence or word; the way to overcome these kinds of errors is to focus on how the ST functions as a text. The translation of cohesive markers is a case in point: these are not words that can be translated easily with the aid of a bilingual dictionary, which is better suited to the codification of content words such as verbs, adjectives and nouns. The reason, as we have seen, is that the function of cohesive markers or connectors is to bind the text together. Their 'meaning' is therefore embedded in the text, not in any external point of reference. Choosing appropriate means of establishing cohesion—maybe dense in closely argued scholarly texts, maybe loose in poems—is one of the factors contributing to a translation which is communicatively successful, i.e. fit for purpose. We should also recall that genre conventions vary between languages: this is especially important for specialised texts. As a relation between the text and its anticipated readers, coherence is, of course, interactive, depending on how successfully the ST author or the TT translator meets the expectations of the readers. Many factors play a role here, not least cultural knowledge and experience (see Chapter 5).

As a translator, you need to ask not just 'what does a word or a sentence *say*', but 'what does it *do*', what is its role within a text? Make sure you can trace the overall argument of what you are translating and that you are attentive to the points at which the direction changes. It is likely that, in fact, you will have thought about many of these questions before but in different contexts; the purpose of literary analysis, for example, is to explore patterns in literary texts which are often subtle, being associative and implied. Even if you have not studied literature, every time you have written an essay, you have reflected on the clarity of an argument, made changes to avoid digression, made vocabulary choices to ensure a consistent register without inelegant repetition. You need to use these skills as a translator too. However, you are not seeking to impose an alien sense of coherence on a text, but rather one which is an appropriate reflection of the ST's own nature and the TT's purpose, according to the translation brief. For example, is it striving to persuade through argumentation (with lots of clear marking) or is it rather presenting statements without marking, as indisputable facts? If there is ambiguity, should it be resolved by interpreting the overall purpose of the text, or preserved? These are some of the issues you should consider in the following exercises.

Further reading

Asher, R.E. and Simpson, J.M.Y. (eds) 1994. *The Encyclopedia of Language and Linguistics*. Oxford: Pergamon [Entries 'Text Linguistics', 'Text' in Vol. 9.].

Baker, Mona 2011. *In Other Words*. London and New York: Routledge [Chapter 6 and Chapter 7 on cohesion and coherence.].

Duden 4: Die Grammatik 2016. 9th edn. Edited by Wöllstein, Angelika. Berlin: Dudenverlag [Has a large section on text, including hypertext, pp. 1073–80.].

House, Juliane 2012. 'Text linguistics and translation', in Gambier, Y. and van Doorslaer, L. (eds) *Handbook of Translation Studies*. Vol. 3. Amsterdam and Philadelphia: John Benjamins, pp. 178–84.

House, Juliane 2015. 'Global English, discourse and translation: Linking constructions in English and German popular science texts', *Target*, 27, pp. 370–86.

Steiner, Erich 2015. 'Contrastive studies of cohesion and their impact on our knowledge of translation (English-German)', *Target*, 27, 351–69.

White, Michael 2015. 'Herder and Fontane as translators of Percy's *Reliques of ancient English poetry*: The ballad "Edward, Edward"', in Robertson, R. and White, M. (eds) *Fontane and Cultural Mediation: Translation and Reception in Nineteenth-Century German Literature*. Germanic Literatures. Vol. 8. Oxford: Legenda, pp. 107–19 [Relevant to the exercise below.].

Practical 8

8.1 COMPARISON: COHERENCE IN POETRY TRANSLATION

Assignment

i   Compare Theodor Fontane's (1852) translation of the first three verses of the Scots ballad 'Edward, Edward' with the text as it is in Percy's *Reliques of Ancient English Poetry* (1765). Demonstrate how the translation creates a closer sense of coherence and how that is marked.

ii   What is the effect of these changes and why might they be problematic?

Note: the spelling is supposed to look historical: 'Quhy' = 'Why'; 'zour' = 'your'.

English Text	*Fontane's Translation*
Quhy dois zour brand sae drop wi' bluid, Edward, Edward?	Was blinket dein Schwert so rot von Blut, Edward, Edward?
Quhy dois zour brand sae drop wi' bluid? And quhy sae sad gang zee, O?	Was blinket dein Schwert so rot von Blut, Und macht so trübe dich schreiten?
5 O, I hae killed my hauke sae guid, Mither, mither:	‚Ich hab' erwürgt meinen Falken gut' Mutter, Mutter
O, I hae killed my hauke sae guid: And I hae nae mair bot hee, O.	Ich hab erwürgt meinen Falken gut Und hatte doch keinen zweiten'.
Zour haukis bluid was nevir sae reid, 10 Edward, Edward:	Deines Falken Blut war nimmer so rot, Edward, Edward,

English Text	Fontane's Translation
Zour haukis bluid was nevir sae reid,	Deines Falken Blut war nimmer so rot,
My deir son I tell thee, O.	Dein Schwert ist dünkler gerötet; -
O I hae killed my reid-roan steid,	‚Ich hab erstochen mein rotbraun Roß,
Mither, mither,	Mutter, Mutter,
15 O I hae killed my reid-roan steid,	Ich hab erstochen mein rotbraun Roß
That erst was sae fair and free, O.	Im Zorne hab ich's getötet'.
Zour steid was auld, and ze hae gat mair,	Dein Roß war alt, das kann es nicht sein,
Edward, Edward:	Edward, Edward!
Zour steid was auld, and ze hae gat mair,	Dein Roß war alt, das kann es nicht sein,
20 Sum other dule ye drie, O.	Was tät deine Wang entfärben;
O, I hae killed my fadir, deir,	Ich hab erschlagen den Vater mein,
Mither, mither:	Mutter, Mutter,
O, I hae killed my fadir deir,	Ich hab erschlagen den Vater mein,
Alas! and wae is mee, O!	Und mir ist weh zum Sterben!
(Percy 1910: I, 101–2.)	(Fontane 1995: I, 370–1.)

8.2 TRANSLATION: COHESION AND COHERENCE IN AN ESSAY

Assignment

You are translating the following text for an anthology of texts by critical intellectuals in German society from 1900–1945. The text will appear as an extract, with an introductory page about the author and the text. The book will have a glossary, but other notes should be avoided. The book is aimed at students on university comparative literature programmes, programmes in European studies, historians and general readers.

i Discuss the decisions that you have to take about your general approach, given the genre and the translation brief, before starting detailed translation of this ST, and outline and justify the approach you adopt. While not ignoring other issues, indicate in particular what you see as the main issues of cohesion and coherence that you will have to tackle.

ii Translate the text, including the title, into English.

iii Explain the main decisions of detail that you took.

iv Compare your TT with a sample translation, which will be given to you by your tutor.

Contextual information

The ST is an extract from Heinrich Mann's essay 'Geist und Tat' (January 1911). In the essay, Mann contrasts the intellectual traditions of Germany and France. In this excerpt, he refers to the failures of Germany's *Literate*. One piece of advice— read the text aloud, translate according to the sense and the flow of the text—do not let the sometimes unusual punctuation throw you off. Note: some of the spelling is historical.

ST

Geist und Tat
Der Letzte aber, dem all diese Verirrung und Feigheit erlaubt wäre, der Mensch des
Geistes, der Literat: gerade er hat sie geweiht und verbreitet. Seine Natur: die Definition
der Welt, die helle Vollkommenheit des Wortes verpflichtet ihn zur Verachtung der
5   dumpfen, unsauberen Macht. Vom Geist ist ihm die Würde des Menschen auferlegt.
Sein ganzes Leben opfert der Wahrheit den Nutzen. Die Erscheinungen löst er auf,
vermag das Grosse klein zu sehen und im Kleinen das durch Menschlichkeit Grosse:
dergestalt, dass ihm Gleichheit zur letzten Forderung der Vernunft wird . . . Gerade aber
er wirkt in Deutschland seit Jahrzehnten für die Beschönigung des Ungeistigen, für die
10 sophistische Rechtfertigung des Ungerechten, für seinen Todfeind, die Macht. Welche
seltsame Verderbnis brachte ihn dahin? Was erklärt diesen Nietzsche, der dem Typus
sein Genie geliehen hat, und alle die, die ihm nachgetreten sind? Ist es der
überwältigende Erfolg der Macht, den diese Zeit und dies Land sahen? Die
Hoffnungslosigkeit, die eigene Natur durchzusetzen, heute und hier? Der Drang zu
15 wirken, sei es gegen sich selbst: durch Steigerung und Verklärung des Feindes, als
bewunderter Anwalt des Bösen? Ist es die perverse Abdankung des allzu Wissenden,
der sich im schlechten, unbewussten Leben wälzt wie ein entflohener Sträfling? Vom
tragischen Ehrgeiz bis zu elender Eitelkeit, von der albernen Sucht, besonders zu sein
bis zum panischen Schrecken der Vereinsamung und dem Ekel am Nihilismus: die
20 abtrünnigen Literaten haben viele Entschuldigungen. Sie haben vor allem eine in der
ungeheuerlich angewachsenen Entfernung, die, nach so langer Unwirksamkeit, die
deutschen Geister vom Volk trennt. Aber was taten sie, um sie zu verringern? Sie haben
das Leben des Volkes nur als Symbol genommen für die eigenen hohen Erlebnisse. Sie
haben der Welt eine Statistenrolle zugeteilt, ihre schöne Leidenschaft nie in die Kämpfe
25 dort unten eingemischt, haben die Demokratie nicht gekannt und haben sie verachtet.
Sie verachten das parlamentarische Regime, bevor es erreicht ist, die öffentliche
Meinung, bevor sie anerkannt ist. Sie tun als hätten sie hinter sich, wofür nur die andern
geblutet haben, und maasen sich die Miene der Uebersättigung an, obwohl sie niemals
weder kämpften noch genossen.

(Mann 2012: 117–18)

8.3 TRANSLATION: CD BOOKLET

Assignment

i   You are translating the following ST for a bilingual CD booklet. Discuss the overall approach that you want to take before starting detailed translation of this ST, and outline and justify the approach you adopt. As always, consider the genre and the brief. Pay special attention to text-level issues, but do not neglect other significant features. (Remember to look for textual features within sentences as well as between sentences.)

ii   Translate the text into English.

iii Explain your overall approach and decisions of detail you took.

iv Compare your TT with the published one, which will be given to you by your tutor. Texts tend to expand in translation. The TT is four lines longer than the

ST: can you identify any reasons for this? How long is your own translation? (Note: word counts are unreliable when comparing the length of English and German texts).

Contextual information

The ST is taken from the booklet provided with a CD of Glenn Gould playing Bach's *Goldberg Variations*. The omitted material concerns earlier recordings of the work. The '*Aufnahme*' referred to in line 15 is Gould's first-ever recording.

ST

Der 22jährige Glenn Gould war in seiner Heimat Kanada bereits eine Berühmtheit, als er am 2. Januar 1955 in der Phillips Gallery in Washington (und neun Tage später in der New Yorker Town Hall) sein USA-Debüt gab. Dennoch war zu den beiden Klavier-Recitals mit ihrem eigenwilligen Programm (eine *Pavan* des englischen Virginalisten
5   Orlando Gibbons, die *Fantasia cromatica* von Jan Pieterszoon Sweelinck, fünf dreistimmige *Sinfonien* und die fünfte Partita von Bach, Anton Weberns Variationen op. 27, Beethovens E-Dur-Sonate op. 109 und zum Abschluß die Sonate von Alban Berg) kaum die 'erste Garde' der nordamerikanischen Musikszene erschienen—glücklicherweise nicht, muß man im Nachhinein wohl sagen: Denn so hatte David
10 Oppenheim—Klassik-Manager der 'Columbia', der auch eher zufällig in das Konzert geraten war, um sich (auf den Rat eines Freundes hin) diesen jungen Mann anzuhören, 'der leider ein wenig *crazy* sei, aber von geradezu hypnotischer Ausstrahlung am Klavier'—das große Glück, Gould *stante pede* und exklusiv für seine Firma unter Vertrag zu nehmen. [. . .]
15 Über das Wunder dieser Aufnahme ist viel geschrieben worden: Über ihr Temperament, über das faszinierende Non-legato-Spiel fast ohne Pedal, über ihren 'Swing'. Über ihren beinahe respektlosen Umgang mit einem sakrosankten Heroen der Musikgeschichte (was manche Kritiker zu dem Bonmot 'Gouldberg-Variationen' animierte). Über ihre atemberaubende Virtuosität, über ihre Innigkeit und Tiefe, über
20 ihr 'Kalkül' und ihre 'Ekstase'—zwei Attribute, die Gould für sich selbst in Anspruch nahm—über ihre Wirkung auf die internationale Musikwelt: Als habe jemand in einem seit hundert oder mehr Jahren nicht mehr gelüfteten Raum plötzlich ein Fenster aufgerissen und frische Morgenluft hereingelassen. Aber Goulds Triumph war nicht nur ein musikalischer: Der 22jährige entsprach auf frappante und ideale Weise dem
25 Zeitgeist. Ein 'Junger Wilder' der Musik, ein *angry young man*, wie ihn John Osborne 1956 mit der Figur des Jimmy Porter in seinem Schauspiel *Look Back in Anger* ('Blick zurück im Zorn') auf die Bühne brachte, eine Inkarnation des Holden Caulfield aus Jerome D. Salingers 1951 erschienenem Erfolgsroman *The Catcher in the Rye* ('Der Fänger im Roggen').

(Stegemann 1992a: 12–14)

References

Primary

Doderer, Heimito von 1995. *Die Strudlhofstiege*. Munich: Beck.
Fähnders, Walter 2010. *Avantgarde und Moderne 1890–1933: Lehrbuch Germanistik*. Stuttgart: Metzler.

Fontane, Theodor 1962–1997. *Werke, Schriften und Briefe* [originally *Sämtliche Werke*]. Edited by Keitel, Walter and Nürnberger, Helmuth. 21 Vols. in 4 Sections. Munich: Hanser.

Fontane, Theodor 1995. *Gedichte*. Großer Brandeburger Ausgabe. Edited by Joachim Krueger and Anita Golz. Berlin: Aufbau.

Fontane, Theodor 2010. *No Way Back*. Translated by Chambers, Helen and Rorrison, Hugh. London: Angel Books.

Lorenz, Dagmar 2007. *Wiener Moderne*. Sammlung Metzler. Vol. 290. Stuttgart: Metzler.

Mann, Heinrich 2012/1911. 'Geist und Tat', in Hahn, M., Fierl, A. and Klein, W. (eds) *Band 2. Essays und Publizistik*. Bielefeld: Aisthesis, pp. 113–9, 117–8.

Percy, Thomas 1910. *Reliques of Ancient English Poetry*. 2 Vols. London: Dent.

Schieder, M. 2006. 'Between *grâce* and *volupté*: Boucher and religious painting', in Hyde, M. and Ledbury, M. (eds) *Rethinking Boucher*. Los Angeles: Getty Research Institute [Only published in English; German ST remains unpublished].

Stegemann, M. 1992a. 'Der Marlon Brando des Klaviers' [CD notes]. *The Glenn Gould Edition. J.S. Bach, Goldberg Variations etc.* Sony (SMK 52 594).

Secondary

Blum-Kulka, Shoshana 1986/2004. 'Shifts of cohesion and coherence in translation', in Venuti, L. (ed.) *The Translation Studies Reader*. 2nd edn. London: Routledge, pp. 290–305.

Halliday, Michael A. K. and Hasan, Ruqaiya 1976. *Cohesion in English*. London: Longman English Language Series.

Neubert, Albrecht and Shreve, Gregory 1992. *Translation as Text*. Kent, OH and London: The Kent State University Press.

Rogers, Margaret 2005. 'Native versus non-native speaker competence in German-English translation', in Anderman, G. and Rogers, M. (eds) *In and Out of English: For Better, for Worse?* Clevedon: Multilingual Matters, pp. 256–74.

9 Sentential issues in translation

In the previous chapter, we examined the translation issues that can arise at the level of textual structure, in particular, aspects of textual coherence and cohesion. From these insights from the field of text linguistics we now move to a related set of problems and translation strategies, this time within the individual sentence. Here we are concerned with two principal decisions, when to maintain the information order of a sentence, and when to amend the information order of a sentence.

Information structure

One factor in the construction of textual cohesion, and contributing to the overall coherence of the text, is the distribution of information at the sentence level. As a rule of thumb, each sentence in a text will build on the information of the previous sentence, typically by first linking in some way with the previously given information and then adding newer information afterwards, so that the sentence can be analysed in terms of the 'theme' or given information, and 'rheme', the comment or new information. The theme/rheme structure can clearly be observed in the first two sentences of Immanuel Kant's famous answer to the question '*Was ist Aufklärung?*' His first sentence picks up the principal term of the question and elaborates on it, and then the second sentence again reprises the final term of the first sentence and, in turn, develops the argument:

> **Was ist *Aufklärung*?**
>
> *Aufklärung* ist der Ausgang des Menschen aus seiner selbst verschuldeten Unmündigkeit. *Unmündigkeit* ist das Unvermögen, sich seines Verstandes ohne Leitung eines andern zu bedienen.
>
> (Kant 2002: 9 [Our italics, MR/MW])

It goes perhaps without saying that the structure of most sentences cannot be so readily analysed as these, and that 'given' and 'new' information are broad categories indeed. Their refinement need not concern us here. Rather, for present purposes it is sufficient to note that the *pragmatic* or communicatively governed ordering of a sentence can play a significant role in the creation of textual cohesion, and thus in the overall functional success of the text, and that the text's information structure itself may merit becoming an object of translation.

The different principles governing German and English word order often confront the translator with a choice: maintain the pragmatically or communicatively determined order of ideas, or maintain the syntax of the source text. We can see this clearly in the excerpt from Doderer's *Strudlhofstiege* that we considered in the previous chapter:

> Freilich, man wußte so halb und halb, worin man lebte, ganz beiläufig, aus dem Augenwinkel gesehen: in Umgebungen, die, an Schweigsamkeit nicht zu überbieten, sich dennoch unaufhörlich mit Übergewalt aussprachen. In den Schluchten und Rissen nah an den Wänden des Bergs, in diesen Wunden des Walds, die jeder Frühling wieder mit dumpf trommelnden Wassermassen neu aufriß, lag jetzt, da sie sommerlich grün zum Teil wieder heilten, der verlassene und trockene feine Sand in den großen Becken zwischen glattgewaschenen Blöcken.
>
> (Doderer 1995: 228)

The first part of the highlighted sentence ('*In den Schluchten*') relates to the previous sentence's announcement of the violent surroundings; the second part of the sentence and indeed the subject of the sentence '*der verlassene . . . Sand*' relates to what comes next, the overgrown stream bed. If we wish to maintain the order of ideas we need to make some amendments to the grammatical structure of the source text. Here the prepositional phrases in the initial position are promoted to become the sentence-initial subject of a main clause by introducing the verb 'to be', making this clause independent of the verb 'to lie':

> The ravines and crevices near the mountain were wounds in the forest that each spring tore open with torrents of low beating water, and, now that they had begun to heal to a summer green, the fine sand lay there, dry and abandoned in the large hollows between rocks washed smooth.

Our principal problem when putting this sentence into English is that this information sequence is made grammatically possible in the ST because German can both readily place the subject after the finite verb in main clauses and have an extended element first in the sentence (here two prepositional phrases in apposition, the second qualified by a relative clause). This is because the underlying structure of modern German sentences is based on the fixed placement of the verb, around which other elements can be moved with relative flexibility. In an earlier chapter (Chapter 2) we drew attention to the fact that the verbal idea is split in a typical German sentence between the second position and the final position, creating a 'bracket' structure (*Satzklammer*), as we can see in the following examples:

Initial element ('Vorfeld')	Opening bracket	Central elements ('Mittelfeld')	Closing bracket
Wir	sind	extra seinetwegen nach Rom	gefahren.
In seiner Antwort	wich	er meinen Fragen	aus
Der Donnerstag	war	trüb und neblig	

As the grammatical subject in German is not associated so closely as in English with the sentence-initial position, the subject in German can often be the 'rheme', newer information, with some other element occupying the 'theme' position in the *Vorfeld*, as the following example from a study of adhesive layers in metal-plastic hybrid materials shows. In both these sentences, the post-verbal subject is 'newer' information than the information in the *Vorfeld*, a structure which, as is clear here, functions to promote textual cohesion:

> Als Adhäsionsschicht [i.e. in the layering of the material] kommt ein im Institut entwickelter Niedertemperatur-Uretdionpulverlack in unterschiedlichen Aushärtungsstufen zum Einsatz. Im Rahmen der Entwicklung dieser Pulverlacksysteme wurde von Lehman für den Fall der Anwesenheit spezieller Katalysatoren ein bis dahin unbekannter Reaktionsmechanismus gefunden.
>
> (Bräuer et al. 2012: 535)

Additionally, provided the verbal bracket is in place, the *Vorfeld* can be considerably extended either for stylistic reasons, as in our Doderer text, or for organisational communicative purposes as in the following example from the metal-plastic hybrid text in which a long noun phrase which is the accusative object occupies the first position:

> Einen Überblick zu aktuellen Trends, Möglichkeiten, Besonderheiten und Grenzen sowie über realisierbare Funktionsintegrationen bei der Herstellung von Metall-Kunststoff-Verbunden mittels Spritzgießen geben Heinle, Ridder, Amacio-Fihlo und Michaeli.
>
> (Bräuer et al. 2012: 535)

While German word order is thus in large measure the product of pragmatic concerns (with the exception of the verb which remains largely fixed), word order in English has a more significant grammatical function, which limits the extent to which it can be manipulated to meet communicative or pragmatic ends, especially in standard English written texts. In English the subject must precede the verb in statements and the order of subsequent elements indicates their function as direct or indirect objects. The translator who wishes to preserve the information structure of a German ST thus often needs to introduce some level of syntactic change which will allow the order of information to fit into natural English sentence patterns, as in the following examples:

- *Active to passive/accusative object to subject*: **Diesen Roman** hat Gunter Grass geschrieben/***This novel** was written by Gunter Grass*

- *Active to passive with change of verb*: **Dieses Produkt** trägt eines der oben gezeigten Recycling-Symbole/***The product*** *is marked with one of the above recycling symbols*
- *Part of main clause to subordinate clause*: **Schon der Name signalisiert** ein sorgfältig durchdachtes Qualitätsprogramm/*As its name suggests, this is a painstakingly devised quality programme* (example from Chesterman 2000: 97)
- *Many rewritings conflate a number of changes*: **Für diese Zubereitungs-weise eignen sich besonders** kleine Fleischstücke (unter 1 kg) und solche mit derber Fleischfaser/***Braising is an excellent method for cooking*** *small joints of less than 2½ lb (1 kg), as well as for the tougher cuts of meat*

The exact strategy will be determined by context, but also genre, which can itself determine word order: perhaps the most common example here are closing formulae for letters, where German frequently uses a placeholder '*es*' or similar, as a way of ending with the subject: '*es grüßt Euch ganz herzlich, XX*'.

It is by no means the case that all information structures need to be maintained, and in practice the choice between information structure and grammatical equivalence is not straightforward. This is partly because English can of course tolerate some adverbials before the subject (tomorrow, I will go shopping), also subordinate clauses, etc. In particular, because pronoun subjects are unlikely to be an object of special focus or have 'communicative value' (Lühr 1986/2000: 283), sentences with pronominal subjects in German often retain them in English translation, with the resulting, but insignificant, change of information structure (Rogers 2006: 50).

Focus, information distribution, directionality

Now we move on to a related but slightly different issue, the effects that the different structures of English and German sentences have beyond the theme/rheme ordering outlined. Not only do German and English differ in that German has a pragmatic word order and English a grammatical word order, but also in the *directionality* of their sentence structures: in English sentences or clauses, the verb occurs relatively early, with development to the right, i.e. English is 'right-branching'; in German sentences, this is essentially the other way around, i.e. German is 'left-branching'. We can get a sense of this difference in simple infinitive structures: '*jede Woche schwimmen gehen*'/'go swimming every week', in main clauses: '*er wollte jede Woche mit seinen Freunden ins Schwimmbad gehen*'/'he wanted to go to the swimming pool with his friends every week', or in subordinate clauses: '... *weil er jede Woche mit seinen Freunden ins Schwimmbad gehen wollte*'/'... because he wanted to go to the swimming pool with his friends every week'. Furthermore, the German bracket structure in main clauses creates an initial point of **focus** around the end of the *Vorfeld* and near the first part of the verbal idea (in second position) and another at the end, creating a kind of 'tension' which presents significant problems for simultaneous interpreters, for instance, as do also subordinate clauses with their verb-final structure.

A great many sentences in German are marked by an announcement and completion pattern, whether that means reading a finite form of '*haben*' or '*sein*' that points to a past participle or infinitive to come, a modal verb that points to an infinitive or a *Funktionsverb* that points to its complement at the end. The same logic applies when the reader encounters a conjunction such as '*wenn*' or '*dass*', or a relative pronoun. There is a certain tautness in the syntactic structure, a stretched line that is quite alien to most forms of English. We can see this principle in action in the following sentence written by a native speaker of German writing in English: 'She **cites** as the reason she includes all ten plays in her analysis **their common theme**'. In general the 'heavier' elements of the *Mittelfeld*, those complements most closely related to the verb will often come nearest the final position: '*Uwe ist gestern mit der neuen Maschine leider zu tief geflogen*'/ 'Unfortunately, Uwe **flew too low** yesterday in the new plane'. In a comparative paper on German and English focus, Doherty (2005) suggests a typical information distribution pattern of '2–3–1' in German, with English closer to '3–2–1', in which 1 is the newest, 3 the most 'given' information (in German, often a subject pronoun tucked in after the finite verb), giving concise expression to the relative importance of the *Vorfeld* and the latter part of the *Mittelfeld*.

But the ends of sentences often follow different patterns too. Whereas the German sentence is marked often by a sense of completion, by a closing bracket, English typically not only requires information after the verb phrase, but in fact typically orders both more important information here (end-focus) and, significantly, more complex syntactic structures too (end-weight). The following German example (the relevant part highlighted) has an extended subject in the *Mittelfeld*, and we feel the focus in the sentence just before the final verb which then completes the sentence; the communicatively weakest element—'*dazu*'— appears in this case in the *Vorfeld*:

Die Schweiz—amtlich heißt sie *Schweizerische Eidgenossenschaft*—ist eines der führenden Reiseländer der Erde. Dazu haben ihre günstige geographische Lage im Herzen Europas, die sprichwörtliche Gastfreundchaft der Bewohner, die sich schon früh auf den Fremdenverkehr eingestellt hatten, und der besondere Reiz ihrer landwirtschaftlichen Schönheiten beigetragen.

(Example from Snell-Hornby 1985: 22)

If we kept the very extended subject in English, we might end up with:

Its favourable geographical position in the heart of Europe, the proverbial hospitality of its inhabitants, who soon adapted to tourism, and the special charm of its scenic attractions, have contributed to this.

(Example from Snell-Hornby 1985: 22)

The weakness of this translation, the unidiomatic ending, is the product both of placing the given information at the end, and, at the same time, having the complex subject come first. A more idiomatic rendering might be:

> This is mainly due to its favourable geographical position at the heart of Europe, the proverbial hospitality of its inhabitants who soon adapted to tourism, and the special charm of its scenic attractions.
>
> (Example from Snell-Hornby 1985: 23)

In short, dealing with the distribution of information at a sentence level involves being aware that German and English sentences typically have different patterns of grammatical focus which constrain the translator's freedom to accommodate theme/rheme patterns between sentences.

Concluding remarks

In this chapter we have examined a number of related issues that arise in translation between German and English at the level of the sentence and which often require syntactic shifts. We have differentiated between information structure broadly (including issues of what could be called the textual flow between sentences), and the related issue of focus in the sentence governed by the different directionalities of German and English syntax. The first step for the translator into English is often simply to accept that syntactic transpositions will be inevitable in many cases. A worthwhile way to explore these sorts of issues is, as so often, to read specifically for them: read looking for sentence structure, thinking first about information structure, then about other, more stylistic or communicative emphasis. Often enough, recognising just how frequently German texts vary word order is enough to help us realise that transferring those structures into English will require thought and a variety of approaches. It is also a good idea to read a range of genres for this; look also at translations critically, and English texts too.

Further reading

Doherty, Monika 2005. 'Topic-worthiness in German and English', *Linguistics*, 43(1), pp. 181–206.

Durrell, Martin 1992. *Using German*. Cambridge: Cambridge University Press [Chapter 5.1, pp. 228–39.].

Johnson, Sally and Braber, Natalie 2008. *Exploring the German Language*. Cambridge: Cambridge University Press [Chapter 7 gives a clear exposition of the basics of German sentence structure.].

Practical 9

9.1 RESEARCH EXERCISE

Assignment

The aim of the assignment is to help you get some sense of the scope of the issue by exploring German texts and reading attentively for the types of sentences that have been discussed here. You can use a text corpus of your choosing, preferably mixing a range of genres and registers:

i   Find sentences with elements in the *Vorfeld* other than the subject—how can you analyse these? How do they function in the textual structure? Which ones offer potential problems of translation?
ii   Find sentences that exemplify focal points of German. Do these present similar or different problems of translation to the first set of sentences?
iii Find sentences with a relatively weak end bracket. Attempting a rough translation of these, can you find anywhere it is useful to consider the principle of 'end-weight'?

9.2 TRANSLATION: LITERARY HISTORY

Assignment

The following extract is from: Johannes Hösle, *Kleine Geschichte der italienischen Literatur*. It is a brief history of Italian literature, which aims to provide an overview for students and the general reader; it is a small paperback, and each author is afforded only a few pages. This section is about Federigo Tozzi.

i   Analyse the sentence into its constituent parts.
ii   Translate into English.

ST

Federigo Tozzi
Während in Frankreich in der zweiten Hälfte des 19. Jahrhunderts mit Léon Bloy, Paul Claudel und verschiedenen anderen eine gegen die im Zeichen des Agnostizismus stehende Literatur des positivistischen Zeitalters gerichtete katholische
5   Erneuerungsbewegung (*renouveau catholique*) die spirituellen Werte von Christentum und Kirche neu entdeckte, war die römische Kurie darauf bedacht, wenigstens in Italien jeden Autonomieanspruch der Intellektuellen bereits im Keim zu ersticken, wie bereits das Beispiel Antonio Fogazzaro zeigte.

(Hösle 1995: 180–2)

9.3 TRANSLATION: TOURIST GUIDE

Assignment

i   You have been commissioned to produce English text for some of the popular mid-market *HB Bildatlas* series of illustrated regional guides, in this case the one entitled *Südlicher Schwarzwald—Hochrhein—Kaiserstuhl*, from which the ST has been taken. Discuss the decisions that you have to take before starting detailed translation of this ST, and outline and justify the approach that you adopt.

ii   Translate the ST into English.

iii   Explain the main decisions of detail you took in connection with grammar.

iv   Compare your TT with a sample one, which will be given to you by your tutor.

Contextual information

The book is in A4 format and includes maps; however, most double-page spreads, including that with the ST, have a 7 cm-wide column, far right, containing about 220 words of text, and about six good-quality colour photographs of various sizes arranged on the remaining area; the terraced vineyards feature prominently.

ST

Mit neuem Gesicht:
der vulkanische Kaiserstuhl
Egal, aus welcher Richtung man sich dem Kaiserstuhl nähert: Schon von weitem ist
diese mitten in der Oberrheinebene aufgebuckelte Erhebung zwischen Vogesen und
5 Schwarzwald zu erkennen. Die bis zu 557 Meter hoch aufragende Hügelgruppe macht
ihrem monumental klingenden Namen alle Ehre, denn die durch längst erloschene
Vulkantätigkeiten entstandenen Bergkuppen sind in der Form eines großen, nach
Südwesten geöffneten Hufeisens angeordnet. Das Ganze sieht aus wie ein riesiger
Lehnstuhl, der einem sonnenhungrigen Fabelriesen bequem Platz bieten würde.
10   Daß die Sonne in dieser Gegend eine überragende Rolle spielt, läßt sich nicht
übersehen. Die überall in großem Maßstab neu angelegten Rebterrassen weisen
darauf hin. Sie haben dem Kaiserstuhl in den vergangenen zwei Jahrzehnten ein
völlig neues Gesicht verliehen, sehr zum Leidwesen der Naturschützer. Im kleinen
verraten aber noch immer zahlreiche aus mittelmeerischen Gefilden stammenden
15 Pflanzen am Wegesrand, daß im Kaiserstuhl südländische Klimaeinflüsse
vorherrschen.
    Es gibt übrigens ganz in der Nähe 'unbearbeitete' Natur: das Altrheingebiet
Taubergießen.
Neue Terrassen, alte Hohlwege
20 Den schönsten Blick auf die Kaiserstuhllandschaft gewährt der Badberg. Man erreicht
diese kahle, von Trockenrasen bedeckte Buckelwelt am besten vom Schelinger Paß
aus, wo ein von langen Tischen und Bänken umgebener Kiosk zur zünftigen Vesper
einlädt. Links erhebt sich das Totenkopfmassiv, leicht zu erkennen an seinem
Sendemast, und im Hintergrund, Richtung Rhein, erkennt man die wie von
Zyklopenhand hingeklotzten, treppenförmig ansteigenden Rebterrassen der
'Oberbergener Mondhalde', eine der bekannten Kaiserstühler Weinlagen.

(Klugmann 1989: 21)

References

Primary

Bräuer, M., Edelmann, M., Häußler, L. and Kühnert, I. 2012. 'Metall-Kunsttoff-Verbunde: Untersuchungen zur Wirkungsweise einer Adhäsionsschicht aus Uretdionpulverlacksystemen', *Materialwissenschaft und Werkstofftechnik*, 43, pp. 535–43.

Doderer, Heimito von 1995. *Die Strudlhofstiege*. Munich: Beck.

Hösle, Johannes 1995. *Kleine Geschichte der italienischen Literatur*. Munich: Beck.

Kant, Immanuel 2002. *Was ist Aufklärung?* Edited by Bahr, Ehrhard. Stuttgart: Reclam.

Klugmann, U. (ed.) 1989. *HB Bildatlas Südlicher Schwarzwald*. Hamburg: HB Verlags- und Vertriebs-Gesellschaft mbH.

Secondary

Chesterman, Andrew 2000. *Memes of Translation*. Amsterdam and Philadelphia: John Benjamins.

Lühr, Rosemarie 1986/2000. *Neuhochdeutsch: eine Einführung in die Sprachwissenschaft*. 6th edn. Munich: Fink.

Rogers, Margaret 2006. 'Structuring information in English: A specialist translation perspective on sentence beginnings', *The Translator*, 12(1), pp. 29–64.

Snell-Hornby, Mary 1985. 'Translation as a means of integrating language teaching and linguistics', in Titford, C. and Hieke, A. E. (eds) *Translation in Foreign Language Teaching and Testing*. Tübingen: Narr, pp. 21–8.

10 Grammatical issues in translation

In this chapter we continue our focus on translation problems that arise from the formal properties of texts. In the previous chapter we considered shifts at the sentential level; in this chapter we discuss what we have called 'grammatical' changes, i.e. those changes that necessarily occur in translation at the level of the word and phrase because the available structural patterns and habits of expression in the two languages are different.

Grammatical shifts

One way of viewing translation is to see it as a series of changes, 'shifts' or 'transpositions', which occur even in literal or close translation. When we move from '*all-abendlich*' to 'every evening' we can analyse that shift as a move from one word class to another, from an adverb to a noun phrase, but also from a compound to a qualified noun. We make these changes without the need for special comment, indeed these pairings are often listed as equivalents in the dictionary, but it is important to be able to analyse what changes have occurred, even in literal translation, to account for, and thus seek to manage, change in meaning or suitability. In this discussion we are interested both in the types of obligatory translation changes that occur when a close translation is impossible owing to formal differences between the source and the target language, but also in optional changes where a direct translation would be inappropriate for pragmatic reasons. We can see how quickly problems of this kind arise in the following well-known passage about the German language:

> Französisch ist ein edler Park, Italienisch ein großer, heller bunter Wald. Aber Deutsch ist beinahe noch wie ein Urwald, so dicht und geheimnisvoll, so ohne großen Durchgang, und doch tausendpfadig. Im Park kann man sich nicht verirren, in der italienischen Waldhelle nicht so leicht und gefährlich; aber im Deutsch kann einer in vier, fünf Minuten im Dickicht verschwinden. Darum, weil der Weg so schwierig scheint, suchen die meisten möglichst gradlinig hindurchzumarschieren, was eigentlich gegen die Natur dieser Sprache ist. Sie will gewiß eine Hauptrichtung, aber ladet durch hundert Pfade und Pfädchen nach links und rechts bald aus ihr heraus, bald wieder in sie hinein.
>
> (Federer 1928: 188f.)

It is obvious that our approach to the first and second sentences must be different. In the first sentence, word-for-word translation is structurally possible. In the second sentence, we encounter '*Urwald*' and '*tausendpfadig*' for which there are no direct equivalents in English, but which might each be rendered as 'primaeval forest', and 'crossed by a thousand paths'. Analysing these transpositions involves being aware of changes in the distribution of meaning between the German original and any English translation. The prefix '*Ur-*' becomes an adjective ('primaeval') in our English version, which collocates well with 'forest'. But the adjectival suffix '*-ig*' ('*tausend-pfad-ig*') which indicates the condition of something, presents more problems. Established words such as '*schläfrig*' or '*klebrig*' have '-y' suffixes in English: 'sleepy', 'sticky', but 'thousand-path-y' does not work, so the meaning of that component has to be represented in a more creative way. Our suggestion is to transpose the suffix into an adjectival phrase, 'crossed by . . . '.

Translation scholars have charted typical shifts or transpositions and classify them according to type as a way of analysing the translation process. One of the pioneers of Translation Studies, the Scottish linguist J.C. Catford, for example, distinguishes between level shifts and category shifts (Catford 1965; see pp. 73–82 for 'translation shifts'). Level shifts involve the replacement of one level of language with another: the translation '*Ur-*' > 'primaeval' can be analysed as a level shift (morphology > lexis). All other kinds of other changes in form, such as change in basic word order (structural shift), change from a phrase to a clause (unit or rank shift), change from a noun to a verb (class shift) and a change within a particular part of the language system such as voice, e.g. active to passive (inter-term shift) Catford groups under 'category shifts'.

A similar, but slightly different approach was adopted by two other early translation scholars, the French-Canadian scholars Jean Paul Vinay and Paul Darbelnet (Vinay and Darbelnet 1958/1995). Apparently prompted by (poor) translations of road-signs in Canada, they proposed a framework through which translation could be systematised. They distinguish *inter alia* between 'transpositions', similar to Catford's 'shifts', and 'modulations', changes which make the TT more idiomatic, such as a change in perspective, often a change in verb. Their work, dating back nearly 60 years, has understandably been the subject of some criticism, as has Catford's. One of the main points which translation scholars have made is that their examples are not authentic i.e. not taken from actual translations or 'idealised' and that they are purely linguistic with the sentence being the highest level of analysis, i.e. decontextualised (Munday 2016: 97). In other words, there is little if any consideration of translation as communication. Nevertheless, Vinay and Darbelnet's model in particular, as well as Catford's, has been popular in translator training through the decades. We would like to present the 'shifts' discussed here in the spirit of linguistic arpeggios: not yet a full performance but useful practice in developing technique. The names of these shifts are not too important; indeed, translation scholars do not agree on them, and they often overlap or are difficult to apply in practice. But these early contributions are useful to our present purpose as this linguistic approach facilitates *formal* analysis within the boundary of a sentence. For you what is important is being able to trace translation changes, thus accounting for potential changes in meaning.

Problem areas between German and English

Affixation and compounding

It should be clear from the previous discussion that it is not possible, nor especially useful to enumerate all possible grammatical changes that occur in translation. We can, however, survey some particular types of difficulty, beginning with small issues, morphemes. There are a number of prefixes and suffixes in German for which we have no direct equivalent in English and which need either partial translation, expansion, or omission, depending on the case. We have already seen the prefix '*ur-*', which we translated with a rank shift (morpheme > word). Now consider the following example. It is the title of an exhibition at the Munich Pinakothek: *Neue Nachbarschaften II* 'New Neighbours II'. Presented as a word-for-word translation (the English printed directly below the German), the English arguably leaves the German suffix '*-schaft*' untranslated. While '*die Nachbarschaft*' can indeed mean 'the neighbours', the sense of the German is arguably 'new neighbourhoods' or in this specific case 'the fact of being new neighbours' as paintings in the museum which would not normally be exhibited together were displayed together because of renovation; here the German word puts as much emphasis on the relationship of the paintings as on the paintings themselves. Another common example is the translation of '*-tum*', in '*Bürgertum*' or '*Beamtentum*'—here a more concrete alternative may be needed, e.g. '*Es ist nicht nur Schöpfung des ökonomischen Mittels, wie das Beamtentum überhaupt, sondern . . .*'/'Not only is this a creation of the economic means, as were the officials themselves, but . . .' (example from Linguee).

Problems involving verbal derivation are perhaps more complex because verbal prefixes can convey shades of meaning, often expressing *Aktionsart*: '*er-*', for example, can express an ingressive aspect ('*erblühen*', '*erklingen*', '*erkranken*', '*erwachen*'), '*ab-*' can be mutative ('*abnehmen*', '*abtragen*') or terminative ('*abwarten*', '*abbrennen*'). Neat progressions such as '*erblühen*', '*blühen*', '*verblühen*' are transparently systematic in German, but often lexicalised and less clear in English ('come into bloom'/'bloom', 'bloom', 'wither'). Other kinds of meaning can be expressed similarly: '*anblicken*', '*ansehen*', '*anlächeln*', '*anlachen*', '*anfahren*', '*anbrüllen*', '*anfauchen*', '*anschnauzen*' correspond to English verbs expressing person-to-person contact, for example, and can be contrasted with, say, '*lachen über*'.

One of the most obvious difficulties posed by the Federer example are its various compounds and derivatives: '*Waldhelle*', '*Hauptrichtung*', '*Urwald*', '*tausendpfadig*', '*Pfädchen*'. Compounding in German is very often parallel with English, but more prolific: English has no compact noun match for e.g. '*Fundort*' or '*Hausrat*'. Most compounds are nevertheless unproblematic: even '*Aschaffenburger Ungeziefervertilgungsanstalt*' (incised over a doorway in that town) is imposing rather than impossible. Elsewhere they can be markers of style: in

Schiller's *Maria Stuart*, for example, '*frischblütend*', '*leichtbedeckt*' and '*rache-fodernd*', occur in close proximity. The difficulties of the compounds and deriva-tives in our initial example are in part the result of their evocative nature, in part their role in maintaining a taut style. Some are relatively straightforward ('*Wald-helle*' might give 'woodland brightness'; '*Urwald*' > 'primaeval forest'); others are trickier: '*tausendpfadig*' is an example both of German's capacity to create neologisms through compounding and derivation and of a tendency in German for adjectives and adverbs to have a significance we more easily see in verbs and nouns in English. '*Pfädchen*' only really presents a problem because it has been preceded by '*Pfade*': 'paths and little paths' is an unacceptable repetition. 'Paths and byways' might be one solution which is rhythmically close and works within the text's semantic field of roads ('*Weg*', '*Durchgang*', '*pfadig*').

Phrases and clauses

A second point emerging from the Federer example concerns the relative semantic import of prepositions in German: '*ohne großen Durchgang*' might, as we have suggested, be rendered 'lacking a great thoroughfare'. What this highlights in German is that a prepositional phrase can express a meaning we might consider verbal in English. In '*er eilte über den Platz*' the verb conveys a sense of pace, while motion and direction are implied and conveyed by the preposition. We can do this in English too, 'he hurried across the square' but the tendency is stronger in German: '*Der Aufruhr im Breidenbacher Hof war groß. Das Grand Hotel befand sich im Ausnahmezustand. Da mußte man durch*' (Pleschinski 2015: 11). Here we would have to supply a verb (expansion): 'you had *to get* through'.

Dealing with German prepositional phrases by substituting a verb in English, often a participle, is perhaps one of the most common transpositions. Indeed, prepositions rarely constitute a unit of translation themselves; they are rarely translated in a word-for-word sense. '*Bei*', for example, may stand for 'near', 'in circumstances of', 'in the event of', 'with', occasionally 'by', and even 'in spite of'. But it is only in a technical or formal context that 'in the event of' will be used in English. Otherwise, when '*bei*' is used in that precise sense, most translators will turn to grammatical rearrangement. For instance, in a text about translation problems in the EU, a sentence begins: '*Selbst bei einer Erweiterung der EU um lediglich fünf Länder . . .* '. It is not beyond the resources of English to ren-der this idea through roughly equivalent grammatical structures, but (as so often with '*bei*') an idiomatic English version can more adequately be produced by replacing *preposition + noun* with an if-clause ('Even if the EU is/were enlarged by . . . '), in other words through a unit or rank shift from a phrase to a clause. Newmark (1988: 85) notes a similar transposition: although the prepositional phrase '*Bei jeder sich bietenden Gelegenheit . . .* ' has its phrasal equivalents in English—'At every opportunity that occurs', 'At every available opportunity'—it also goes quite naturally into a clause: 'Whenever the opportunity occurs'.

Making morphological or syntactic changes is often a question of style as much as necessity. For instance, German relative clauses almost always *can* be rendered with a closely matching English relative clause; and as a consequence, they too often *are* so rendered. The result is not by any means always an unidiomatic calque: examples (1) to (3) that follow could just as well use a TL relative. But English has a range of other ways of handling information contained in a ST relative clause. Participial constructions are perhaps the solution most often overlooked by translators, but, as the examples show, there are other possibilities. The examples show two types of relative clause: those which modify a preceding noun phrase (examples (1) and (5)), and 'wer' as a relative (examples (2), (3) and (4)) which can be understood as 'the one who' although 'the one' is not specified. The 'wer'-type can be more problematic to translate closely.

1a   Kunden, die auf sofortiger Erstattung bestehen, werden an Schalter 10 verwiesen.
1b   Customers *insisting* on immediate refunds are referred to Desk 10. (Rank shift, clause > phrase)

2a   Wer auf den Ausflug lieber verzichtet, meldet sich bitte bei meiner Kollegin.
2b   *Anyone preferring not to take* the excursion should see my colleague. (Rank shift, clause > phrase)

3a   Wer sich von so was beleidigt fühlt, möge einfach wegbleiben.
3b   *Those offended* by such things should just stay away. (Rank shift, clause > noun phrase)

4a   Wer in [der Politik] Machtpositionen behauptet, ausbauen oder erringen will, wer nur die eigenen Zwecke verfolgt, [. . .]. Wer dagegen Politik auch als Aufgabe versteht, [. . .].
4b   *If I* use politics to assert, consolidate or win power, *if I pursue* my own aims exclusively [. . .]. *If on the other hand I see* politics as involving a task that is given to me [. . .]. (Modulation, relative clause > conditional clause)

5a   [*From a swimwear blurb*] Das Badethema 'Magische Zauberwelten' hat Felina in vier faszinierende Farbgruppen aufgeteilt, die Sie je nach Anlass und Stimmung durch die Sonne begleiten.
5b   [. . .] four fascinating colour tonalities *to suit* your mood and the occasion all summer long. (Modulation, relative clause > infinitive phrase)

The need to think sensitively and flexibly about possible solutions that use the full resources of English is perhaps nowhere more obvious than in dealing with the extended attributive phrase. This one is representative of the many difficult and complicated cases which test the ingenuity of the translator. The source is an account of Robert Koch's bacteriological research. It may take a little thought to produce an accurate, reasonably idiomatic English rendering of the clause beginning at 'Dem—' in the following text:

Selbst die berühmten Postulate entpuppen sich bei näherem Hinsehen als historiographisches Konstrukt der Schüler Kochs: Dem—wie erwähnt—von Loeffler geprägten Begriff der Postulate standen von Fall zu Fall variierende Nachweiskriterien bakterieller Ätiologien bei Koch selbst gegenüber.

(Gradmann: unpublished)

As often happens with this construction, there is no obvious best translation. In the TT extract reproduced below for discussion, the relative clause that is probably the nearest thing to a conventional solution has been avoided in dealing with the first of the two problems (*Dem—wie erwähnt—von Loeffler geprägten Begriff der Postulate*) and adopted—after a fashion—in the second (*von Fall zu Fall variierende Nachweiskriterien bakterieller Ätiologien bei Koch selbst*):

Having become a recognized concept thanks to Loeffler, as already mentioned, they nonetheless must be seen in the context of criteria set up by Koch himself for demonstrating bacterial aetiology—criteria which vary from case to case.

(Gradmann 2003: 87)

The essential issue here is recognising the function of the structure in the original: encapsulation is typical of German academic prose, a characteristic thus of a particular register. English academic prose generally conforms to slightly different norms (it is less dominated by noun phrases, for example), so that the syntactic structure becomes less important in itself, and indeed needs to be replaced with target-language appropriate forms.

German adverbial constructions

Now we move on to explore in more detail one area where word-for-word translations are often possible, but where an optional grammatical transposition may lead to a more idiomatic, more 'natural' text (Newmark 1988: 24ff.), namely thinking about the frequent correspondence between German verb + adverb constructions and English verb + verb constructions. Consider the following, in which two possible translations are offered:

6a [. . .] bis allmählich die Liebenden [. . .] aus den Seidengründen dämmerten.
6b [. . .] until the lovers [. . .] gradually became visible in the silken depths.
6c [. . .] until the lovers [. . .] began to materialise out of the silken depths.

7a Seine Besuche wurden allmählich seltener und hörten zuletzt ganz auf.
7b His visits gradually grew less frequent and eventually stopped altogether.
7c His visits began to grow fewer, and eventually stopped altogether.

While the TTs marked (b), taken individually, are not particularly 'strange' in English, and are not mistranslations, they do not take up an option that is in spontaneous English used readily and often: the double-verb construction. That is to say, the STs' '*allmählich*' + finite verb combination might have been replaced by 'begin' + infinitive, as in the (c) translations. Are the (c) versions less good? Or just less likely to be suggested by the ST's syntactic structure? The decision here is whether to stick to the German construction, which is possible in English, or whether to favour a more typically English formulation. While in the previously mentioned cases the adverbs were certainly an option, let's consider some of the drawbacks of using the verb + adverb construction elsewhere.

To remain with the pair '*allmählich*'/'begin', literal translation of '*allmählich*' as 'gradually' may limit the scope for translating surrounding text because of the collocations available. In the following sentence, for instance, the ST verb '*sich abzeichnen*' offers the translator a choice of renderings. Some, for instance 'emerge', are a collocative match for the adverb 'gradually'; others are not. Should this adverb be allowed to determine the choice of TL verb for '*sich abzeichnen*'? Why limit the choice? TT (c) shows an alternative way:

8a   Eine neue Gefahr zeichnete sich allmählich ab.
8b   A fresh danger became/was becoming gradually apparent.
8c   A fresh danger began/was beginning to loom.

The constraints arising from the use of 'gradually' in this example indicate how the translator cannot treat words in isolation. For example, a reason for avoiding 'begin' in translating '*allmählich*' may be euphony ('*begin to become*'), or it may be unconscious retention of ST structures by a translator working quickly—at the expense of TT alternatives.

That there is indeed a disparity between the two languages, with English favouring many more two-verb structures, is sharply apparent to translators working *into* German. Here, certain frequently used English structures, such as the pseudo-cleft structure in example (9a), do not travel well into German. The solution here is a rank shift from clause > adverb:

9a   But that wasn't how he went about it. What he did was to write to Mr Smith asking for more time.
9b   Diesen Weg hat er jedoch nicht gewählt. Er schrieb vielmehr an Herrn Smith und bat um mehr Zeit.

The following example poses difficulties over the verb combination 'come to appreciate'. The most straightforward solution is to report, not the completed 'journey' ('has come'), but the new position arrived at ('now appreciates') with the sense of a change in attitude being expressed through the adverb + verb structure in German, an example of a 'reversal of terms' modulation (Vinay and Darbelnet):

10a He has come to appreciate that money alone is not the answer to his problems.
10b Er sieht inzwischen ein, dass seinen Problemen nicht mit Geld allein beizukommen ist.

This solution points to the significant potential of adverbs of time; some, such as '*früher*' have a role in German that tenses might have in English (er hat *früher* viel geschrieben > he *used to* write a lot); some such as: '*schon*', '*noch*', '*nicht mehr*', convey ideas of change, continuation and cessation often covered in English by verbs such as 'begin', 'go on', 'give up'.

The next example presents major problems which cannot be easily handled with a literal translation:

11a There, without bothering to light the lamp that stood ready with its box of matches, I tried one key after another in the door until I had found the right one.
11b Dort, ohne die samt Streichholzschachtel bereitstehende Lampe erst anzuzünden, probierte ich . . .

The English sentence is complex (containing five clauses, including two non-finite ones), and translations involving '*sich die Mühe geben*' are unwieldy and implausible here: they miss the point that 'without bothering to' is a stock formulation that modalises the negative much as a German modal particle ('*erst*') might. And the use of the extended attribute allows the same information order to be retained in the German while actually reducing the number of clauses.

Our final example in this group presents two separate verb-on-verb combinations, 'continued . . . to see' and 'came no nearer to deciding'. The first finds a grammatical counterpart in German in '*fuhr fort . . . zu sehen*', and thus could tempt the translator towards a stylistically infelicitous TT. The second is patently resistant to literal translation, and thus may guide the translator, usefully, to the underlying principle: namely that in German this is adverb territory. A solution covering both problems might be:

12a Meanwhile, I continued occasionally to see something of Quiggin, though I came no nearer to deciding which of the various views held about him were true.
12b Ich hatte auch weiterhin noch gelegentlichen Kontakt zu Quiggin, nur stand ich so ratlos wie eh und je vor der Frage, welche der verschiedenen Ansichten über ihn denn eigentlich zuträfen.

Concluding remarks

The aim of this chapter has been in the first instance to explore some common difficulties that arise in translating between certain German and English words and phrases, that is to consider how German constructs meanings at a level below the sentence in ways that often cannot satisfactorily be done in English in the same way. The translation strategies that we have introduced, the way of thinking about and improving our translation procedures have been those of comparative stylistics, that is considering systematically the function of parallel sets of structures in German and English and the series of small grammatical changes that moving between two different structural patterns imposes. The danger is that in so doing we look for a list of ready-made solutions; really what the student of translation can take away from this approach is the very empowering ability to be able to create their own sets of observations, their own categories, and to use those observations to inform and support their own translation decisions.

Further reading

Baker, Mona 2011. *In Other Words*. 2nd edn. London: Routledge [Chapter 4 'Grammatical equivalence', pp. 92–130.].

Grabski, Michael and Stede, Manfred 2006. '*Bei*: Intraclausal coherence relations illustrated with a German preposition', *Discourse Processes*, 41(2), pp. 195–219.

Hansen, Sandra and Hansen-Schirra, Silvia 2012. 'Grammatical shifts in English-German noun phrases', in Steiner, E., Hansen-Schirra, S. and Neumann, S. (eds) Cross-*Linguistic Corpora for the Study of Translations: Insights from the Language Pair English-German*. Berlin: De Gruyter, pp. 133–45.

Munday, Jeremy 2016. *Introducing Translation Studies: Theories and Applications*. 4th edn. London and New York: Routledge [See Sections 4.1, Vinay and Darbelnet's model, pp. 88–95, and 4.2 Catford's translation 'shifts', pp. 95–7.].

Practical 10

10.1 TEXT FOR DISCUSSION: POEM

Assignment

Read the following poem, 'Der Werwolf' by Christian Morgenstern. What translation difficulties does the text raise that are relevant to our discussion? What solutions might you propose?

ST

Ein Werwolf eines Nachts entwich
von Weib und Kind, und sich begab
an eines Dorfschullehrers Grab
und bat ihn: Bitte, beuge mich!

5 Der Dorfschulmeister stieg hinauf
auf seines Blechschilds Messingknauf
und sprach zum Wolf, der seine Pfoten
geduldig kreuzte vor dem Toten:

'Der Werwolf',—sprach der gute Mann,
10 'des Weswolfs'—Genitiv sodann,
'dem Wemwolf'—Dativ, wie man's nennt,
'den Wenwolf'—damit hat's ein End'.

Dem Werwolf schmeichelten die Fälle,
er rollte seine Augenbälle.
15 Indessen, bat er, füge doch
zur Einzahl auch die Mehrzahl noch!

ST

Der Dorfschulmeister aber mußte
gestehn, daß er von ihr nichts wußte.
Zwar Wölfe gäb's in großer Schar,
20 doch 'Wer' gäb's nur im Singular.

Der Wolf erhob sich tränenblind—
er hatte ja doch Weib und Kind!
Doch da er kein Gelehrter eben,
so schied er dankend und ergeben.

(Morgenstern 1990: 87–8)

10.2 TRANSLATION COMPARISON: INTERNATIONAL AGREEMENT

Contextual information

The following text extracts are taken from a European Council decision in late 2002 on international co-operation against terrorism. It is not clear which of the texts, if either, is the ST.

Assignment

Analyse the language of the two texts contrastively, focusing on grammatical differences at word- and phrase-level.

DER RAT DER EUROPÄISCHEN UNION—
[. . .]
BESCHLIESST:

Artikel 1
5 **Schaffung des Mechanismus für die Begutachtung:**
(1) Es wird ein Mechanismus geschaffen, mit dem im Rahmen der internationalen Zusammenarbeit zwischen den Mitgliedstaaten die einzelstaatlichen Vorkehrungen zur Terrorismusbekämpfung gegenseitig begutachtet werden sollen; die Einzelheiten sind nachstehend geregelt.
10 (2) Die Mitgliedstaaten verpflichten sich zur engen Zusammenarbeit ihrer jeweiligen Behörden mit den Gutachterausschüssen, die im Rahmen dieses Beschlusses im Hinblick auf dessen Anwendung eingesetzt werden; hierbei sind die einzelstaatlichen Rechts- und Standesvorschriften zu beachten.

Artikel 2
15 **Gegenstand der Begutachtung**
(1) Für jede Begutachtungsrunde werden der genaue Gegenstand der Begutachtung sowie die Reihenfolge der zu begutachtenden Mitgliedstaaten auf Vorschlag des Vorsitzes vom Ausschuss 'Artikel 36' festgelegt.
Ferner legt der Ausschuss 'Artikel 36' je nach dem genauen Gegenstand, der
20 für die Begutachtung ausgewählt worden ist, fest, welche dem Ausschuss 'Artikel 36'

(*Continued*)

(Continued)

---

nachgeordnete Arbeitsgruppe des Rates die Begutachtung durchführen soll oder ob er diese selbst durchführt.

Der Ausschuss „Artikel 36" legt darüber hinaus für jede Begutachtungsrunde die Häufigkeit fest.

(Europäische Gemeinschaften 2002: L 349/1)

THE COUNCIL OF THE EUROPEAN UNION,
[...]
HAS DECIDED AS FOLLOWS:

Article 1
5 **Establishment of the evaluation mechanism**
  1. A mechanism for peer evaluation of the national arrangements in the fight against terrorism within the framework of international cooperation between Member States shall be established in accordance with the detailed rules set out below.
10 2. Each Member State shall undertake to ensure that its national authorities cooperate closely with the evaluation teams set up under this Decision with a view to its implementation, with due regard for the rules of law and ethics applicable at national level.

Article 2
15 **Evaluation subjects**
  1. For each evaluation exercise, the specific subject of the evaluation as well as the order in which Member States are to be evaluated shall be defined by the Article 36 Committee, on a proposal from the Presidency.
     Depending on the specific subject chosen for the evaluation, the Article 36
20 Committee shall also decide whether to designate a Council Working Party subordinate to it to carry out the evaluation or to carry it out itself.
     In addition, the Article 36 Committee shall decide the frequency of each evaluation exercise.

(European Communities 2002: L 349/1)

10.3 TRANSLATION: ESSAY

Contextual information

The following excerpt is from an essay by Joachim Fest, 'Die Intellektuellen und die totalitäre Epoche. Gedanken zu einer Geschichte der Täuschungen und Enttäuschungen', republished in a collection of Fest's essays in 2007. In this excerpt, Fest seeks to trace the intellectual background of totalitarianism in the eighteenth and nineteenth centuries.

Assignment

i   Translate the text into English.
ii As you are working through the text, make notes on the grammatical changes you are making, and, especially perhaps when revising the text, make notes on any optional modulations you make for pragmatic reasons.

ST

Auch eine kursorische, nur die gröberen Linien nachzeichnende Betrachtung muß bis ins 18. Jahrhundert zurückgehen. Im weiteren Sinne war die Aufklärung nichts anderes als die Machtergreifung des Gedankens, der sein Vorrecht gegenüber den bis dahin geltenden, auf bloßer Herkunft [. . .] beruhenden Herrschaftsverhältnissen behauptete
5 und schließlich durchsetzte. [. . .] Das hat der Epoche den großen, überschwenglichen Aufbruchston verschafft, dessen Nachhall bis ins unsere Tage reicht. [. . .]

Das gesamte 19. Jahrhundert tut sich groß im Erdenken immer neuer Entwürfe für eine nach den Prinzipien der Vernunft geordnete Welt: die Philosophen gaben sich diesen Planspielen ebenso hin wie die Dichter und die Schreibenden überhaupt, und die
10 Leidenschaft dafür erfaßte selbst die Künstler mit den Träumen einer endlichen Versöhnung von Kunst und Leben. Unversehens verwandelte sich die Welt in ein Labor abgemachter Zwecke und mit Menschen, die ein beliebig formbares, auf die reine gesellschaftliche Funktion reduziertes Material abgaben. In den Marschsäulen der totalitären Systeme, drei oder vier Menschenalter später, ist dieser Sachverhalt noch
15 symbolisch ausgedrückt, in den opferreichen Arbeitseinsätzen und den Umsiedlungsaktionen bis hin zu den Massenausrottungen dann mit allen Konsequenzen des realen Vollzugs.

Es ist das eigentümlich experimentelle Verhältnis zur Welt, das den radikalen Bruch zur voraufgegangenen Zeit ausmacht. Weder gewachsene Ordnungen noch die Ansprüche
20 auf Leben, Recht und Glück des einzelnen hemmen die großen Kalküle, die sich in zusehends kühneren Konzepten sei es der Neuordnung, sei es der Erlösung der Welt über dergleichen hinwegdenken.

(Fest 2007: 164–5)

References

Primary

Europäische Gemeinschaften 2002. 'Beschluss des Rates vom 28. November 2002', *Amtsblatt der europäischen Gemeinschaften* No. L 349, 24 December. Brussels: Commission of the European Communities.

European Communities 2002. 'Council Decision of 28 November 2002', *Official Journal of the European Communities* No. L 349, 24 December. Brussels: Commission of the European Communities.

Federer, Heinrich 1928. *Aus jungen Tagen*. Berlin: Grote.

Fest, Joachim 2007. *Bürgerlichkeit als Lebensform: Späte Essays*. Reinbeck Bei Hamburg: Rowohlt.

Gradmann, C. 2003. 'Experimental life and experimental disease: The role of animal experiments in Robert Koch's medical bacteriology', *Futura*, 18(2), pp. 80–8 [Only published in English; German ST remains unpublished.].

Morgenstern, Christian 1990. 'Der Werwolf', in *Band III: Christian Morgenstern Werke und Briefe. Kommentierte Ausgabe. Humoristische Lyrik*. Stuttgart: Urachhaus, pp. 87–8.

Pleschinski, Hans 2015. *Königsallee. Roman*. Munich: DTV.

Secondary

Catford, J.C. 1965. *A Linguistic Theory of Translation*. London: Oxford University Press.

Newmark, Peter 1988. *A Textbook of Translation*. New York: Prentice Hall.

Vinay, J-P. and Darbelnet, J. 1958/1995. *Comparative Stylistics of French and English: A Methodology for Translation*. Amsterdam and Philadelphia: John Benjamins [Translated and edited by Sager, Juan and Hamel, Marie-Jo from Vinay, J.-P. and Darbelnet, J. 1958. *Stylistique comparée du français et de l'anglais: Méthode de traduction*. Paris: Didier.].

Lexical and related resources

Linguee n.d. Available at: www.linguee.com/ (Accessed: 2 March 2018) [Provides parallel contextualised examples from existing translations].

11 Phonological issues in translation

As you have worked through this book you will probably have considered translation and your translated texts from the point of view of phonology as a matter of course: we may decide one translation '*sounds*' better than another, often as an intuitive means of justifying a decision which we are unable to justify in another way. In this chapter we will address the significance of phonology for translation, the meaning that sound patterns can have in the source texts and our translations, and how an awareness of that meaning can influence our translation decisions.

Phonology and text production

Perhaps the first thing we need to think about is the need to reflect on sound at all. In the standard *Handbuch Translation*, Dieter Huber summarises:

> Innerhalb der Translationswissenschaft nehmen phonologische Fragestellungen naturgemäß eine vergleichsweise untergeordnete Stellung ein; übersetzt beziehungsweise verdolmetscht werden letztlich nicht einzelne Laute oder prosodische Merkmale, sondern Texte, Inhalte, Äußerungen.
>
> (Huber 1999: 47)

One early translation theorist, J.C. Catford, goes so far as to exclude phonology from the realm of 'what is usually meant by translation' (1965: 22). Catford's model distinguishes between objects which stand in a relationship of sameness, which are grammar and lexis, and objects which stand in a relationship of necessary difference created by the act of translating, which are graphology and phonology. We replace 'meaning', we replace words and grammatical forms with equivalents, but we do not aim to do this at the level of phonology, i.e. the sounds of what we are translating. We can therefore talk about the translation of words, '*Luft*' is 'air', phrases '*kalte Luft*' ('cold air') and clauses '*Die Luft ist kalt*' ('the air is cold'), but in no helpful sense can we say that /e/ (the British English pronunciation of the first vowel of 'air') is a 'translation' of /l/. When we translate '*Luft*' into English 'air', it is indeed obvious that we will lose the sounds of the German word in translation, which is not problematic in most circumstances. Catford does foresee moments when a TL form might be replaced by a phonologically equivalent or near equivalent expression in the SL (e.g. '*Grammatik*' > 'grammar'), but this he sees as accidental, or a special case (in the translation of poetry). Phonological translation, in Catford's model can exist as a kind of restricted translation—such as a German actor speaking German with an English accent (i.e. English phonology).

Theoretically, it is not possible to divide speech and writing this neatly. Psycholinguists investigating the processes of reading and writing suggest that when we read, we 'hear' what we are reading (in our inner voice), something we also do when we are writing, in short, that we deal with written information in a text at a phonological level. This may be because our memories which we use to process, plan and produce language are predisposed to phonological data because we learn to speak or understand spoken language before we learn to read and write (Wolf, Velluntino and Berko Gleason 1998: 429). In one sense then, this means that all texts need to be considered at the level of phonology, because phonological form may play a constituent role in all textual production and reception. What is more, because the inner voice supports comprehension, the argument has been made that the phonological representation of written material is more relevant for difficult texts (such as scientific articles) than for easier ones (such as a light novel) (*ibid.*: 441f.). For translators, this is potentially significant, because it means that it is not only poetry, drama or other obviously oral forms that need to be considered when thinking about the role of sound in translation; readers attend to the phonological representation of texts in which, normally, we might assume the sound patterns to be unremarkable or neutral.

Essentially, the heart of the problem and cause of vagueness in the discussion surrounding the significance of the phonological level is the complex and opaque relationship between speech and writing. On the one hand, it is obvious that both speech and writing are different types of discourse, regulated by different sets of conventions, often fulfilling different roles, and governed to a large extent by what the physical and other circumstances of their production allow. At the same time, in literate societies, the importance of literacy in the education process means that the two modes influence each other. Certainly, many of the structural patterns which characterise formal writing such as anaphora, have their roots in oratory, and there is broader evidence that intonation patterns influence syntactic decisions in writing (Chafe 1992). As such, when we talk about 'style' we are often enough talking primarily about creating textual patterns that appeal to our auditory sense as readers—both to create an attractive piece of writing, to persuade, or merely to make ourselves understood.

Whatever the theoretical explanations, most writers know that thinking about the sound of what they are writing plays some role in the composition process—and that goes from writing a PhD thesis in Biology to writing a poem—albeit at very different stages of importance and meaning. For us as translators, we have then two questions to ask: firstly, am I dealing with a text in which the sound patterns are meaningful enough to warrant specific attention? Secondly, even if the answer to question one is no, has the act of translating caused interference, caused me either to punctuate a text in a way which is unclear (rules for commas are grammatically governed in German, usually prosodically in English), or wrought a rather ridiculous series of redundant repetitions? These are questions of style. Before going on to think about the relative importance of these questions, we'll proceed to analyse the different sound patterns our texts may create.

Types of sound patterns: phonemic and prosodic patterns

Let us approach the discussion of what *kinds* of structures are relevant at the phonological level by considering a translation into German of a famous advertising jingle:

> Washing machines live longer with Calgon!
> Waschmaschinen leben länger mit Calgon!

This jingle is, in English and in German, characterised by repetition of sounds at the beginning of words (*live longer/leben länger*), i.e. **alliteration**; perhaps more striking is its **assonance**, or the repetition of sounds within words (wa*sh*ing ma*ch*ines/Wa*sch*ma*sch*inen: /ʃ/). This translation is one example of where it is easy to achieve almost identical patterning at the level of individual sound **segments**, or **phonemes**, though obviously there are still differences—the alliterated 'w' (/w/) in '**w**ashing' and '**w**ith' is lost, but a correspondence is established in terms of assonance in the German between ('*Waschmaschinen*', /a/ /a/) which is not the case in English ('washing machine', /ɒ/ /ə/). The brand name 'Calgon' itself is an interesting example of phonological translation in Catford's sense, as not only is the term pronounced with a long 'o' (/oː/) in the second syllable in German, it of course loses its meaning (calcium gone). A similar example, only this time lost in the move from German to English, is provided by the German range of domestic cleaning products, 'Vileda', the brand name originally suggesting a similarity of function between its synthetic cleaning cloth and (chamois) leather.

Anyone who has heard, or even just read the Calgon advertising jingles will know, the tunes are different, both in the television advertisements and in terms of the natural melody of the language. This is because even though the individual sound patterns correspond closely, sentences are different in terms of their **prosody**, or **suprasegmental** structures. Both English and German have a tonic accent, which means in individual words and across sentences some syllables are stressed, and some have a weaker stress: thus one says *Da*vid, *Ma*rgaret, *gin* and *ton*ic, *whis*key and *so*da, trans*late* this *in*to idio*ma*tic *Ger*man. There are other models for representing stress and intonation in Linguistics (in tree diagrams for example). In Literary Studies, these patterns are traditionally analysed in terms of **metre**, and because these patterns are relevant to the analysis of poetry, this is what we shall present here.

The difference between our two Calgon sentences is that the distribution of stress is different. The English has a pattern which involves a stressed syllable being followed by two unstressed, or weaker ones, then one stressed syllable and one unstressed, or weaker one (*Wa*shing ma*chi*nes live *lo*nger with *Ca*lgon), which we can represent as follows, with '-' indicating a stressed, and 'v' an unstressed syllable:

—v v—v—v v—v

The German one scans differently; in it, a stressed syllable is followed each time by just one unstressed syllable (*Wasch*ma*schin*en *le*ben *läng*er *mit* Cal*gon*), which we can represent like this:

—v—v—v—v—v—

The best way to scan a piece of writing (such as a poem) for its underlying metrical pattern is to read it unemotionally and blandly, this is because there is a difference between rhythm and metre which we will come onto shortly. The stress patterns of a piece of writing can be divided into sections, or feet, and commonly occurring feet and metrical patterns have specific names. The most common ones are perhaps the iamb (v - = *Es schlug mein Herz, geschwind, zu Pferde!*), the trochee (- v = *Kleine Blumen, kleine Blätter, streuen mir mit leichter Hand*), the dactyl (- v v = *Alles Vergängliche ist nur ein Gleichnis*) and the anapaest (v v - = *Und es wallet, und siedet, und brauset und zischt*). Dactyls and anapaests are often interspersed with the shorter iambs and trochees without that affecting the overall metrical pattern of the line. Thus, in our initial example, the difference is that the English line is dactylic, while the German line is trochaic. In a sense, the names are not important; what is important is being able to identify, trace and account for the different prosodic patterns in the two sentences.

Metre is a formal, conventional and external way of tracing basic stress patterns, and really is most important in the analysis of verse where poems meet conventional forms (such as the sonnet). We have said *basic* stress patterns, because it is important to distinguish between metre and rhythm. Metre is, in a sense, the framework; rhythm is the natural property of language, and arises both from the intonation patterns of sentences (and thus syntax), but also from other considerations, such as the length of vowels, and indeed the meaning of the words themselves. While we might normally expect, say, a line of iambic pentameter to have a pacy, forward-moving rhythm, as in 'Willkommen und Abschied' by Goethe ('*Es schlug mein Herz, geschwind zu Pferde!*') it can have a slow rhythm, as in Eichendorff's 'Der Einsiedler' ('*Komm Trost der Welt, du stille Nacht*'). Here the line is slowed by the long vowel in '*Trost*' but also because the initial imperative '*Komm*' is syntactically important and thus receives emphasis (compare the unstressed 'dummy' subject, '*es*'). In other words, there is a tension between the overall metrical pattern, and the rhythm of the line. Similarly, when we read for rhythm, we find that not all words are accented equally in a sentence—here '*Trost*' and '*Nacht*' have a greater prominence than '*Welt*', for example.

In general, verse (with the exception of free verse) is written to match (or engage with) established patterns which are measured and analysed metrically; within this framework the rhythm of the text has an expressive function. Prose is not governed by a metrical pattern, but it still has a rhythmical quality, which can be expressive—it can be fast, or slow, periodic and ceremonial, or broken and turbulent. Consider the following aphorism by Nietzsche, and note how especially in the final two sentences, Nietzsche modulates the pace of the text, slowing us down at the end to make the contrastive ending all the more emphatic:

> *Der langsame Pfeil der Schönheit.*—Die edelste Art der Schönheit ist die, welche nicht auf einmal hinreißt, welche nicht stürmische und berauschende Angriffe macht (eine solche erweckt leicht Ekel), sondern jene langsam einsickernde, welche man fast unbemerkt mit sich fortträgt und die Einem im Traum einmal wiederbegegnet, endlich aber, nachdem sie lange mit Bescheidenheit an unserm Herzen gelegen, von uns ganz Besitz nimmt, unser Auge mit Tränen, unser Herz mit Sehnsucht füllt.—Wonach sehnen wir uns beim Anblick der Schönheit? Darnach, schön zu sein: wir wähnen, es müsse viel Glück damit verbunden sein.—Aber das ist ein Irrtum.
>
> (Nietzsche 1967: 316f.)

Nietzsche is of course a rather unusual case, but a sense of balance, a sense of an ending is often created in similar ways in more general prose. Martin Swales ends the introduction to a newly published translation of Goethe's *Iphigenia* in a way which is not dissimilar to Nietzsche's measured periods:

> Although one hesitates to claim immediate contemporary relevance for a literary text that is over two hundred years old, it is hard to resist venturing that few works can have such purchase on our contemporary concerns as Goethe's *Iphigenia*. The Tantalid curse, the endless bloodletting of the play's prehistory, the desperate cycle of outrage followed by acts of retribution that fuel the flames; above all, the play's understanding of the notion of sacrifice that conjoins the sacred and the violent into a poisonous brew—all these preoccupations speak with incomparable urgency to us today. The times have caught up with, indeed perhaps they have never lost contact with, Goethe's *Iphigenia*.
>
> (Swales 2014: 29)

Finally, it is useful to distinguish rhythm in the sense we have used it here (which is stylistic) from intonation. In linguistic studies of prosody, the term intonation is used more specifically to refer to variations in vowel pitch and voice modulation that make up typical sentence patterns and which distinguish 'you're not coming in?' posed as a question, from 'you're not coming in' intended as an instruction. Intonation can have a cohesive function in a text, and as such the relationship between intonation and syntax is an object of text-linguistic analysis (Halliday and Hasan 1976: 271); furthermore, intonation is specifically important to us as translators into English because English is a language in which 'a heavy semantic load is carried by rhythm and intonation' (Halliday 1985: 271). Having made a survey of some of the ways we can think about the sounds of a text, we can now discuss the conditions in which they become significant for translation.

Stylistic choices and genre issues

In order to decide (a) whether to translate individual sounds or patterns and (b) how much attention we need to pay to the sound of our translation, we need to differentiate the degree and type of significance that the phonological level has for a text, and the relative freedom that a writer and translator has to attend to this level.

Consider the following sentence from a Biology article about angiogenesis. Here, the initial alliterative pairs could be described as negligible and probably accidental: '*Die Bildung neuer Blutgefäße ist bei einer Vielzahl von Vorgängen, wie zum Beispiel der Embryogenese, dem weiblichen Reproduktionszyklus, der Wundheilung, dem Tumorwachstum und der Neovaskularisation ischämischer Gewebe, von Bedeutung*' (Kalka et al. 2000). Certainly, the patterns here cannot be said to have any intrinsic meaning: they neither symbolise anything, nor are they part of a rhetorical strategy. A scientific or academic article arguably works by presenting evidence that needs to be perceived as fact, not argument, and as such scientific articles adopt a neutral tone, usually eschewing affective rhetoric. In other, more obviously persuasive or affective texts or parts of texts, such as speeches, the closing paragraphs of essays, newspaper articles etc., rhetorical strategies which create prosodic effects (climax through postponement, groups of three, structural repetition etc.) are clearly important, and thus warrant the translator's attention. That is not to mention genres such as advertising slogans, jokes, or parts of texts which seek to attract attention, such as book or film titles. There is a distinction to be made between rhetorical strategies and expressive ones: if we end an essay, for example, with a short, memorable phrase, we do that for reasons of argumentation; an advertisement, however, may wish to evoke a mood, create an association. Finally, in literature, we might distinguish between say, a realist novel, a ballad, and a symbolist poem: in the latter, individual sounds may be symbolically significant and need preservation; a ballad is a relatively loose form of verse which allows irregularities of rhythm and rhyme; in a realist novel it is likely to be the overall tone which is important.

These generalisations can, as always, mask important nuances, however unusual. The norm is for a writer to think, at least in some way, about the way a text sounds, whether in a scientific article, or a set of instructions, or a text which is to be read aloud such as a sermon. We have already suggested in a previous chapter that one might avoid 'begin to become' for euphonic reasons. Similarly, we may guard against unnecessary repetitions of the same word, we might avoid writing 'of' too frequently in essays, or we may wish to check that the intonation pattern of an utterance is going to be clear from the context or whether we need to restructure a sentence to avoid ambiguity. These considerations can even enter into the translation of terminology in certain circumstances. In the glossary to their 1967 translation of Schiller's *Über die ästhetische Erziehung des Menschen in einer Reihe von Briefen*, Elizabeth M. Wilkinson and L.A. Willoughby conclude a lengthy note under '*Trieb*' as follows: 'Where *Trieb* is used in Schiller's own technical sense, we have usually translated by "drive"—though in the case of "Trieb des Lebens" [. . .] euphony forbade it' (Schiller 1982: 332).

We close our discussion by looking at three examples. Broadcast in the 1970s and 1980s, the American TV series *Hart to Hart* is about a successful husband and wife, Mr and Mrs Hart, who fight crime together while maintaining a romantic marriage. The title is alliterative to be catchy, but it works also through association, recalling the phrase 'heart to heart', and as such characterising the whole show, which concentrates on the love between the glamorous couple. The German translation, *Hart, aber herzlich*, contains translation strictly at the phonological level (the name Hart), but then has to deal with the consequences of the meaning of '*hart*' in German, which creates a sense of antagonism between the immutable name 'Hart' and the quality of the two characters. The solution here, which is very good, is to include '*aber*' which validates the semantic import of '*hart*' (presumably their crime fighting) and to spell out some sense of what is implied by the English title using the alliterative '*herzlich*'.

That these sorts of difficulties need to be addressed on a case-by-case basis is exemplified by the following text, seemingly very similar to our previous example. The politics section of the *Frankfurter Allgemeine Sonntagszeitung* ran the following headline and by-line in an article about the CDU politician Wolfgang Schäuble:

HERZLOS, HERRISCH HÄSSLICH

Die Grünen schimpfen auf Schäuble. Ihr Held heißt Helmut Kohl. Ernsthaft? Na ja.

Certainly, the headline works both alliteratively and through the prosodic correspondence of each of its terms (they all have the same number of syllables with the same stress pattern). The layout, in which the final word '*hässlich*' is much larger than the others, underlines too the rhetorical importance of the tricolon (group of three). An initial translation, say for the European page of a quality English newspaper, might thus try to keep this alliteration, at the expense of the precise meanings of the words ('heartless, haughty, hideous'). As we read on in the article, however, this solution becomes problematic, because in fact these are terms taken from a statement made by a politician about Schäuble. While that statement, too, certainly played on the alliteration of the three terms, translating the statement of such a politician requires clarity about his precise meaning, and the translator cannot afford to put words in his mouth. One solution here would be to translate the quotation closely, and use those words in the headline, but enclosing them in quotation marks. The translator would have much more freedom in the by-line, and arguably preserving the alliterative effect here would give some indication of the source text's tone.

What should be becoming clear, then, is that in part what is at issue is the freedom of the translator (and writer) to attend to the sound of what they are writing. In a scientific article, the writer has to use specific terms, whether that creates alliterative patterns or not, whether that means conspicuous repetition or not. The translator in the previous example is faced with similar constraints.

The previous two examples were alliterative. Spotting the function of prosody is often more difficult. In the following description of the '*Baiersbronner Himmelsweg*' from a tourist website about the Black Forest, the writer seeks to evoke a mysterious atmosphere. This is especially present in the last section marked, again by alliteration and assonance, but also by a series of polysyllabic noun phrases with frequent anapaests that create a sense of gentle movement:

> Abseits von Autos und Straßenverkehr hinein mitten in den tiefsten Nordschwarzwald führt diese Wanderung zum sagenumwobenen Huzenbacher See. Eine Wanderung, welche die ganze Schönheit der Region beinhaltet: entlang plätschender Bäche, an mystisch anmutenden Baumriesen vorbei zu einem eiszeitlichen Karsee mit abschließendem Ausblick auf Schwarzenberg und Schönmünzach.

(Schwarzwald-Tourismus n.d.)

The lower part of the page is the factual description of the journey and is related in more down-to-earth prose. The challenge for the translator in tackling the more lyrical passage—say, for an English-language version of the website—would be to retain the sense of a peaceful and relaxing place far from the jarring noise of cars and traffic. One way of doing this would clearly be to replicate as far as possible both the segmental and suprasegmental features of the ST passage, even if this means restructuring or rewriting the original text.

Concluding remarks

The main purposes of this chapter have been to draw your attention to the significance of the phonological level in the composition and effects of texts, and to give you some tools for the analysis of sound patterns, primarily derived from and relevant to the analysis of verse. As we have seen, being attentive to the function and relative importance of sound patterns in texts is, however, relevant to a wide range of genres. The following practicals focus on verse translation, because that is obviously one of the forms in which sound patterns contribute to the meaning of the text most significantly. However, it is worthwhile reflecting on some of the practicals you have done already and thinking about texts or sections of texts where sound and your awareness of the sound patterning in the text influenced or guided your translation decisions: the practicals in the chapter on cultural issues, for example, contain many such examples.

Further reading

Fox, Anthony 2005. *The Structure of German*. 2nd edn. Oxford: Oxford University Press [Chapter 2 'Phonology', pp. 22–100.].

Huber, Dieter 1996. 'Prosodic transfer: Non-verbal language in intercultural communication', in Drescher, H. W. and Hagemann, S. (eds) *Scotland to Slovenia: European Identities and Transcultural Communication*. Frankfurt am Main: Peter Lang, pp. 259–77.

Kayser, Wolfgang 1975. *Kleine deutsche Versschule*. Berne: Francke.

Wagenknecht, Christian 2005. *Deutsche Metrik: Eine historische Einführung*. Munich: Beck.

Practical 11

11.1 TRANSLATION AND DISCUSSION: VERSE

Assignment

Translate the first verse of Lewis Carroll's 'The Jabberwocky' into German. What changes do you make and what motivates those changes? Do all of the sounds have the same effects in German?

ST

Twas brillig, and the slithy toves
Did gyre and gimble in the wabe:
All mimsy were the borogoves,
And the mome raths outgrabe.
                    (Carroll 2012: 208)

11.2 ANALYSIS AND TRANSLATION: VERSE

Assignment

i   Analyse the function of sound patterns in Theodor Storm's 'Abseits' (1847), paying attention to the mood evoked by the poem.
ii Translate the final stanza. Your translation must rhyme and be formally and metrically comparable to the original.

ST

Abseits

   Es ist so still; die Heide liegt
   Im warmen Mittagssonnenstrahle,
   Ein rosenroter Schimmer fliegt
5 Um ihre alten Gräbermale;
   Die Kräuter blühn; der Heideduft
   Steigt in die blaue Sommerluft.

   Laufkäfer hasten durchs Gesträuch
   In ihren goldnen Panzerröckchen.

ST

---

10 Die Bienen hängen Zweig um Zweig
Sich an der Edelheide Glöckchen,
Die Vögel schwirren aus dem Kraut —
Die Luft ist voller Lerchenlaut.

Ein halbverfallen, niedrig Haus
15 Steht einsam hier und sonnbeschienen,
Der Kätner lehnt zur Tür hinaus,
Behaglich blinzelnd nach den Bienen;
Sein Junge auf dem Stein davor
Schnitzt Pfeifen sich aus Kälberrohr.

20 Kaum zittert durch die Mittagsruh
Ein Schlag der Dorfuhr, der entfernten;
Dem Alten fällt die Wimper zu,
Er träumt von seinen Honigernten.
—Kein Klang der aufgeregten Zeit
25 Drang noch in diese Einsamkeit.
(Storm 1978: I/110)

11.3 TRANSLATION: VERSE

Assignment

Translate Klopstock's 'Die frühen Gräber' (1764). Which of the features of the poem are most important for you to maintain in your translation?

ST

Die frühen Gräber

Willkommen, o silberner Mond,
Schöner, stiller Gefährt der Nacht!
Du entfliehst? Eile nicht, bleib, Gedankenfreund!
5   Sehet, er bleibt, das Gewölk wallte nur hin.

Des Maies Erwachen ist nur
Schöner noch, wie die Sommernacht,
Wenn ihm Tau, hell wie Licht, aus der Locke träuft,
Und zu dem Hügel herauf rötlich er kömmt.

10 Ihr Edleren, ach es bewächst
Eure Male* schon ernstes Moos!
O wie war glücklich ich, als ich noch mit euch
Sahe sich röten den Tag, schimmern die Nacht.

*Male—graves

(Klopstock 1962: 108)

References

Primary

Carroll, Lewis 2012. 'Jabberwocky', in Beer, G. (ed.) *Jabberwocky and Other Nonsense*. London: Penguin, pp. 208–9.

Kalka, C., Asahara, T., Krone, W. and Isner, J. M. 2000. 'Angiogenese und Vaskulogenese. Therapeutische Strategien zur Stimulation der postnatalen Neovaskularisation', *Herz*, 25(6), pp. 611–22.

Klopstock, Friedrich Gottlieb 1962. 'Die frühen Gräber', in Klopstock, F.G. *Ausgewählte Werke*. Edited by Jünger, Friedrich G. Munich: Hanser, p. 108.

Nietzsche, Friedrich 1967. *Werke*. Edited by Frenzel, Ivo. 2 Vols. Munich: Hanser.

Schiller, Friedrich 1982. *On the Aesthetic Education of Man, in a Series of Letters, English and German Facing*. Translated and edited by Wilkinson, Elizabeth M. and Willoughby, L.A. 2nd edn. Oxford: Clarendon Press.

Schwarzwald Toursimus n.d. Available at: www.schwarzwald-tourismus.info/10-Tipps-fuer/romantische-Stunden/Baiersbronner-Himmelsweg-Romantik-Tour (Accessed: 30 July 2015).

Storm, Theodor 1978. 'Abseits', in Storm, T. *Sämtliche Werke*. Edited by Goldammer, Peter. 4 Vols. Berlin and Weimar: Aufbau, I, p. 110.

Secondary

Catford, J.C. 1965. *A Linguistic Theory of Translation*. London: Oxford University Press.

Chafe, Wallace 1992. 'Writing vs. speech', in Bright, W. (ed.) *Oxford International Encyclopedia of Linguistics*. Vol. 4. New York: Oxford University Press, pp. 257–9.

Halliday, Michael A.K. 1985. *An Introduction to Functional Grammar*. London: Arnold.

Halliday, Michael A.K. and Hasan, Ruqaiya 1976. *Cohesion in English*. London: Longman English Language Series.

Huber, Dieter 1999. 'Phonologie', in Snell-Hornby, M., Hönig, H., Kußmaul, P. and Schmitt, P.A. (eds) *Handbuch Translation*. 2nd edn. Tübingen: Stauffenburg, pp. 47–8.

Swales, Martin 2014. 'Introduction', in Goethe, J.W. von *Iphigenie in Tauris*. Translated by Pascal, R. London: Angel Classics, pp. 1–29.

Wolf, Maryanne, Velluntino, Frank and Berko Gleason, Jean 1998. 'A psycholinguistic account of reading', in Berko Gleason, J. and Bernstein Ratner, N. (eds) *Psycholinguistics*. 2nd edn. Fort Worth, TX: Harncourt Brace, pp. 409–51.

Section D

The translation process and translation specialisms

Throughout this book, we have included practical examples and exercises in the belief that engagement with actual translation problems is essential if new translators are to develop a systematic understanding of how to set about any translation task. In the current section, the perspective shifts to particular fields of translation, but starts with preparation for translation and finishes with final checks.

The opening chapter presents some of the preparatory research which the translator needs to carry out in terms of subject matter, background and language, detailing a range of available resources—online and paper—using worked examples (Chapter 12). At the end of the translation process comes the stage where final checks are carried out (Chapter 16). Here we distinguish between 'revision', 'review' and 'proofing', terms that are often confused. The three middle chapters deal specifically with particular subject areas of translation. The selected areas are exemplars, covering what we hope are a wide range of problems with accompanying analysis and possible solutions. These central chapters focus on translating consumer-oriented texts (Chapter 13), scientific-technical texts (Chapter 14) and literary texts (Chapter 15). Depending on students' own experience and interests, these chapters may open up new opportunities for development. However, what we aim to show here is that despite differences in subject matter, all translation requires analysis, imagination and perseverance.

12 Research and resources for translation

In this chapter we survey another technique in translation that, at first glance, may not seem like 'translation' at all—research. Most translation projects require research of some kind, as we have already seen in the discussion of genres (Chapter 4) or cultural issues (Chapter 5), for example. The purpose of the following discussion is twofold. Firstly, we explore the importance of research in relevant subject areas and the availability and optimal use of resources. Secondly, we map out the ground for the following chapters which present, very broadly, the challenges and particularities of different topic areas of translation, namely the translation of consumer-oriented texts, scientific/technical texts and literary texts. Two case studies are presented, illustrating some techniques for using online and print resources to solve terminological problems in both scientific and literary translation.

The importance of research

Many students are surprised when they undertake their first translation assignments how much of their time is taken up by vocabulary research. There are many estimates of how much time is devoted to research—much but not all of which is concerned with terminology, including in some literary translation—but two empirically based sets of figures are worth noting. A recent survey conducted with over 500 professional translators in many different countries revealed that the time spent on research in familiar subject fields was estimated to be over 20% of the time spent on a job; for unfamiliar subject fields, the figure was understandably higher, at just over 40% (Gough 2011). A later observational study of professional translators (Gough 2017) based on a much smaller sample concluded that 30% of time is spent on research in familiar subject fields, and 36% in unfamiliar subject fields. For trainees or novitiates, these figures are, of course, likely to be higher. The best advice to student translators therefore is to understand that research is a necessary part of the job: conducting effective and targeted research is a part of translator competence.

Resources for translation

The next question is, of course, what is 'effective' research? Apart from 'dictionaries' (to which we return below), useful sources of subject-related information include text books (first-year university level books often give useful subject overviews, including a chapter-by-chapter mind map), abstracting and indexing journals, periodicals, yearbooks, encyclopaedias, standards and trade literature, subject-specific literature, previous translations, and occasionally theses and dissertations. Many of these—particularly in English—are now available online, but good browsing skills are essential. More recently, other resources have been added to the translator's portfolio of research materials, such as corpora (understood here as digital collections of texts) and tools such as concordancers (for analysing digital texts), more of which below.

For specific projects, it is important to find and to familiarise yourself with SL and TL material of a similar TC genre dealing with similar subject matter, or by the same author, and, depending on the purpose of the translation, written contemporaneously. Such sources serve both as a key source of information and as a stylistic model. For instance, a professional translator tackling the technical text in Practical 14.1 (*'Tunnelauskleidung'*) would regard it as essential to refer in detail to at least one of the following resources: (a) a TL description of an actual tunnel or project under construction (Internet or paper), i.e. a 'parallel text'; (b) a specialist publication of the Institution of Civil Engineers or the British Tunnelling Society and/or (c) a subject expert. The Internet, including both email and www, is an essential tool for fast access to up-to-date information. Major firms and organisations often maintain their own glossaries or termbases, containing centrally agreed translations of relevant expressions. Two examples can be mentioned here.

The European Union's multilingual terminology database—IATE (InterActive Terminology for Europe since 2004)—incorporates all previous EU terminology resources, including the most well known, the Commission's Eurodicautom, and has been publicly available since 2007. One of the advantages of online resources is that they can be regularly updated, a feature which is especially important in subject fields which undergo rapid developments, and as decisions are made about company or organisation preferences for equivalent terms sometimes even as a translation project proceeds.

Our second example of a major terminology database is the United Nations Multilingual Terminology Database, now 'UNTERM' (United Nations Terminology Database). As with IATE, UNTERM brings together several local terminology collections of the UN. Although German is not an official UN language, some German entries are available. The subjects covered include Science and Technology, as well as Disarmament, Human Rights, Shipping and Transportation.

The inventory of online resources which are now available—often without cost—to translators is growing rapidly. But the increase in quantity is accompanied by other, qualitative changes as the distinction between 'tools' and 'resources' becomes blurred. For example, some so-called 'Translation Memory' tools now incorporate terminology databases, and some dictionary-type tools incorporate search engines linked to large bilingual corpora of texts.

'Translation Memory' (TM) is a type of 'computer-assisted' or 'computer-aided translation' (CAT) software tool which facilitates the consistent use of terms and repetitive phrases by storing translations for re-use. It is typically used for genres such as manuals which need to be regularly updated. TM is a database—there are a number on the market—which can store previously translated STs and their translations, usually segmented into sentence-size chunks. The 'memory' can be created as the translator works their way through a new translation, or an existing ST-TT pair of texts can be loaded into the database and 'aligned' so that ST and TT segments correspond. The translator—or a team of translators working on different parts of the same document—can access a termbase directly through the memory tool in order to improve consistency of terminology, and accept or edit segments proposed by the system as it matches an updated version of a ST to a previously translated ST-TT pair stored in the memory. Various help mechanisms are also available to help convert dates, currency, decimal markers and so on (see also Chapter 14). To describe the current state of the art in Translation Memory would go beyond the scope of this book, and any comments would rapidly date. Suffice it to say that employment as a professional translator in technical fields and genres more often than not requires training in TM systems, and most Master's programmes now offer such training, including evaluative as well as operational skills. For more on Translation Memory, see Byrne 2012: 133–4; Olohan 2016: 42–5.

In addition to the resource of 'heritage' translation data for technical translation, online resources are often freely available. A recent stock-take of online resources for translators (Gough 2017) includes:

- dictionaries and glossaries
- terminology databases (term banks or termbases)
- corpora
- thesauri (dictionaries of related meanings)
- concordancers
- knowledge-based resources (encyclopaedia; wiki media, allowing users to collaborate in creating a resource)
- discussion forums
- search engines (allowing the www to be used as a giant 'corpus')
- web pages as parallel texts and subject-related documents
- Translation Memories and Machine Translation

As with paper resources, of course, caution is recommended when choosing particular solutions from the rather bewildering array of possibilities generated from the www (not 'by' the www: it is the user who marshals the resources and shapes the search). This means checking and double-checking e.g. between bilingual and monolingual terminology resources, between terminology resources and texts, and between dictionaries/glossaries and encyclopaedia or wikis.

Subject knowledge: avoiding conceptual translation errors

A factor which is inherent in the very project of acquiring expertise in many areas of specialised knowledge concerns underlying conceptual problems. Getting to grips with a new subject field, or updating current expertise, means understanding not only what the words 'say', but how the subject works. 'Non-literary' translators in particular have even been described as 'personal knowledge managers' (Kastberg 2009: 97–8); and as we point out below, literary translators can be even more challenged as many literary works engage—often unpredictably—with external worlds ranging from bird watching to the law.

Any knowledge gaps may concern the *facts* known and taken for granted—and so never spelt out—by specialists in a given discipline. Or they may be to do with the discipline's *logic*, its way of working, in particular the relationships between concepts; this too tends to be simply taken for granted, a part of the culture, only coming to the surface if a dispute arises.

To take the 'facts' gap first: we have already seen in Chapter 7 how the 'testing of steel for homogeneity'—explicit in the German ST—could become simply 'testing of steel' in the English TT, because the industry practice in the UK is to take the purpose for granted when referring to this process.

To illustrate the importance for the translator of understanding how the concepts of a discipline relate to one another, we can use the abstract of an article published in a German-language medical journal. As is the normal convention for learned journals, the abstract appears at the head of the article, alongside its English translation that we print below. Spellings are as found. We omit the headings:

ST

Das Ginkgo-biloba-Extrakt wird aus grünen Blättern des Ginkgobiloba-Baumes gewonnen. Präparate mit diesem Wirkstoff werden u. a. zur Behandlung von Hirnleistungsstörungen und arteriosklerotischen Erkrankungen genutzt. In In-vitro- und In-vivo-Studien wurden Radical Scavenger- und PAF (platelet activating factor)-
5   antagonistische Wirkungen beschrieben. In dieser Arbeit konnte eine konzentrationsabhängige Superoxiddismutasenaktivität des Ginkgo-biloba-Extraktes rökan-flüssig nachgewiesen werden.
Code: Gingko biloba—Superoxiddismutasenaktivität—freie Sauerstoffradikale

---

TT

The Ginkgo biloba extract is obtained from green leaves of the Ginkgo biloba tree. Preparations with this active substance are among others used for the treatment of disturbances of the cerebral function and arteriosclerotic diseases. In in-vitro- and in-vivo studies antagonistic effects of radical scavenger and PAF (platelet activating
5   factor) were described. In this study a concentration-depending superoxide dismutase activity of the Gingko biloba extract rökan® liquid could be made evident. **Code: Ginkgo biloba—superoxide dismutase activity—free oxygen radical**
(Diwok, Kuklinski and Ernst 1992: 308)

Apart from errors in handling *u.a.* ('among others', incorrectly indicating that the Ginkgo biloba extract is one of several preparations that can be used to treat the condition rather than that the said preparations can be used for other purposes) and '*konnte . . . nachgewiesen werden*' ('could be made evident' instead of 'was demonstrated'), the TT goes seriously wrong on the crucial issue of the research results (in the sentence beginning '*In In-vitro* . . . ', ST lines 3–5). The problem has arisen in the compounding of terms. While the hyphenation—always a key indicator in German texts—in the ST makes clear (at least to a subject expert) the relationship of the phrase '*Radical Scavenger-*' to the head noun '*Wirkungen*', confusion may arise for the unwary reader in so far as the adjectival phrase referencing one of the two named types of effect, i.e. '*PAF* (platelet activating factor)-*antagonistische*', itself contains a hyphen. It is easy to see how a translator without any subject knowledge could imagine '*antagonistische*' to mean 'directed against radical scavengers *and* PAF', even though this adjective is in fact attached to '*PAF*' and its parenthetical explanatory English equivalent, but this reading lacks subject-field coherence. The TT sentence (lines 3–5) should read: 'A number of in-vitro and in-vivo studies have described free radical scavenger and PAF-antagonist effects'.

It should be clear then that the attempt to translate unfamiliar specialised material even into the mother tongue, and even with the current array of terminological reference help, can take the translator onto thin ice. Yet linguists from a non-scientific background do, of course, develop into fully proficient sci-tech translators. Acknowledging the importance of subject knowledge, as well as knowledge concerning core resources, some Master's programmes offering specialised translation provide introductory courses into the basic concepts of, say, Science and Technology, or Economics and Finance. Reading around the subject matter in both languages is very important, as is the nurturing of links with subject experts wherever possible. Interpersonal skills are clearly essential here. Literary translators may dip in and out of specialised subject areas according to need but still need to undertake research.

The translator's profile

Initiatives such as the European Commission's European Master's in Translation (EMT) Network bear witness to the increasing co-operation between European universities on language matters and an awareness of what constitutes high-quality translator training. Programmes gaining entry to the Network need to demonstrate a proven track record in delivering a number of 'competences' for their graduates. These competences—'the combination of aptitudes, knowledge, behaviour and knowhow necessary to carry out a given task under given conditions' (Gambier 2009: 1)—comprise Language and Culture; Translation (strategic, methodological and thematic competence); Technology (tools and applications); Personal and Interpersonal; Service Provision (EMT Board 2017). Of immediate relevance to this chapter are the following three skills; the first two belong to the set of Translation competence skills, the third to Technology (sometimes known as 'information mining'). Students should know how to:

- Evaluate the relevance and reliability of information sources with regard to translation needs

- Acquire, develop and use thematic and domain-specific knowledge relevant to translation needs (mastering systems of concepts, methods of reasoning, presentation standards, terminology and phraseology, specialised sources etc.)
- Make effective use of search engines, corpus-based tools, text analysis tools and CAT tools

Clearly, for students new to the task of translation as a text-creation activity rather than as a language-learning device, these skills are aspirational. Nevertheless, they provide a useful initial orientation point and a sense of direction.

Beyond the dictionary?

A particular problem which faces translators of specialised texts—and translators of any texts which include specialist terms—concerns the identification of terms which need to be researched. Words and expressions which are unfamiliar e.g. 'labellum' (Botany), can be assumed, at least in the first instance, to be terms. But there are many terms whose ordinary uses are familiar to the translator but which are used in some other subject-specific specialised way in the ST e.g. 'work' (Physics), 'negligence' (English Law). These forms have been described as doing 'double duty' (Sager 1990: 19). For example, the apparently ordinary word 'platform' has a variety of meanings—i.e. it is polysemous (see Chapter 3)—with which most of us would be familiar; both literal and figurative meanings are derived from the original sixteenth-century French borrowing: 'A surface or area on which something may stand, *esp.* a raised level surface' (*OED*). Modern meanings include: the place where you stand to catch a train or to give a speech, and figuratively, a set of beliefs indicating allegiance to a particular political group. But, through another extension of its meaning, 'platform' is also used in specialised subject fields such as Information Technology ('hardware platform', 'software platform'), the oil industry ('drilling platform'), as well as in Construction, the Military and Geology (see, for instance, www.dictionary.com for definitions). While the basic meaning is shared and extended in this way in English, we cannot assume that German will mirror this distribution of form and meanings, as we saw in Chapter 3. In German therefore we have a range of forms, with the influence of English particularly evident in (c) to (e): (a) '*Bahnsteig*' or '*Gleis*'; (b) '*Podium*'; (c) '*Plattform*'; (d) '*Hardwareplattform*'; '*Softwareplattform*'; (e) '*Bohrplattform*'.

A bilingual dictionary or online terminology database is usually a good starting point in such cases, but this preliminary research will need to be followed up using more specialised TL resources in order to check that the equivalent/s given for the relevant domain is/are in current use i.e. they are not 'dictionary words', and to check how they are used in context. You therefore need to think beyond the use of dictionaries, or even online termbases.

The use of the electronic medium to create and store texts (often referred to as a combination of 'format' and 'content' in the IT world) has changed the way translators—and many others—work over the last 40 years. Digital text is widely available on the www, meaning that we can search for information both widely and quickly. While some languages are more fully represented than others, resources in lesser used languages are becoming more common. As a translator, you will need to develop your 'info mining competence'—as outlined previously—in order to identify relevant textual resources which will tell you 'something about the terminology and phraseology of that genre' as well as the 'patterns of language usage, frequencies of use and information about likely co-occurrence of words, terms and phrases' (Olohan 2016: 28). As you would expect, now that what is called 'corpus-based' analysis has moved from the research lab to the commercial market, tools are readily available to execute the task, including, for example, Sketch Engine, Wordsmith and AntConc. (see Lexical and related resources for all URLs). AntConc is freeware, Sketch Engine and Wordsmith are licensed, although free trials are often available. These tools allow you to create a corpus, which is simply a collection of texts which you have identified and selected as appropriate to your purpose, e.g. in a certain subject field and genre for a given language. The corpus—which has the advantage of size over individual texts—can then be processed in a number of ways. The principal outputs are:

- word lists (sorted alphabetically or by frequency)
- Key Word in Context (KWIC); i.e. concordance, a technique which goes back to medieval analyses of the Bible to list all words in alphabetical order in their immediate context

Table 12.1 shows an example of what a concordance might look like, based on texts in the British National Corpus (BNC), an existing but early online resource consisting of 100 million words of 'written and spoken language from a wide range of sources, designed to represent a wide cross-section of British English, both spoken and written, from the late twentieth century'(BNC, n.d.). The corpus—now a little dated (1980s–1993)—contains 'extracts from regional and national newspapers, specialist periodicals and journals for all ages and interests, academic books and popular fiction, published and unpublished letters and memoranda, school and university essays, among many other kinds of text' (*ibid.*).

Table 12.1 A concordance of 'platform' based on a 'simple search' using the BNC concordance function ('BNC Source' shows the text identifier)

Context to the left	Keyword	Context to the right	BNC Source
1	the fire on the Piper Alpha oil	platform	the spillage from the Exxon *Valdez*	ABH
2	on a range of hardware	platforms	while others, such as Microsoft,	CBX
3	Kinnock takes time away from the	platform	limelight by MALCOLM PITHERS	A3G
4	as well as on an Intel/MS-DOS	platform	depending on intensity of use	CTD
5	basinwards of the marginal	platform	in deeper marine, slope and base of	B2J

This small sample provides contextual examples of the search or 'key' word in Economics/Finance, Accounting, Politics, Computing and Geology. The BNC website provides a link from each text source directly to the full text. In Table 12.1 the concordance is randomly ordered, but most concordancers allow the user to sort alphabetically to the left or to the right, so that recurring patterns can be identified e.g. multiple occurrences of 'hardware platform' or 'platform limelight' respectively. Other more up-to-date ready-made accessible corpora of English include the Corpus of Contemporary American English (COCA: 560 million words, 1990–2017, last update) and the enTenTen (20 billion words of US and UK English available through Sketch Engine). Mark Davies of Brigham Young University has an excellent webpage presenting up-to-date information on corpus-based resources, some running into billions of words.

Turning to German documentary resources, a wide array of texts has been assembled and made digitally available by the Institut für Deutsche Sprache (IDS)—'*die zentrale außeruniversitäre Einrichtung zur Erforschung und Dokumentation der deutschen Sprache in ihrem gegenwärtigen Gebrauch und in ihrer neueren Geschichte*'—in a large collection entitled COSMAS II (IdS n.d.). In total, the collection contains over 44.5 billion words organised in 366 different corpora including historical, literary, LSP (*Fachsprache*), newspaper and other texts. Concordance results can be presented as KWIC and/or as full text versions. Sketch Engine also includes a large German corpus (deTenTen). Another useful and easy-to-use website is the DWDS (*Digitales Wörterbuch der deutschen Sprache*). Here you can find a number of monolingual dictionaries of different types, easy access to a range of corpora (contemporary and historical) as well as statistical information on word frequency and collocative patterns.

A detailed, very useful account of how to create and process your own corpus for terminological research, covering both the ST and the TT, can be found in Olohan 2016: 27–41. A number of readily available online corpora are also listed there, to add to the BNC, COSMAS II and those in DWDS, all of which could be equally useful for specialised and literary translation.

We go on here to illustrate in two case studies the use of selected online and paper resources. We leave you to explore the exciting opportunities offered by others.

CASE STUDY 1:   Literary translation as detective work

Because literary texts, but particularly novels and plays, represent a world, they often include a great deal of what we might term factual information, although the extent to which it corresponds to reality, or is accurate, varies. Uwe Tellkamp's *Der Turm* (2008), a novel set in East Germany, is a good example of a literary text in which the inclusion of factual material functions to create the realistic experience of a whole world, and exists in the novel alongside a huge range of culturally specific terms and discourses to recreate lived experience: difficulties for translators here include everything from Saxon dialect to the terminology of paper production. But, of course, the range of worlds represented in novels is vast and constantly evolving. The *Europäisches Übersetzer-Kollegium*, a specialist library for literary and specialised translators, describes the problem of providing resources for literary translators succinctly:

> Literarische Übersetzer bilden eine spezifische Benutzergruppe in Bibliotheken. Anders als die meisten Benutzer interessieren sie sich nicht für ein klar definiertes Fachgebiet oder einen bestimmten Themenkreis. Ihre Recherchen decken fast den gesamten Wissenskosmos ab: je nach der im Roman abgebildeten—oder konstituierten—Wirklichkeit müssen sie sich in verschiedenste Fachsprachen einarbeiten. [. . .] (www.euk-straelen.de/deutsch/das-kollegium/die-bibliothek/, 30 July 2018)

As a result, students translating literary texts also need to be adept researchers, and almost more importantly, able to evaluate how much research is necessary to solve a particular problem within the scope of their translation project. Like all literary scholars—and all translators—they need to be able to chase up clues. Thinking in this vein, we may take as a simple example some of the research that could be involved in translating a historical crime novel such as Volker Kutscher's *Der nasse Fisch* (2016), set in 1920s Berlin. One difficulty the translator has to deal with here are terms specific to the police at the time, notably the names for officers and officials ('*Wachtmeister*', '*Kriminalassistent*', '*Kriminalsekretär*', '*Oberkommisar*', '*Regierungsdirektor*').

The first decision to be made is whether to translate these terms or not, and here looking at other translations and TL texts provides guidance. Michael Hofman's translation of Hans Fallada's *Jeder stirbt für sich allein* does translate them ('*Kommisar*' > 'Inspector', '*Kriminalassistent*' > 'Deputy Inspector'), though it retains short forms of address such as '*Herr*' and '*Frau*' in German and German names for titles in institutions clearly part of the Nazi state lacking English equivalents, such as the '*SS Obergruppenführer*' (Fallada 2009: 172). Interestingly, Philip Kerr's English-language novels set in Berlin in the Nazi period, however, use borrowings such as '*Kripo*' and '*Kriminalinspektor*' (Kerr 2012). In Kutscher's text, the novel creates, even for its German readers a world which is unfamiliar, and we note that some terms are glossed, especially where knowledge about the rank of the person and their experience is relevant to the reader's understanding of the plot: '*ein einfacher Kriminalassistent, seit wenigen Wochen erst das Abschlusszeugnis der Polizeischule in der Tasche, hatte diese Nummer wie selbstverständlich in seinem Notizbuch stehen*' (Kutscher 2016: 387). This suggests we could proceed in a similar way in our translation, and for present purposes we will suggest that these job titles will be borrowed. But finding out more precisely what these officers' roles were is still important because it informs their personal relationships and their characterisation.

Let us take one of these terms which seems innocuous, '*Kriminalsekretär*', as our example. Our initial reaction might be to try an Internet search:

Table 12.2 Online resource Google U.K. search engine: results for search term '*Kriminalsekretär*'

Resource	Outcome	Evaluation
Google using search term	Discussion forum on Proz.com: suggests 'detective sergeant'	How dependable? No overview to place term in context
Google using search term	Wikipedia entry on the '*Ordnungspolizei*', giving useful indication of different ranks' relations to each other	Needs to be double checked, not least because it describes police roles after 1933, whereas novel set in 1929
Google using search term	Google Books: *Foundations of the Nazi Police State: The Formation of Sipo and SD* (Browder 1990) incl. appendix of police titles	More dependable but comparison is to U.S. Army ranks (pp. 250–1); much of the book unavailable online—definitions of roles hard to find

At this point we become aware that more systematic library research may be required, and indeed may shed light on other aspects of the text. We begin our search this time with a search in a *Brockhaus* encyclopaedia and other dictionaries with some encyclopaedic entries, including a reference work published at around the time the novel was set:

Table 12.3 Brockhaus and related results for search term '*Kriminalsekretär*'

Resource	Outcome	Evaluation
Brockhaus Encyklopädie 1970	No individual entry, but entry for '*Kriminalpolizei*' includes reference to '*Kriminalbeamter*' with a very useful hierarchy of terms depending on training: '*Kriminal(ober)assistenten, Kriminal(ober)-sekretäre, Kriminal(ober)inspektoren; in dem leitenden kriminalpolizistischen Vollzugsdienst: Kriminalkommissare, Kriminalräte, (Ober-)Regierungs-und Kriminalräte und Regierungs-und Kriminaldirektoren*'	Could be enough to solve immediate problem, but worth further exploration
Brockhaus online 2014	Entry for '*Kriminalpolizei*': hierarchy of posts omitted; no entry for '*Kriminalbeamter*'	Historical information removed from later edition
Wahrig 1984	No relevant entries	Ordinary general-purpose dictionaries not specialised enough
Duden Großes Wörterbuch 1994	No relevant entries	
Brockhaus Encyklopädie 1928–1935	Entry for '*Kriminalbeamter*': describes duties incl. two career paths, confirms plain clothes. Establishes that terms vary regionally	Where possible, contemporaneous sources optimal

Knowing now that a '*Kriminalsekretär*' is a second-rank position allows us a rough comparison with U.K. police ranks, which seems to confirm that '(detective) sergeant' would be an equivalent if we decided to translate these titles. Establishing the fact that these are plain clothes policemen is important as this is an issue which emerges in the first chapter of the novel, but perhaps more so also are the details on the two career paths, '*Kriminalsekretär*' belonging to the lower one, implying a difference in background between the '*Kriminalsekretär*' and the main character, the '*Kommisar*'. To make this research more useful in the longer term, we may also use the 1928–1935 *Brockhaus* to research contemporaneous reference books on policing: the entry '*Kriminalpolizei*' lists several volumes that would be useful background for anyone translating this series of crime novels. More academic sources can be sourced in the standard *Handwörterbuch zur deutschen Rechtsgeschichte* (Cordes et al. 2004.).

It is worth noting that the first *Brockhaus* search was by far the most efficient: one of the most important skills as a researcher is being able to choose where you are going to research a term, and get a feel quickly for whether a certain resource is going to help you quickly or not. Encyclopaedias and authoritative reference works are often invaluable aids for translators and literary scholars as they give overviews of terms and topics, are written by specialists, and, perhaps most importantly, often provide short but useful bibliographies that allow us to continue our research if necessary. Obviously, the amount of time a translator (or a scholar) can spend on this kind of research depends on the task in hand, the time available (not to mention remuneration), the amount of research that has already been done in the field and that is readily available, and the requirements of the particular translation problem.

CASE STUDY 2:　Online resources and medical science

The expression which will serve as the basis of our next case study is the medical term *Hirnleistungsstörung* from the Ginkgo biloba text. The purpose is to show you some of the possibilities of online research, not to prescribe definitive procedures. In any particular case, the number, sequence and combination of searches will vary, according to the nature of the translation problem and—not to be underestimated—the predisposition of the user, i.e. you, as, for instance, an 'economical' researcher or an 'explorer' (Gough 2017).

The online resources which are illustrated below are the dictionary websites Lexicool, Leo, Linguee and Reverso Context, all of which have additional functionality of various kinds. The search engine Google is also used, in its ordinary monolingual mode, but also as a bilingual resource, 2Lingual.

Lexicool provides access to hundreds of bilingual dictionaries across a range of language pairs and directions, as a kind of 'metadictionary'. For the direction German>English, there is a choice of six dictionaries. The results for our chosen ST term from two well-known German<>English dictionaries are shown in Table 12.4:

Table 12.4 Online resource Lexicool: results for query term '*Hirnleistungsstörung*'

Resource	Gloss of function/s	Outcome
Lexicool www.lexicool.com/	Online dictionaries in multiple language pairs and direction. Offers the user a range of possible dictionaries once the language pair/direction is selected (includes access to Leo and Linguee)	*Collins*: No results. Search term too specialised. Offers related words e.g. '*Leistungsstörungen*' ('defective performance') *PONS*: As for Collins

This shows us that bilingual general-purpose dictionaries—*Collins* and *PONS* have been among the favourite bookshelf items of German-language students for many decades—are unsurprisingly not able to cover the wealth of specialised vocabulary necessary for many areas of translation. We therefore need to look for more specialised resources.

Leo is a popular dictionary resource with the added functionality of a discussion forum, where translators describe their problem (usually ter-minological but also concerned with word combinations such as which verb goes with which noun) and invite responses. From Leo, the follow-ing rather straightforward picture emerges:

Table 12.5 Online resource Leo: results for search on the query term '*Hirnleistungsstörung*'

Resource	Gloss of function/s	Outcome
Leo www.leo.org/	Online dictionaries in multiple language pairs; bidirectional in each pair. Offers: - dictionary equivalents; - discussion forum: users can post questions about translation problems related to a particular word, phrasing or term	'brain deficiency' [med.] 'brain disorder' [med.] No questions posted

As both English equivalents given by Leo are labelled as specialised medical terms and therefore potentially usable, one simple way of pro-ceeding is to use a search engine to check which seems to be more frequent: 'brain disorder' turns out to be nearly 80 times as frequent as 'brain deficiency', but, whilst indicative, this is a crude measure for a number of reasons. Useful information to check further at this point would be definitions (to confirm the meaning: are the terms really synonymous?) and examples of how the terms are used in texts (and in which text genres). As most bilingual dictionaries include neither definitions nor contextual examples, we must look elsewhere.

Ideally, to confirm equivalence of meaning, we need to compare authoritative definitions of the German ST term and of the suggested English dictionary equivalent/s. In the present case, this proved fruitless: although both the German and the English terms were found in many medical or medical-related texts, no useful definitions were found, as Table 12.6 records:

Table 12.6 Online resource Google: results of search for German and English definitions of English dictionary equivalents and of German ST term

Resource	Search technique	Outcome
Google www.google.co.uk/	Search terms: 'medical dictionary'	Wikipedia provides links to free online medical dictionaries and encyclopaedia but no definitions were found.
	'brain disorder' definition 'brain deficiency' definition	Many occurrences of 'brain disorder' in hits, including many types of brain disorder, but no definition except a circular one: 'any disorder or disease of the brain'
Google Deutschland www.google.de/	Search terms: 'medizinisches Wörterbuch'	Some free online medical dictionaries identified but no definition found.
	Hirnleistungsstörung Definition	Many occurrences of 'Hirnleistungsstörung' in hits, including many types, but no definition except a circular one: 'Störungen der geistigen Leistungsfähigkeit'

If no definitions can be found, contextual examples can sometimes be helpful with respect to meaning, as well as usage. The next resource, Linguee, provided no dictionary equivalents for the ST search term, but did identify a number of German and English texts in which the

ST term and potential TT equivalents appear. One example is shown in Table 12.7:

Table 12.7 Online resource Linguee: results of search for the query term '*Hirnleistungsstörung*' showing contextual examples of ST search term and English equivalents

Resource	Gloss of function/s	Outcome
Linguee www.linguee.com/	Online dictionaries in multiple language pairs; bidirectional in each pair. Offers: - dictionary equivalents; - examples of word/term in context from bilingual corpus of parallel texts; - gives link to fuller version of the contextual examples	- No result for the compound. - Bilingual parallel contextual examples: [. . .] eine gezielte, ursächliche Be-handlung der schweren **Hirnleis-tungsstörung**, an der weltweit Millionen von Menschen erkrankt [. . .] *Full clickable version*: [not shown here] [. . .] points for a targeted, causative treatment of this severe **brain disorder** which affects millions of people worldwide, as reported [. . .] *Full clickable version*: [not shown here] Nine further bilingual contextual examples [not shown] are given, yielding the English terms (sometimes plural): 'degenerative disorder of the brain' 'cerebral disturbances' 'cognitive brain dysfunctions' 'brain disorders' 'brain disorder' 'brain fog' [term omitted in English] 'cerebral disorders' 'cerebral disorder'

The dictionary equivalent 'brain disorder' has more than one confirmation in the translations identified by Linguee of German texts in which '*Hirnleistungsstörung*' occurs, whereas 'brain deficiency' does not, providing support for its relative rarity, as in the earlier Google frequency search. We could at this point decide to opt for 'brain disorder', but in order to expand the range of resources illustrated in this case study, let's continue with our exploration, turning first to another resource—Reverso context (Table 12.8)—which, as Linguee, produces 'parallel' contextual examples, i.e. an extract from a German text and its English version. Immediately we see that the number of possible translation equivalents for our ST term has increased.

Table 12.8 Online resource Reverso context: results for search on the query term '*Hirnleistungsstörungen*'

Resource	Gloss of function/s	Outcome	
Reverso context http:// context .reverso. net/	Customisable for many language pairs/directions. Offers: - word/term in context in two columns from a range of textual sources, incl. 'official' documents; - gives link to fuller version of the contextual examples from parallel texts	[. . .] Verwendung von substituierten Aminen zur Behandlung von **Hirnleistungsstörungen** *Full clickable version*: [not shown here]	Use of substituted amines for the treatment of **cerebral insufficiencies**. *Full clickable version*: [not shown here]
		Seven further bilingual contextual examples [not shown] are given, yielding the English terms (sometimes plural): 'cerebral insufficiency disorders' 'cerebral insufficiency disorder' 'cerebral disorders' 'mental disorders' 'mental disorder' 'disturbances of brain function' 'brain deficiencies'	

It is worth noting that although both Linguee and Reverso contexts produce texts which are related by translation, we don't necessarily know whether the German or the English text is the original ST. Pairs of translated texts are clearly very useful in identifying possible equivalents but confirmation from an original authoritative source can strengthen the case for a particular choice.

The bilingual search engine 2Lingual operates in the same way as the monolingual Google, but produces hits in two specified languages based on a query term or expression in one of these languages. The English texts produced as hits alongside the German hits for the German search term are not translations of the German: we can assume that in the majority of cases they are texts originally written in English. This search produces one more term: 'brain failure', as in Table 12.9:

Table 12.9 Online resource 2Lingual: results of search on the query term '*Hirnleistungsstörung*'

Resource	Gloss of function/s	Outcome
2Lingual www.2lingual. com/	Bilingual Google search engine. Presents—in two columns— the results of a Google search in each specified language	Search on '*Hirnleistungsstörung*' produces many websites for the German term and a range of terms in English, including 'brain failure'

The 2Lingual search alerts us to a particular danger when using Google: it operates on character strings and 'knows' nothing about the content of what it is retrieving. It turns out that only some of the hits for 'brain failure' are medically related; the others are referencing a Chinese punk band called 'Brain Failure'.

So, to take stock, the consolidated list of English terms resulting from our various searches (excluding repetitions) is as follows:

'brain deficiency'/'brain deficiencies'
'brain disorder'/'brain disorders'
'brain failure'
'brain fog'
'cerebral disorder'/'cerebral disorders'
'cerebral disturbances'
'cerebral insufficiencies'
'cerebral insufficiency disorder'/'cerebral insufficiency disorders'
'cognitive brain dysfunctions'
'degenerative disorder of the brain'
'disturbances of brain function'
'mental disorder'/'mental disorders'

In addition to 'brain disorder', our original lead term so far, and the less likely 'brain deficiency', there are two other possible English terms with 'brain' as the modifier ('brain failure' and 'brain fog'). We have also identified four terms with the modifier 'cerebral' and one with 'mental'. Finally, we have 'cognitive brain dysfunction', 'degenerative disorder of the brain' and 'disturbance of brain function'. The preferred head clearly seems to be 'disorder', followed by 'deficiency'/'insufficiency'. All together then, there are 12 terms (if we conflate singulars and plurals), demonstrating that the range of terms used in texts can be much wider than the solutions offered in dictionaries, especially where compounds and multiword terms are concerned. This has both advantages and disadvantages for the translator. On the one hand, the translator enjoys the possibility of nuancing the choice of terms according to register e.g. 'cerebral insufficiency disorder' versus the intuitively informal 'brain fog'. On the other hand, this kind of research is time-consuming and ultimately, potentially confusing. Choosing between an array of apparent synonyms is a common problem for translators. In the case here, we can probably rule out 'mental disorder' as this seems to be a broader term incorporating psychological as well as neurological disorders. Let us also rule out the three terms which occur only once in the Linguee search and bear little formal resemblance to the other candidate terms ('cognitive brain dysfunctions', 'degenerative disorder of the brain', 'disturbances of brain function') as well as 'brain deficiency', which seems rare.

If we focus on 'brain disorder' and 'cerebral disorder', a further Google search in English (looking at the first 20 hits) indicates that the former (alongside 'mental disorder') tends to appear more in news items and texts for the general public on health, whereas the latter appears in more specialised texts such as journal articles. As our ST is part of a learned article for specialists, compounds with 'cerebral' look more promising. That leaves us with four candidates: 'cerebral disorder', 'cerebral disturbance', 'cerebral insufficiency' and 'cerebral insufficiency disorder'.

At this point, having narrowed down our selection on the basis of genre, it is time to consider the subject matter of the ST, to see if any of our four candidate terms occurs in English-language texts which are concerned with the medicinal herb Ginkgo biloba. A Google search on each of the four terms together with 'Gingko biloba' produces the following results in Table 12.10:

Table 12.10 Online resource Google U.K. search engine: results for four candidate English terms with 'cerebral' as modifier for the ST term '*Hirnleistungsstörung*'

Resource	Search Technique	Outcome
Google www.google.co.uk/	Search terms: (One page of hits for each search term analysed to identify learned papers with a focus on Ginkgo biloba as a medicinal herb)	Relevant hits/hits per page
	"cerebral disorder" "Ginkgo biloba"	3/16 hits
	"cerebral disturbance" "Ginkgo biloba"	0/11 hits
	"cerebral insufficiency" "Ginkgo biloba"	8/13 hits
	"cerebral insufficiency disorder" "Ginkgo biloba"	0/13 hits (most overlapped with 'cerebral insufficiency')

Based on the frequency of relevant hits, the term 'cerebral insufficiency' is the best fit in this context. Two of these hits—both learned articles—actually use the term in their title: 'Ginkgo biloba for cerebral insufficiency' and 'Efficacy of Ginkgo biloba in 90 outpatients with cerebral insufficiency caused by old age' published in the *British Journal of Clinical Pharmacology* and in *Phytomedicine* respectively (Kleijnen and Knipschild 1992; Vesper and Hänsgen 1994).

That is not to say that the term in the published translation of the 1992 abstract—'disturbances of the cerebral function'—is incorrect. The many possibilities revealed by our exploration using online resources has simply demonstrated that even in Medical Science, ways have to be developed to deal with rich displays of synonymy, a phenomenon which is not exclusive to literary translation but for which a different basis has to be established for decision-making. If in the end you decide to test your choice with a subject expert, you need to be well prepared with specific questions and a limited range of choices: they are busy people.

Concluding remarks

We hope to have shown in this chapter how important good research techniques are in order to solve certain translation problems, whether they occur in literary or specialised texts. You may start out with a lexical problem in mind, but it should soon become apparent that what lies behind the words—as well as how they are used in context—is equally important in interpreting and evaluating the information gleaned from both online and paper resources. Dictionaries—even specialised ones—are rarely adequate in this respect. In setting out our two illustrative stories of long searches for possible equivalents of German terms, there is no intention to imply that such intensive searches are always necessary or even desirable. However, it is hoped that the details of the case studies will stimulate your interest in developing research techniques using some of the resources described here. The following chapters— on translating consumer-oriented and sci-tech texts—illustrate some further techniques.

Further reading

Chan, Sin-wai 2004. *A Dictionary of Translation Technology*. Hong Kong: The Chinese University Press.

Practical 12

12.1 COMPARING RESOURCES

Assignment

The aims of this exercise are: to familiarise you with some of the resources discussed in the chapter; to help you judge their value; and to understand the different types of information you can glean to best solve particular problems in the future.

i   Choose a *compound* German term e.g. from one of the texts set in a previous practical or from a relevant website such as BASF: any subject field will do.
ii Follow the procedures—at least some of them—outlined in the chapter to see which of the searches, or which combination of searches, leads you to a satisfactory result.

12.2 RESEARCHING TERMINOLOGY FOR TRANSLATION

Assignment

As demonstrated in this chapter, one of the decisions facing translators is having to choose between an array of apparent synonyms when trying to find an equivalent for a term in the SL in a particular subject field. Dictionaries, termbases and so on often do not go beyond a broad subject label, providing little information on contextual use, with all that implies for readership and degree of specialisation. The terms listed below all belong to the field of Automotive Engineering dealing with catalytic converter technology. Using as many resources as you can, try to respond to the following points:

i   Gather as much further information as possible in order to narrow down (a precise alignment is probably not possible) the genres in which the following terms are found.

ii Find as many examples as you can of how each term is used in context (these 'contextual examples' can consist of a phrase, a clause or a sentence showing a typical use such as which verbs the term combines with, which adjectives modify it, etc.).

iii Establish:

    a whether any definitions you can find agree on the main characteristics (as they should for denotative synonyms) and what to do if they don't;

    b whether any of the terms are used in other subject fields and if so, whether the sense differs;

    c which terms are the most frequent e.g. across a range of genres, and therefore have a potentially wide distribution;

    d whether any of the terms seem to be company-specific;

    e whether any of the terms are specific to a particular variety of English (e.g. UK English or US English);

    f whether any of the terms are no longer in use ('deprecated').

iv And discuss:

    a how best to store the information and make it retrievable for future use (advantages/disadvantages of Word table? Excel spreadsheet? Terminology Management System*?).

---

catalytic converter
automotive catalyst
automotive catalytic converter
exhaust catalyst
exhaust catalytic converter
catalytic exhaust converter
catalysor
catalyst
exhaust gas catalytic converter
cat

---

*Note: Terminology Management Systems—customised databases—are commercially available but some companies offer demo versions. If you google 'Terminology Management Systems', you can learn more about what is an essential tool for professional sci-tech translators (and Language Service Providers, as well as service and manufacturing companies) for creating their own termbases. You could try creating a couple of entries for the data which you have gathered.

References

Primary

Browder, George C. 1990 *Foundations of the Nazi Police State: The Formation of Sipo and SD*. Kentucky: University Press of Kentucky.

Diwok, M., Kuklinski, B. and Ernst, B. 1992. 'Superoxiddismutasenaktivität von Ginkgo-biloba-Extrakt', *Zeitschrift gesamte Inn. Medizin*, 47, pp. 310–3.

European Commission's European Master's (EMT) in Translation Network n.d. Available at: https://ec.europa.eu/info/resources-partners/european-masters-translation-emt/european-masters-translation-emt-explained_en (Accessed: 22 March 2018).

Fallada, Hans 2009. *Alone in Berlin*. Translated by Hofmann, Michael. London: Penguin.

Kerr, Philip 2012. *Berlin Noir*. London: Penguin.

Kleijnen, J. and Knipschild, P. 1992. 'Ginkgo biloba for cerebral insufficiency', *British Journal of Clinical Pharmacology*, 34(4), pp. 352–8.

Kutscher, Volker 2016. *Der nasse Fisch*. Cologne: Kiepenheuer & Witsch.

Tellkamp, Uwe 2008/2010. *Der Turm: Geschichte aus einem versunkenen Land*. Frankfurt am Main: Suhrkamp.

Vesper, J. and Hänsgen, K-D. 1994. 'Efficacy of Ginkgo biloba in 90 outpatients with cerebral insufficiency caused by old age: Results of a placebo-controlled double-blind trial', *Phytomedicine*, 1(1), pp. 9–16.

Secondary

Byrne, Jody 2012. *Scientific and Technical Translation Explained: A Nuts and Bolts Guide for Beginners*. London and New York: Routledge.

Cordes, Albrecht et al. (eds) 2004. *Handwörterbuch zur deutschen Rechtsgeschichte*. Berlin: Schmidt.

EMT Board 2017. *EMT Competence Framework 2017* [Online]. Available at: https://ec.europa.eu/info/resources-partners/european-masters-translation-emt/european-masters-translation-emt-explained_en#documents (Accessed: 13 February 2018).

Gambier, Yves 2009. *Competences for Professional Translators, Experts in Multilingual and Multimedia Communication*. Brussels: DGT, European Commission.

Gough, Joanna 2011. 'An empirical study of professional translators' attitudes, use and awareness of web 2.0 technologies, and implications for the adoption of emerging technologies and trends', *Linguistica Antverpiensia, New Series—Themes in Translation Studies (LANS—TTS)*, 10, pp. 195–217 [Online]. Available at: https://lans-tts.uantwerpen.be/index.php/LANS-TTS/issue/view/14 (Accessed: 13 February 2018).

Gough, Joanna 2017. *The Patterns of Interaction Between Professional Translators and Online Resources*. PhD Thesis. University of Surrey, UK [Online]. Available at: www.surrey.ac.uk/library/ (Accessed: 13 February 2018).

Kastberg, Peter 2009. 'Personal knowledge management in the training of non-literary translators', *JoSTrans*, Issue 11/January 2009, pp. 88–102 [Online]. Available at: www.jostrans.org/issue11/art_kastberg.pdf (Accessed: 13 February 2018).

Olohan, Maeve 2016. *Scientific and Technical Translation*. London and New York: Routledge.

Sager, Juan 1990. *A Practical Course in Terminology Processing*. Amsterdam and Philadelphia: John Benjamins.

Lexical and related resources

2Lingual n.d. Available at: www.2lingual.com/ (Accessed: 1 March 2018).

AntConc n.d. Available at: www.laurenceanthony.net/software.html (Accessed: 1 March 2018) [Tools for concordancing and text analysis.].

British National Corpus n.d. Available at: www.natcorp.ox.ac.uk/ (Accessed: 1 March 2018) [Provides access to 100m words of written and spoken English and to other corpora of English such as the extensive Brigham Young BYU/BNC corpus.].

Brockhaus Encyklopädie 1970. Wiesbaden: Brockhaus.

Brockhaus-Enzyklopädie-Online 2013. Munich: Brockhaus.

Corpus of Contemporary American English (COCA) n.d. Available at: http://corpus.byu. edu/coca/ ['[T]he largest freely available corpus of English'.].

Der Große Brockhaus 1928–1934. Leipzig: Brockhaus.

Dictionary.com n.d. Available at: www.dictionary.com (Accessed: 1 March 2018) [Includes definitions and synonyms in English.].

Duden: Das große Wörterbuch der deutschen Sprache 1994. Mannheim: Bibliographisches Institut.

DWDS (Digitales Wörterbuch der deutschen Sprache) n.d. Available at: www.dwds.de/ (Accessed: 1 March 2018) [Very useful options to consult monolingual dictionaries, corpora and information on patterns of word behaviour.].

Europäisches Übersetzer-Kollegium (EÜK) n.d. Available at: http://euk-straelen.de/ deutsch/das-kollegium/ (Accessed: 1 March 2018).

Google n.d. Available at: www.google.co.uk (Accessed: 22 March 2018).

Google Deutschland n.d. Available at: www.google.de (Accessed: 22 March 2018).

IATE (InterActive Terminology for Europe) n.d. Available at: http://iate.europa.eu/ (Accessed: 2 March 2018) [European Union term bank.].

Institut für deutsche Sprache (IdS) n.d. *COSMAS II*. Available at: www.ids-mannheim.de/ cosmas2/ (Accessed: 2 March 2018) [Corpus of German texts; full online access to the collection can be obtained by registering at https://cosmas2.ids-mannheim.de/cosmas2-web/. Using the *Anmeldung* button, you will be asked to enter your details as well as a username [*Kennung*] and a password [*Kennwort*]. For background on *Projekt Korpusrecherchesystem* see http://www1.ids-mannheim.de/direktion/kl/projekte/recherche system.html.].

Leo n.d. Available at: www.leo.org/ (Accessed: 2 March 2018) [Provides a range of equivalents in bilingual lists with some information on subject field and the possibility of an interactive discussion list for queries.].

Lexicool n.d. Available at: www.lexicool.com/ (Accessed: 2 March 2018) [Claims to offer 'a directory of "all" the online bilingual and multilingual dictionaries and glossaries freely available on the Internet'.].

Linguee n.d. Available at: www.linguee.com/ (Accessed: 2 March 2018) [Provides parallel contextualised examples from existing translations.].

Oxford English Dictionary (OED). Available at: http://public.oed.com/about/free-oed/ (Accessed: 2 March 2018) ['offers many tasters and routes into the dictionary's 600,000 words and 3 million quotations': accessible through local or university libraries.].

ProZ n.d. Available at: http//www.proz.com/ (Accessed: 2 March 2018) [Claims to provide 'tools and opportunities that translators, translation companies, and others in the language industry' can use to network and to improve their work. For terminology resources see www.proz.com/about/overview/terminology/.].

Reverso n.d. Available at: www.reverso.net (Accessed: 2 March 2018) [Provides parallel contextualised examples of equivalents.].

Sketch Engine n.d. Available at: www.sketchengine.co.uk/ (Accessed: 2 March 2018) [Includes ready-made text corpora in German and English at www.sketchengine.co.uk/ documentation/tenten-corpora/ and text-analysis tools.].

UNTERM n.d. Available at: https://unterm.un.org/UNTERM/portal/welcome (Accessed: 2 March 2018) [United Nations Terminology Database: includes some entries for German.].

Wahrig, Gerhard et al. 1984. *Deutsches Wörterbuch*. Munich: Mosaik.

Wordsmith n.d. Available at: www.lexically.net/wordsmith/version6/index.html (Accessed: 2 March 2018) [Includes text-analysis tools for several languages.].

13 Translating consumer-oriented texts

Most texts, including translations, are produced for a specific purpose. The purpose, as we have seen, is a major factor in deciding how to approach the translation. Translating consumer-oriented texts makes the importance of purpose especially clear, as the intended readership plays a dominant role in the translation decisions taken. This, together with the fact that many translators earn their living with these sorts of text, is why we are giving them a chapter to themselves.

Scope of the chapter

'Consumer-oriented texts' in our understanding for this chapter include acts of communication that try to persuade the public to buy something, whether a product or a service, but also extend to other texts of a non-commercial nature which are in the public domain and aim to influence or guide behaviour. They can be functionally categorised as what we have called—after Reiß (Chapter 2)—operative or persuasive texts. As these texts are reader-focused, the translator has to keep criteria such as readability in mind, even in texts that have some technical content: compare, for example, the concise and straightforward subject-verb 'if'-clause 'If your battery goes flat' with the wordier and more nominal 'In the unlikely event of your battery going flat'.

This chapter, like others, emphasises that part of the translator's preparation must be to study examples of appropriate TL texts so as to become familiar with the requirements of the genre in the target culture. It is just as important, however, to be aware that there is considerable scope in many consumer-oriented genres for stylistic variation reminiscent of literary writers. Compare, for instance, the rather didactic style of Delia Smith's cookery books with Jamie Oliver's matey tone (see Chapter 4). The language of contracts and other legal texts—also aiming to regulate human behaviour—is by contrast highly conventionalised and will not be discussed here.

We have pointed out earlier in this book that text classifications serve the purpose of allowing certain generalisations, which can in turn help to set priorities for the translator in making translation decisions in a relatively systematic way. But all classifications are a kind of abstraction: in practice, we are faced not only with hybridity but also with a range of possibilities within any category. In what we have called 'consumer-oriented texts', given the dominant textual function of influencing or guiding behaviour, and hence the usually dominant influence of the target reader/recipient, there is considerable scope for variation in content, form and tone depending on age, education, social group and so on. If the readership is very broad, e.g. as in party-political election leaflets, the task is challenging.

It would be impossible to deal with the whole range of genres which have an operative function and so we are focusing here on a selection. In the first half of the chapter we deal predominantly with advertising and promotional texts of various kinds. In the second half of the chapter, we present two case studies which extend the notion of 'consumer' to the readers of a set of instructions on acceptable behaviour in swimming pools and of a promotional tourist brochure for a well-known *Schloss*.

Translating advertisements

Translating adverts is often as much a question of creating or 'rewriting' copy as of 'translation' in the conventional sense, a niche part of the translation market now often referred to as 'transcreation', a kind of admixture of translation and copywriting. One way for international companies and organisations to deal with the cultural specificities of their local target markets is for marketeers to start with a relatively neutral brief, a process known as 'glocalisation' as the basis for 'internationalisation', often through translation (see Adab 2000: 224). But translators are also asked to translate 'unglocalised' advertisements, and intra-trade publicity is commonly translated. Many multinationals, keen to ensure a distinctive brand image worldwide, commission all their translations from one translation company with which they work closely through their marketing department in ensuring presentational brand norms of all kinds. But translators beware: marketing professionals, especially those who consider themselves to be proficient in the TL (as is often the case for English in German-speaking areas) do not always easily defer to the expertise of translators, sometimes taking a fairly literal view of the translation task. For our needs in this course, translating advertising material is certainly a good way of focusing attention on the dimension of purpose in textual genre. If you did not do Practical 6.1, we recommend that you at least look at this for this chapter.

Translating advertising material also obliges the translator to consider carefully the central question of cultural differences between SL public and TL public: probably no other genre makes it so brutally clear how intercultural differences can make a too-close translation unwelcome, even where it is possible. For example, a French bath product for men was labelled '*bain moussant relaxant*' in French, but adjusted to 'foaming muscle soak' in English, suggesting a functional post-exercise necessity rather than an indulgent sensual experience. While the manufacturer of the bath foam demonstrated a rather refined cultural awareness, this is not the case for an English-language print advert in an in-flight magazine for investing in Bavaria. The text praises the 'Bavarian way of life', whether it is 'in the state's architecture, culture or economy'. For Bavarians, '*der Staat*' is for historical reasons likely to be the federal state of Bavaria, not the country, Germany. But an English-speaking readership is unlikely to know this, leading to possible confusion, not to mention the alienating effect of the awkward use of the possessive 'the state's architecture. . . '.

A particular feature of advertisements—whether in print, on the www or on the street—is their multimodality: the integration of verbal and non-verbal text means that in any translation or transcreation, the functioning of the text as a whole needs to be considered alongside the cultural specificities of the target locale. Colours are powerful indicators of certain emotions, but may vary between languages and cultures. Yellow is, for instance, associated with envy (cf. '*gelb vor Neid*') and cowardice in German but only with cowardice in English (cf. 'green with envy'). The actual use of a particular colour in a text can therefore symbolise different emotions in different cultures. Animals too can symbolise very different characteristics: in the western world, owls are wise, but elsewhere, they can be associated with death. A web-based project, say in a metropolitan UK locale, to promote adult education evening classes in a multicultural community might therefore give out entirely the wrong message if 'branded' with an owl, which might be linked thematically and linguistically with verbal content such as 'night owl'. Caution also needs to be exercised when assuming that certain social values, such as cleanliness (see Torresi 2004), are universal.

Different cultures value different things, have different taboos and stereotype consumers differently. These sorts of differences are just as important in consumer handbooks as in advertisements. As noted earlier, texts are rarely of a 'pure' type. Many handbooks, for example, whose primary function is to give users instructions for use also have an important publicity function as well, flattering purchasers and trying to cement their loyalty to the brand ('Congratulations! Now that you are the proud owner of . . . ', etc.). Linguistic and cultural mistakes, mistakes, that is, in terms of target audience norms, threaten that loyalty.

Style and appeal

Apart from such cultural factors as religion, race, diet, attitudes to sex, and so on, it is also vital to choose the right style. For instance, while the language of consumerism is relatively relaxed today in the West, the degree of formality observed between customers and traders varies from country to country. While serious comparisons are difficult without large-scale sampling, translators should not assume that the relaxed style now predominant in American and British consumer texts is universal. It is always worth checking the intended tone with the client: a fairly faithful translation into English might come across as over-careful or too ornate, while a similar approach in translation out of English might alienate TL customers by an appearance of flippancy. Humour does not, for instance, always travel well. But it is worth remembering that differences within market sectors in a particular locale, such as that between different age groups, might be greater than those which operate *inter*culturally. In today's digitally connected world, young people in the UK and in Germany might have more in common with each other in terms of social attitudes and experience than they do with the post-war baby-boomer generation in their own country.

The appropriate language for selling upmarket shoes or downmarket sofas is conditioned by a combination of social and broad cultural expectations specific to the product range on offer and its target market. As with sci-tech texts (see next chapter), therefore, the translator needs to have made close comparisons of the language used by at least a representative sample of SL and TL product literature. If significant changes to wording and/or to images are, in the translator's judgement, necessary for cultural—and ultimately commercial—reasons, then the client needs to be advised accordingly. As we point out in Chapter 14, it is rare for the cost of image replacement to be covered, but the translator still has a responsibility to point out possible consequences, as failure to make adjustments could have a strong counter-productive effect of which the client is not aware (see Tercedor et al. 2009 for some relevant examples of verbal text-image relations in French and Spanish in a translation context).

Beyond the issues of potentially inappropriate style, the appeal of a consumer-focused text can be seriously endangered by translation errors, such as those which can be unwittingly made by non-native speakers of the TL. An example is provided by the front page of a leaflet promoting the *Deutsches Pferdemuseum* in Verden, featuring laughing young people on an antique rocking horse, under the words, in enormous print: 'Hold yourself tight . . . '. While translation errors—especially those which evoke *double entendres*—can damage the serious communicative purpose of any text, they are especially damaging for reader-focused texts where the text's authors are reaching out to the target readers. In cases where the wording of the text is creative as opposed to fairly routine, the translation is best left to a trained translator for whom the TL is the language of habitual use. And yet this is no guarantee of a successful translation. It is often clear in advertising copy and product or services literature that the translator has been constrained—whether through inexperience or haste or by the client's insistence on 'accuracy'—to import foreign linguistic structures or cultural assumptions from the source material. If such foreign features are not to be seriously counter-productive, there are only two ways of proceeding. Either they must be avoided altogether, so that the copy reads as truly 'domesticated'; or else they must be consciously and skilfully designed—by translators and copywriters conversant with the target culture—to appeal to that culture's perceptions of desirable/interesting foreignness (perhaps with a lacing of humour and irony, depending on market segment and locale). The following section begins with some examples of advertising slogans which aim to appeal to their potential market—not always successfully—through the use of German in English texts and English in German texts: the ultimate 'foreignisation'.

To translate or not to translate?

It may seem counterintuitive in a coursebook on translation to advise you *not* to translate on occasion. But there are cases such as certain advertising slogans where this is required. For example, in the automotive industry, Audi's '*Vorsprung durch Technik*' marketing campaign in Britain, attempting to appeal to the positive perception of German technology as of high quality, as also the '*Das Auto*' campaign of the Volkswagen brand, are well known. More than just a slogan, these phrases are integral to the overall branding of the company: a recently published Volkswagen Group public-facing document—*Drive*—also switches languages to include particular expressions. The document has the form of a report (A4 40-page booklet available in both German and English and printed on high-quality paper) but clearly has a promotional purpose, as evidenced, for instance, by its use of superlatives: '*Volkswagen hat sich das Ziel gesetzt, bis 2018 der innovativste und nachhaltigste Volumenhersteller der Automobilwelt zu werden*'. The German version includes a reference to an environmental initiative named in English: '*die Initiative "Think Blue"*': the English is intended to distinguish VW from its competition, becoming a Unique Selling Point according to Volkswagen (*personal communication*), although other companies such as Daimler use 'Blue' in a similar way. The English slogan is also used in the French and Spanish versions of the website, as well as in many others. So not everything needs to be translated: 'The car' and '*blau denken*' would be serious errors here.

While we must leave it to the marketeers to decide whether these particular marketing slogans are successful, other cases have been reported which are clearly not successful, as the ability of the broader German public to understand English has been misjudged, resulting in some consumers feeling excluded from the market. One example reported in the *Spiegel Online* (2008)—which could have been flagged up by a competent translator—concerns the Vodaphone slogan 'Make the Most of Now': hard to fathom for many Germans who might associate the English 'most' with the German '*Most*' (a kind of grape juice). Another more damaging example is German television station Sat1's catchphrase 'Powered by Emotion'. *Spiegel Online* reports that this 'was taken by many to be a modern version of "*Kraft durch Freude*," the Nazi party's leisure organisation, often translated into English as "strength through joy"' (2008: online). Again, a competent translator might have been able to anticipate this unfortunate allusion. In such cases, then, the translator can act as expert consultant on the implications of using foreign slogans.

Checkpoint Charlie is a well-known tourist spot in Berlin. Flyers are available in both English and German promoting an on-site exhibition. The front page of the two-sided text (about one third of an A4 sheet) is shown in monochrome format in Figure 13.1 (German) and Figure 13.2 (English) (source: Berliner Forum für Geschichte und Gegenwart e.V. n.d.).

As can be seen, the main heading 'COLD WAR' is displayed in large font in both language versions under an image of a soldier leaning on a tank and looking into the distance through binoculars. 'COLD' is printed in white, 'WAR' in a larger font underneath in red (not reproduced here). But two lines below the heading, the German changes to '*Kalter Krieg*', where the English sticks, of course, to 'Cold War'. Three possible reasons might account for the use of English as a main heading in a German-language text. Firstly, the English has fewer characters, so the font for the main heading would have to be reduced in size if in German ('Cold war' has eight characters including the space, '*Kalter Krieg*', 12) in order to fit

Figure 13.1 Front of two-sided flyer advertising the Ausstellung BlackBox Kalter Krieg at Checkpoint Charlie, Berlin-Mitte (German version). The full colour figure is available at www.routledge.com/9781138920989.

the space available, producing a less striking effect. Secondly, the producers of the flyer may have wanted to have a 'look-alike' feel to the flyers, regardless of language. And thirdly, English is a global *lingua franca*.

Figure 13.2 Front of two-sided flyer advertising the Exhibition BlackBox Cold War at Checkpoint Charlie, Berlin-Mitte (English version). The full colour figure is available at www.routledge.com/9781138920989.

In the case of the Checkpoint-Charlie flyer, we can safely assume that a considered decision was made not to translate the header. There are cases, however, in which text must not be translated, but rather modified. Brochures of various types often contain information relating to versions available in other languages, e.g. '*auch im Englischen erhältlich*'. Clearly, it would be nonsense to include this in the English version: what is needed instead is 'also available in German'. A similar example is evident in a bilingual tourist leaflet advertising an exhibition concerning the Berlin wall. The German and the English information concerning admission charges and special events are presented side by side. The German lists a German-language guided tour on Saturdays. In the English-language column, '*Samstag*' becomes 'Thursday'. But this is not an error, as the English-language tour takes place on Thursdays, not Saturdays. Although these examples are not 'translations' in the traditional sense, handling them in an appropriate way clearly belongs to translation competence.

Byrne (2012: 138–42) details some other interesting cases of when not to translate, for example, when an official translation already exists (and must be used) or when certain proper nouns are used.

CASE STUDY 1:   Public information notice

Controversy concerning the alleged behaviour of some young male migrants in public places in certain European countries hit the headlines early in 2016. One German city authority responded to local complaints by producing a multimodal public information leaflet on '*Baderegeln*' in German, English ('Pool Rules') and French ('*Règles de comportement en piscine*') (A4, double-sided, folded in three, see SWM 2015). More versions are available in Arabic and other languages. The leaflet is arranged as a series of 13 coloured cartoon-type pictures, each with a caption in all the chosen languages supporting the message about what is considered acceptable behaviour in swimming pools. Two have been selected for discussion as they highlight certain issues about a suitable register for this type of public information leaflet, as well as sensitive intercultural issues concerning not only the content but also the leaflet itself. A third example has been chosen as it illustrates what is perhaps a more subtle point about perspective. The following discussion is based on the assumption that the various injunctions are aimed at children and young adults.

The first caption—shown below in Figure 13.3 with its English translation as printed beneath the image—concerns what to wear at the pool. The image [not shown here] shows two young boys, one in bathing trunks, one in underwear. The male pool attendant (we assume) is saying 'YES' (in English!) to the former, and 'NO' to the latter. The expressions on the boys' faces (smile, puzzlement) resonate with approval and prohibition.

Keine Alltagskleidung im Schwimmbad.
Badehose, Badeanzug oder Bikini aus
schwimmtauglichen Materialien sind Pflicht!

No street clothes are allowed in the pool area.
Proper swim attire is mandatory.

Figure 13.3 German caption with English translation for image showing appropriate and inappropriate clothing to wear in the pool.

The elliptical '*Keine Alltagskleidung im Schwimmbad*' is very direct and bossy, but we could also ask why '*Alltagskleidung*' has been used when the point concerns underwear. Instead of adjusting this rather odd choice in the TT, the ST's ambiguity is made worse in the translation: given the image of the boy in his underpants, 'street clothes', instead of something like 'everyday wear' or even 'ordinary clothes', implies that people walk on the street in their undergarments. The German continues in a very specific way, listing different types of swimwear, emphasising the particular material they should be made from, just to make sure. The concise English translation ignores all the detail—which seems rather explicit and legalistic for this genre in any case—but then opts for an inappropriately high register through the choice of 'attire' and 'mandatory'. An alternative would be: 'You must wear proper swimwear'.

The second example concerns advice on how to treat women, regardless of their mode of swimwear: the image [not shown here] shows three young women, one in a bikini, one in a swimsuit and one in a burkini. The German starts informally ('*Egal*') but concludes quite formally with a passive infinitive construction embedded in a main clause. The passive avoids a direct approach to the reader, although the structure is still functionally a command, and has the effect of being impersonal i.e. has a bureaucratic tone.

Egal, welche Badekleidung eine Frau trägt, sie
ist zu achten und zu respektieren!

Regardless of the swim attire of a female patron
she has to be treated with respect and dignity.

Figure 13.4 German caption with English translation for image requiring respect for women.

The English starts in a neutral register but then shifts to high-register vocabulary: 'swim attire' and 'female patron'. The translator has missed a chance here to improve on the original (given its purpose) by addressing the public directly and simply: 'No matter what swimwear a woman is wearing, treat her with respect and dignity'.

The third example illustrates the need to research carefully in the TL to establish the relevant conventions in parallel situations. The image [not shown here] shows a boy dive-bombing into the pool with his knees pulled up to his chest, with another boy standing by cheering him on. A female pool assistant is shown in an insert holding up her left hand with the forefinger extended, saying 'NO!'. In the following, the English reads rather awkwardly, starting with the gerund 'diving'.

Nur ins Wasser springen, wenn es tief genug
ist!

Diving only at the deep end.

Figure 13.5 German caption with English translation for image aimed at prohibiting jumping in the shallow end.

The reason the English formulation is so odd is because such warnings tend to be expressed *negatively* in English: 'No diving', which then requires mention of the shallow end, not the deep end. Hence, a much more natural translation would read: 'No diving in the shallow end', except, of course, that '*springen*' is different from 'diving', meaning that the English command is not consistent with the image (lack of coherence).

CASE STUDY 2:   Tourist brochure

The purpose of the text in this second case study is to attract visitors to a well-known *Schloss* in Bonn: *Schloss Augustusburg*. The text is overtly persuasive through its use of well-chosen vocabulary ('*Bravourstück*', '*eine hinreißende Schöpfung*', '*von höchstem Rang*', and so on), but also informative, giving lots of historical background, attractive in itself to many visitors. The text comes in both German and English versions. The readership can be assumed to be relatively well-educated adults with an interest in culture. As a case study, this text illustrates an issue of coherence in so far as there are evident tensions between the specialised knowledge—and hence terms—surrounding the principal subject matter and readers' general knowledge: how can they be reconciled in a text which is aiming to attract a wide range of tourists?

The English TT printed below is taken from an old well-illustrated brochure, comprising the middle third of the text. The German text is still available on the official website, but the English web version of the text is a little different from the print version shown below (items in bold are for later discussion). We return to this second version in the Practicals at the end of this chapter.

ST	TT
Bis [. . .] [. . .] 1768 wirkten hier namhafte Künstler von europäischem Ruf. Beispielhaft sei **Balthasar Neumann** genannt, der den Entwurf für das 5 **Prunktreppenhaus** anfertigte, ein Bravourstück, eine hinreißende Schöpfung voller Dynamik und Eleganz. Durch die Zusammenführung von Architektur, Plastik, Malerei und 10 Gartenkunst entstand ein **Gesamtkunstwerk** des deutschen Rokoko von höchstem Rang. Die **UNESCO** würdigte dies 1984 durch die Aufnahme des Schlosses Augustusburg 15 —zusammen mit Schloss Falkenlust und den Brühler Gärten—in die Liste des **Weltkulturerbes** der Menschheit. Ab 1949 wurde Schloss 20 Augustusburg viele Jahrzehnte lang als Repräsentationsschloss des Bundespräsidenten und der Bundesregierung genutzt. (Schlösser Brühl n.d.)	Famous artists known throughout Europe worked on the palace until [. . .] 1768. One of the most noteworthy of these was **Balthasar Neumann**, who designed the ceremonial staircase. This exceptional creation is both elegant and innovative. By bringing together architecture, ornamentation, painting and horticulture, a **comprehensive work of art** was created which is a fine example of the German rococo period. This was taken into consideration by **UNESCO** in 1984. Since then Augustusburg, the Hunting Lodge Falkenlust and the palace gardens were added to this organisation's **cultural world heritage list**. For many decades after 1949, Augustusburg was used for representational purposes by the Federal Republic of Germany.

The TT has its successes such as the free but idiomatic rendering of the Balthasar Neumann reference, despite its rather strong interpretation of '*Beispielhaft*'. But it also misleads at one point, and runs into difficulties of a type often met in texts about architecture which are targeted at non-experts such as the tourists visiting the *Schloss*. In such cases, the architectural features have to be described in terms that hover somewhere on the complex interface between specialised language (including that of aesthetics) and consumer-oriented language addressed to the visiting public. This is arguably more challenging for the translator than dealing with specialised expert-to-expert texts where terms are more likely—as labels for condensed shared knowledge—to be immediately understood. The kind of discourse that has established itself in German architectural descriptions—'*Dynamik*', '*Plastik*', '*Gesamtkunstwerk*', '*Repräsentation-*'—brings translators up against a cultural gap less easily bridged than, for example, differences involving metrication.

Of these four ST terms, perhaps '*Gesamtkunstwerk* has least of the *faux ami* about it; to use that German term in English as a loan word is often (and in Music certainly) the best solution in more specialised texts. Here, though, it is problematic, as not every likely TL tourist will make the necessary extrapolation from Music; even then, it has a strong associative meaning of 'Wagnerian opera'. In this context, 'total work of art' is perhaps the nearest to a conventionally accepted rendering. The special status of the phrase could be indicated by using scare quotes in the TT. In this case, and in many of the following points such as the use of Fine Art terms, the role of UNESCO and the naming/history of *Schloss Augustusburg*, we draw your attention to the need to conduct background research.

An alternative translation for '*Dynamik*' ('innovative') is 'vibrant', commonly used in promotional texts and creating euphony with 'elegant', a welcome feature for the genre. The standard equivalent of '*Plastik*' in this context is 'sculpture', alongside '*Malerei*' and '*Architektur*', all three belonging to the Fine Arts; the choice of 'ornamentation' tends to trivialise here rather than enhance. The translation of the UNESCO recognition of the site—'cultural world heritage list'—captures the essence of the ST phrasing but is rather clunky. Dropping '*der Menschheit*' avoids making the phrase even heavier in English and the concept is easily inferred. A more natural wording in English would be: 'have been on the UNESCO list of world heritage sites', thereby also correcting the error in the TT 'were added to' and moving 'UNESCO' to later in the paragraph, while at the same time avoiding the rather clumsy use of 'organisation' to co-refer. Whether 'cultural' needs to be made explicit in a promotional text of this kind is debatable: UNESCO recognises three types of site— cultural, natural and mixed—but the point of visiting Augustusburg is self-evidently cultural. The final phrase—'for representational purposes'—is particularly odd. Omitting mention of the German President and the federal government in favour of 'the Federal Republic of Germany' compounds the opacity of the meaning in so far as a more natural—albeit lengthier—translation such as 'Augustusburg was used by the German President and the government to host visiting dignitaries' focuses on the personal.

If asked to translate '*Schloss*' out of context, dictionary favourites such as 'castle' (or even 'chateau') come to mind, but seem inappropriate here, evoking images of medieval ramparts or French elegance; the published TT choice of 'palace' (TT line 2)—an explicitation of '*hier*' (ST line 1)—is preferable, capturing some of the history and grandeur of the building. Another possibility such as 'country house' (cf. the UK Prime Minister's residence Chequers) is not grand enough and 'stately home' is embedded in British culture. The use of a truncated form in the English, i.e. 'Augustusburg'—for the full name in German: '*Schloss Augustusburg*'—is a neat way of avoiding the issue.

A final point is to note the short paragraphs, consisting mostly of just one sentence. As consumer-oriented texts, brochures of this kind—and later web-based versions—need to be accessible and easily read.

Concluding remarks

All the issues covered in this chapter relating to a selection of consumer-oriented text genres are part of the translator's intercultural competence, one of the six competences specified in the European Commission's European Master's in Translation scheme (see Chapter 12): it is the translator's responsibility to advise and act on such matters, including: 'Knowing how to identify the rules for interaction relating to a specific community, including non-verbal elements [. . .]' (Gambier 2009: 6).

In this chapter, we have tried to raise awareness of how crucial the target readership is in shaping many translation decisions. Firstly, the importance of language variation between social groups—also part of intercultural competence, according to Gambier—is of particular note for reader-focused genres (in the present case, texts aimed at 'consumers' of various kinds), the function of which is in many cases to influence behaviour, an aim which requires a nuanced approach to linguistic, cultural and social issues. Secondly, the example of the swimming pool instructions demonstrates how the verbal and non-verbal content of a text must be treated holistically in translation, also bearing in mind the particular target readership, in this case groups of young people from different linguacultures. And thirdly, the issue of register—also mentioned by Gambier— has featured not only in the swimming pool text, but also in the tourist brochure example, where judgements had to be made regarding the translation of terms from specialised domains in the context of arguably different reader expectations.

Further reading

Adab, Beverly and Valdés, Cristina (eds) 2004. *The Translator*. Vol. 10/2 (special issue *Key Debates in the Translation of Advertising Material*).

Cruz García, Laura (ed.) 2016. *Revista de Lenguas para Fines Específico*. Vol. 22/2 (special issue *New Perspectives on the Translation of Advertising*). Available at: https://ojsspdc. ulpgc.es/ojs/index.php/LFE/issue/view/53. Articles mainly in English, also French and Spanish.

Snell-Hornby, Mary 1999. 'The "ultimate confort": Word, text and the translation of tourist brochures', in Anderman, Gunilla and Rogers, Margaret (eds) *Word, Text, Translation: Liber Amicorum for Peter Newmark*. Clevedon: Multilingual Matters, pp. 95–103.

Torresi, Ira 2014. *Translating Promotional and Advertising Texts*. London and New York: Routledge.

Practical 13

13.1 ANALYSIS AND EVALUATION: TOURIST BROCHURE/WEBSITE

Assignment

i   Through a local tourist office or website, identify a tourist brochure translated into German promoting your local area (town, city or region)—German is often one of the languages provided in the UK.

ii Using Internet research, identify an original text in German promoting a similar locale in a German-speaking area.

iii Select three criteria from this chapter as a basis for evaluating the translated text, referring to the original German text as appropriate.

iv Discuss your analysis with your class or in a group.

13.2 TRANSLATION: IN-FLIGHT MAGAZINE

Assignment

i   You are translating material for an in-flight magazine, including the ST here. Discuss the approach that you decide to take before starting detailed translation of this ST, and outline and justify the method you adopt.

ii Translate the text into English.

iii Discuss the main detailed decisions you took.

iv Compare your TT with the published one, which will be given to you by your tutor.

Contextual information

The ST appeared side by side with the official TT in the Lufthansa in-flight magazine. They formed part of a promotion encouraging passengers to register for the
Lufthansa air miles scheme published in *Lufthansa Magazin*.

ST

**AUTOS MIT STIL, PRESTIGE UND PRÄMIENMEILEN—DANK
MILES & MORE**

**Unterwegs Prämienmeilen sammeln—
Mit vier großen Mietwagenpartnern**

5   Wo immer Lufthansa Sie hinfliegt—einer unserer Mietwagenpartner wartet bereits auf
Sie. Mit Avis, Europcar, Hertz und Sixt als Partner von Miles & More können Sie an
nahezu jedem Ort der Welt das Auto Ihrer Wünsche nicht nur am Flughafen mieten—
und kommen stets komfortabel, günstig und sicher an Ihr Ziel.
     Aber Flexibilität und Mobilität sind nicht Ihre einzigen Vorteile. Bei allen vier
10   Mietwagenpartnern sammeln Sie bei der Anmietung eines Fahrzeugs Prämienmeilen—
im gesamten Netzwerk der Mietwagenpartner. Und besondere Aktionen ermöglichen
Ihnen darüber hinaus, in regelmäßigen Abständen ein Vielfaches der üblichen
Prämienmeilen zu sammeln. Die aktuellen Sonderaktionen finden Sie immer im
Internet unter ***www.miles-and-more.com***

15   **Prämienmeilen z.B. gegen automobile Träume tauschen**
     Sie können aber auch Ihre gesammelten Meilen bei Avis, Europcar, Hertz und Sixt
gegen das Auto Ihrer Träume eintauschen und mit ihm ein Wochenende oder sogar
den Urlaub genießen. Oder Sie lösen Ihre Prämienmeilen in attraktive Flug-, Reise-,
Erlebnis- oder Sachprämien ein. Sie sehen, die Teilnahme an Miles & More lohnt
20   sich!
     Detaillierte Informationen zu den Miles & More Mietwagen- und allen weiteren
Partnern, Prämien und Privilegien erhalten sie unter ***www.miles-and-more.com***

Meilen sammeln und Prämien genießen—Mit Miles & More
Miles & More ist das führende Vielfliegerprogramm in Europa. Dank über 30 Partner-
25   Airlines steht Ihnen ein weltumspannendes Netzwerk mit idealen Flugverbindungen
zur Verfügung, auf dem Sie Meilen sammeln können—in der Business Class sogar
doppelte und in der First Class dreifache Meilen. Außerdem lassen unsere Hotel- und
Mietwagen-Partner sowie zahlreiche weitere Partner am Boden Ihr Meilenkonto
wachsen. Die gesammelten Meilen können Sie dann in attraktive Flug-, Upgrade-,
30   Reise-, Erlebnis- oder Sachprämien eintauschen.
     Mehr Informationen zu allen Partnern, Prämien und Privilegien von Miles & More
finden sie unter ***www.miles-and-more.com***. Am besten gleich hier anmelden und
direkt Ihre ersten Meilen sammeln.

(Miles and More 2004: 70–1)

13.3 ANALYSIS AND EVALUATION: UNIVERSITY WEBSITE

Assignment

Universities in both the UK and Germany are keen to attract students. The
university website has therefore become an essential marketing tool. In this

assignment you should draw on your own knowledge and experience—as well as other resources as appropriate—to evaluate the English translation of webpages from a German university website aimed at prospective students. The task raises challenging questions about the scope of translation and of the expertise of the translator.

You can search for any suitable German university website for this assignment. Most universities have an internationalisation policy, often meaning an English version of selected information is available.

13.4 TRANSLATION: MARKETING SLOGAN

A German multinational company was celebrating its 100th anniversary. The marketing department came up with the slogan: '*Die Zukunft hat Geburtstag*'. As part of the celebrations, the CEO was scheduled to give a presentation in English at which the slogan would be displayed on a large banner above the podium, also in English. The translation department came up with a creative solution which they considered fit for purpose (upbeat, constrained by the space available, accessible to an audience for whom English was not their mother tongue, and conveying the message of building the future on past achievements). Unbeknown to the translators, the marketing colleagues intervened, changing the English translation to 'The future has a birthday', as they considered the proposed solution not to be a 'real translation'. The marketeers' English slogan was not a success and the translators were blamed.

How would you have translated the slogan to meet the promotional purpose of the grand occasion? Brainstorming in a small group might be the best way to release your creative thoughts.

13.5 COMPARISON AND EVALUATION: PROMOTIONAL
TEXT FOR VISITORS

For some reason which is not explained, the older brochure translation of the *Schloss Augustusburg* text differs from the English version on the official website, although the original German remains the same except for one explicitation ('*Die UNESCO würdigte dies 1984 . . .*' becomes '*Die UNESCO würdigte die Geschichte und Gegenwart der Barockschlösser 1984 . . .*'). Your task here is to compare and evaluate the two translations, bearing in mind their readership and content.

Web version of the *Schloss Augustusburg* text extract:

TT

Until [. . .] 1768, numerous outstanding artists of European renown contributed to its beauty. A prime example of the calibre of artists employed here is Balthasar Neumann, who created the design for the magnificent staircase, an enchanting creation full of dynamism and elegance.

5   The magical interplay of architecture, sculpture, painting and garden design made the Brühl Palaces a masterpiece of German Rococo.

TT

UNESCO honoured history and present of the Rococo Palaces by inscribing Augustusburg Palace—together with Falkenlust Palace and their extensive gardens—on the World Heritage List in 1984.

10 From 1949 onwards, Augustusburg Palace was used for representative purposes by the German Federal President and the Federal Government for many decades.

(Schlösser Brühl n.d.)

References

Primary

Berliner Forum für Geschichte und Gegenwart e.V. n.d. *Cold War: Checkpoint Charlie* [Leaflets in German and in English obtained December 2015 in Berlin].

European Commission's European Master's (EMT) in Translation Network n.d. Available at: https://ec.europa.eu/info/resources-partners/european-masters-translation-emt/european-masters-translation-emt-explained_en (Accessed: 22 March 2018).

Miles & More 2004. *Lufthansa Magazin*, March [Advertisement]. Hamburg: Lufthansa.

Schlösser Brühl n.d. *Schloss Augustusburg* [Online]. Available at: www.schlossbruehl.de/Schloss_Augustusburg (Accessed: 23 March 2018).

SWM 2015. *Baderegeln (M/Bäder)*. Available at: www.stadtwerke-buchen.de/images/baeder/baderegeln-edb.pdf (Accessed: 23 March 2018).

Secondary

Adab, Beverley 2000. 'Towards a more systematic approach to the translation of advertising texts', in Beeby, A., Ensinger, D. and Presas, M. (eds) *Investigating Translation*. Amsterdam and Philadelphia: John Benjamins, pp. 223–34.

Byrne, Jody 2012. *Scientific and Technical Translation Explained: A Nuts and Bolts Guide for Beginners*. London and New York: Routledge.

Gambier, Yves 2009. *Competences for Professional Translators, Experts in Multilingual and Multimedia Communication*. Brussels: DGT, European Commission.

Spiegel Online 2008. '"Come in and find out": How Germans really see English Ad slogans' [Online]. Available at: www.spiegel.de/international/germany/come-in-and-find-out-how-germans-really-see-english-ad-slogans-a-596128.html (Accessed: 14 February 2018).

Tercedor, Maribel, Alarcón-Navío, Esperanza, Prieto-Velasco, Juan A. & López-Rodríguez, Clara I. 2009. 'Images as part of technical translation courses: implications and applications', *JoSTrans*, Issue 11, January 2009, pp. 143-68.

Torresi, Ira 2004. 'Women, water and cleaning agents', *The Translator*, 10/2, pp. 269–89.

14 Translating scientific and technical texts

Much professional translation today is concerned with what is variously called 'technical' or 'commercial' or 'specialised' translation—as opposed to literary or Bible translation—all umbrella terms which mask both similarities and differences. 'Specialised' texts, or *Fachtexte*, encompass more than just sci-tech texts, extending to legal, medical, financial, administrative, political, economic and so on, as well as covering texts in the Arts and Humanities. Estimates for the market share of specialised translations at the beginning of the millennium were calculated at around 80%–90% of the world's translations (see Rogers 2015: 20 for a summary). The importance of sci-tech translation in particular as a part of the growing languages service sector is evidenced by the fact that 'the sectors of industry that spend most on translation globally include manufacturing, software and healthcare, alongside defence in the USA' (Olohan 2016: 8; citing Kelly 2012). Many students reading this book will have specialised outside Science and Technology: this is therefore an important chapter for you to judge whether this area of translation is a potential area of development, or not.

Sci-tech translation and specialised translation

What does specialised translation entail? Any specialist field has its own special vocabulary, and communicative norms, whether in the world of Healthcare, Construction, or Theoretical Linguistics; in this chapter we will concentrate on scientific and technological texts because these are unfamiliar for many language students and as such illustrate very well some important points in the translation of all specialised texts. Firstly, the translator must be—or become—familiar with salient aspects of the subject field as an area of knowledge which is mapped out by its own terminology, as well as learning how to research further information effectively using linguistic, encyclopaedic and other resources (see Chapter 12). Secondly, many of the problems met in translating specialised texts are the same as those met in translating any text, including decisions relating to communicative purpose, audience, genre conventions, closeness of the translation, equivalence, and so on. For instance, the number of different genres which sci-tech translation covers is vast, from technical reports through safety instructions to academic research articles, each genre being closely associated with a particular communicative purpose and linguistic register.

While many sci-tech or any other specialised texts are relatively inaccessible to non-specialist readers (e.g. a patent application, instructions for repairing a photocopier, a technical data sheet), ultimately this inaccessibility is conceptual in nature: the expert in any scientific or technical subject has, over a period of years, absorbed a mass of knowledge that has become part of the background and so does not become explicit in texts. Judging the level of knowledge of the new readers, i.e. of the TT, is therefore a crucial aspect of establishing coherence when translating. But not all sci-tech texts are written by and for experts. It is not only the authors of sci-tech documents—including, for instance, journalists and technical writers—that vary in the degree and type of knowledge they bring to their understanding of such texts, so do the readers of such texts. One writer on 'technical communication', when considering who might read sci-tech texts, distinguishes between the 'expert', 'the 'technician', the 'manager' and the 'general reader' (Markel 2004). Some texts need to be accessible to experts only (e.g. a presentation at an academic conference to describe new knowledge) or to 'techies' only (e.g. a manual for an HGV mechanic to repair lorries), both fairly well-defined groups with relatively clear communicative purposes. Writing for managers (e.g. a report outlining recommendations on operational issues of a technical or financial nature as the basis of future policy), or for the general reader (e.g. an encyclopaedia entry or a feature article in a quality newspaper) is in some respects more challenging, as judgements have to be made by the author concerning readers' knowledge of the subject field. Communication between professionals, for whom the language of the text is often a *lingua franca*, typically, English, is usually conducted by the experts themselves (e.g. scientists, engineers), sometimes writing in a second or third language, sometimes writing for later translation. Other levels of communication are nowadays often dealt with by technical authors. Translators can be called in to translate at any of these levels. Given the wide variety of text genres, as well as subject fields and levels of communication, it is not surprising that such texts can sometimes be poorly written, thus posing interesting challenges for the translator. Procedures differ here from those usually applied in literary translation: the translator has a duty to spot factual inaccuracies or other problems in the ST and, ideally in consultation with the commissioner of the translation (who may or may not be the author of the document), to try to resolve those problems in a way which is appropriate to the communicative purpose.

Terminology

Terms, which together make up the terminology of a particular subject field or domain, are items of specialised vocabulary which, if they are to be used appropriately, usually require some kind of familiarity with the subject field in question, either through formal training or experience. They have different formal properties depending on the features of the language concerned. A large number of nominal terms in English consist of at least two words; in German, compounds are, of course, usually written as a single word: e.g. 'auto-immune disorder'/'*Autoimmunkrankheit*' (Medicine). Adjectives can also occasionally be terms e.g. 'acute'/'*akut*'; 'chronic'/'*chronisch*' (Medicine), and even more rarely, adverbs (formally identical to adjectives in German) e.g. 'therapeutically'/'*therapeutisch*') (Medicine) and verbs e.g. 'to download'/'*herunterladen*' (Information Technology). Any specialised text is likely to carry a great deal of information in the noun phrases; the more specialised the text, the denser it becomes.

In what follows we look at some lexical problems arising from the use of specialised terms. In illustrating these, we shall refer to two rather different texts, one scientific, one technical: an extract from an ornithologist's research paper on birdsong, and the ST of Practical 14.1 here ('*Tunnelauskleidung*', a specification of works). These are two quite different genres but each contains terminological problems to solve. We'll start with the research paper:

Hinweise auf Funktionstrennung bei *Parus*-Arten ergeben sich wie folgt:
    1) Bei Territorialgesang: Bestimmte Strophentypen wurden besonders bei Auseinandersetzungen (bei Anlockung mit Klangattrappen), jedoch nicht so oft spontan gesungen (z.B. Smith 1972; Martens 1975; Ficken et al. 1978). Hier liegt
5 also eine Funktionstrennung im Sinne von Revierverteidigung im Gegensatz zu Revierproklamation vor.
    2) ♀-bezogene Strophentypen: Eine Trennung des Repertoires in ♀-bezogene und revierverteidigungsbezogene Strophentypen ist nachzuweisen (vgl. z.B. Romanowski 1978; Schroeder and Wiley 1983b; Gaddis 1983).

(Goller 1987: 306)

In looking at lexical issues, we can start with the obvious problem of terms not used in everyday, ordinary language ('Language for General Purposes' or *Gemeinsprache*), and consequently unfamiliar to the layperson. In the birdsong text, a term such as '*Klangattrappen*' stands out at once as belonging only to a specialised scientific context. Without any research the translator will have almost no chance of coming up with the appropriate TL rendering ('playbacks'). The birdsong extract also highlights the issue of how terms relate to each other, ideally in a systematic way both within and between languages. So '*Revierverteidigung*' ('territory defence') is contrasted with '*Revierproklamation*' ('territory proclamation'). While a close translation of the German terms would in this case produce the correct English terms, we cannot rely on that.

The second problem concerns so-called double-duty terms (see Chapter 12): these can be the most dangerous sort of case for the translator, especially if new to the field, as you may fail to recognise the word as a term, and instead translate its ordinary sense. For example, '*Auseinandersetzung*' has many equivalents, according to its use in general language or in a number of specialised languages. The European Union terminology database IATE (see Chapter 12) lists the general senses 'discussion' and 'examination', but also gives equivalents in four subject fields: Defence, Civil Law, Family Law and Finance (but not Ornithology) (IATE n.d.). In a well-structured entry with appropriate indicators and subject-field labels, the old faithful *Oxford-Duden* (1999) also gives a range of possible equivalents: 'examination'; 'debate', 'discussion'; 'argument', 'dispute'; 'clash'; 'partition'. The label attached to 'dispute' links it to Industrial Relations but in fact, it is also the correct specialised equivalent in Animal Behaviour.

But how would you be able to make that link without specialised knowledge or access to an ornithologist? One way is for the translator to be rather imaginative. In these kinds of situations, it is often helpful to hypothesise about the most likely equivalent of the available possibilities, in the present case, for instance, choosing among those listed in the *Oxford-Duden*: 'clash' or 'dispute' seem the most likely for the discourse of ornithology. As the ST concerns territoriality, two online searches were made using the candidate search terms: (a) "Animal Behaviour" "territory clash" and (b) "Animal Behaviour" "territory dispute". The former produced several hits but these were not from scholarly articles, whereas the latter brought to light several learned articles dealing with the behaviour of a range of animals, including fish, squirrels and birds, as well as a Wikipedia article on 'Territory (animal)'. This all supports hypothesis (b).

Our second example, the '*Tunnelauskleidung*' technical text below, also shows how the translator has, as always, to look beyond bilingual and monolingual dictionaries: the term '*Röhre*' tempts us towards 'pipe' or 'tube'. But *Oxford-Duden* gives explicit advice on 'bore' as the appropriate equivalent under the subject label '*Tunnel~*'. Subject labels are essential to distinguish between the array of apparent synonyms offered as equivalents; the online dictionary *Leo* (see Chapter 12) offers English equivalents for four subject fields including Construction, but does not include 'bore' relating specifically to tunnel construction. The term '*Ausbau*' is also not used here in its commonest semi-technical sense of 'extension'/'development', but rather to mean 'construction'. The technically oriented *Leo* does come up with the correct term, namely, 'construction', although many other terms are also offered, also with the subject label '*Bauwesen*'. So even subject labels do not always indicate a unique choice. One possibility here would be to post a query on the *Leo Diskussionsforum* linked to the entry for '*Ausbau*'. Researching a third term, '*Angriffspunkt*', even in a specialised online dictionary of Civil Engineering (*E&S Dictionary* (online)) is translated as 'point of application', but what the professional translator finds in TL specialist literature is 'break(ing)-out point' or 'cutting-out point'.

On such specific items, generalist bilingual dictionaries cannot be expected to offer comprehensive solutions; nor, in some cases, do specialised terminology resources. However, they can offer a starting point indicating the beginning of a research trail for the translator to pursue, taking into account the huge number of terms in each field, and the fact that scientific and technological fields and their terminologies are constantly developing. As shown in the examples discussed in this and the earlier chapter on research and resources, reference material does not always give a single unambiguous equivalent for a particular scientific or technical term. Translators often have to make an informed choice between alternatives. They can only do this if they have a firm grasp of both the textual context and the wider subject-related context, and are also able wherever possible to check the relevant literature and/or to consult an expert in the field.

So far in our discussion of terminology, we have been ignoring the issue of how specialised the text is and who the intended readers are. One issue associated with different author-reader relations concerns the use of alternative terms or, in a sense, synonyms i.e. terms which refer to the same thing but with different linguistic expressions, depending on whether the communication is, say, expert-to-expert, or expert-to-layperson/layperson-to-expert. It is well known, for instance, that common medical terms often have two variants: a specialised term and a popular term. Examples include: 'myocardial infarction'/'heart attack', 'hypertension'/'high blood pressure'. There are even websites to train doctors in the use of popular terms in order to improve their communication with patients. Doctor-patient communication in German also exhibits similar problems to those in English (see, for example: DocCheck News 2012). Many German medical terms are also based on classical languages e.g. *'Appendizitis'*, although German equivalents exist as in the etymologically more transparent and popular variant *'Blinddarmentzündung'*. Translators therefore need to distinguish in their choice of TL terms between communications directed at patients and those directed at doctors, or more generally, between those targeting laypeople and those aimed at experts.

Having so far outlined some terminological considerations, we will now look at a few practical points specific to sci-tech translation, before going on to consider different approaches to training and skills development, the treatment of errors and of numbers.

Priorities in sci-tech translation

In the previous section we discussed a scientific text and a technical text. The distinction can be an important one. Some useful generalisations about the ways in which these different subject matters are handled in discourse suggest that the primary function of technical texts, whose readers actually want to do something else, is informative, whereas science-based texts '*discuss, analyze and synthesize* information with a view to explaining ideas, proposing new theories or evaluating methods' (Byrne 2012: 2, *emphasis in the original*). The readers of these texts are also interested in information but from a quite different perspective. Technical information or instructions are unlikely to include any persuasive elements, whereas the authors of scientific texts may seek to demonstrate that their arguments are convincing and significant. Scientific texts such as journal papers or even popular science books and articles usually have named authors whereas technical texts such as technical data sheets, manuals of various kinds and instructions for use are usually anonymous. Scientific texts share their lack of anonymity with literary texts, even to the point where some authors may be well known, at least within their discourse community. The inference to be drawn here is that the style of the ST, i.e. the style of the author/s, is more important in shaping translation decisions for scientific texts than for technical texts.

Nevertheless, scientific and technical texts do share some special characteristics that need to be actively considered by students whose first- and second-language experience has been general and/or literary. Scientific and technical language, particularly if between experts, *tends* to be precise and compact. Accuracy and clarity, and therefore consistency, are clearly important.

Consistency is a more important requirement than literary translators might imagine if schooled in the importance of lexical variation for stylistic reasons. As clarity and precision are priorities in sci-tech communication, synonyms can be problematic: how does the reader know that the same object is being referred to in all cases? Is 'catalytic converter' the same as 'automotive catalyst'? Is '*Autoabgaskatalysator*' the same as '*Kraftfahrzeugkatalysator*'? And which term is preferred by the client? One technological development which helps to address the issue of consistency and is now extensively used in the translation industry is the Translation Memory tool mentioned in Chapter 12.

TM is best suited to the translation of technical texts, notably technical instructions, as they are routinely updated when new versions of products are released onto the market. Manufacturers and developers worldwide are constantly updating their documentation, so there has to be a parallel process of updating the operating instructions, descriptive literature, and so on in all relevant languages (as a legal requirement). This implies that features in a 2018 model that are *not* new must be described using the same terminology and set expressions that were used in 2017. Technical translation in particular can in fact often be repetitive, usually for reasons of clarity.

While technology in the form of tools and resources is playing an increasingly prominent role in the world of the twenty-first-century professional translator, it remains the responsibility of the translator to produce a translation which is fit for purpose. Both sci-tech and literary translators are, of course, seeking to build or guard their reputation and are held responsible for their work. But more than this, the implications of mistranslation where a simple error can cause financial loss and even endanger structures or lives, must be borne in mind. Literary translators on the other hand may have to deal with problems such as risky ideological, religious or political issues, depending on the material they are working with and where they are working or being published.

Getting started

Making a start on sci-tech translation without a scientific or technical background is challenging, often involving intensive study of a single aspect within a broader discipline. While translators can build their reputation—as in any other business— by specialising in a particular subject field, few sci-tech translators can afford to offer their services over a spectrum narrower than, say, Medicine, Construction Engineering or Information Technology. Some Master's programmes in translation offer a starting point in different specialisms, and many modern-language students now choose to undertake further training before entering the professional translation market. Unfortunately, the career option for graduate translators—still trainees in most professionally related respects—to work in-house as a member of a supervised translation team is no longer widely available: the business model of delivering translation services has changed considerably over the last two decades or so. Many manufacturing or service-based companies have closed their in-house translation departments, and even so-called 'Language Service Providers' (LSPs) i.e. dedicated translation companies, now employ very few in-house translators. Instead, they build extensive networks of freelance translators to whom they outsource the work according to need. From the LSP's perspective, this allows greater flexibility with regard to subject field, translation pair and direction, availability for fast turnaround, and so on. The translators usually have access to resources such as termbases, previous translations (usually in the form of Translation Memories) and some consultation e.g. in case of errors in the ST, issues of comprehensibility or doubts about specific terminology use for the client.

Freelancers also have functioning networks that provide peer advice, either through mentoring schemes or training courses (often accredited as part of 'Continuing Professional Development') run by professional associations such as the Institute of Translation and Interpreting in the UK, or through translation-related websites such as ProZ (ProZ n.d.). No sci-tech translator, in-house or freelance, can afford to ignore the golden rule, which is in truth a good one for all translators: never be too proud or embarrassed to ask for help or advice. More detailed advice and information—including many weblinks—are given in the Postscript to this course.

Many of the points dealt with in the following sections on errors and units of measurement are not, of course, exclusive to sci-tech texts.

Dealing with errors in the source text

Supplying a text on which people will rely for operating machinery or for prescribing medicines involves responsibility for ensuring accuracy. In a literary text, the translator may be accustomed to a certain trade-off between literal accuracy and other qualities such as mellifluousness or an associative echo; even in the special language of Business and Finance, or in some consumer-oriented texts, the importance of subjective factors may warrant a flourish of rhetoric (cf. Practical 6.1), but exact Science and Technology allow less latitude. In taking every precaution to ensure the accuracy of the TT, it might be necessary for the translator to consult the client—directly or indirectly through their LSP—in cases where:

i   the meaning of the ST is unclear, e.g. where the text is poorly expressed as in cases where it is not clear which noun a pronoun is linked to;
ii   a factual error is suspected but is not immediately checkable;
iii   a factual error is identified e.g. an incorrect date or measurement.

In cases (i) and (ii) the translator will have to wait for the client's response—the client is often not the author—in order to proceed. Where a factual error is definitely detected (case iii), the translator should still notify the client that a correction has been made. These are all cases in which the translator somehow improves on the ST, a move that would usually be considered inappropriate in most literary translation, although editors can and do intervene. Advice on dealing with errors in STs which are technical in nature can be found in Byrne (2012: 161–2) and in Mossop (2014: 84–8).

Using an interesting scale of decreasing saliency, translation scholar Peter A. Schmitt (1999a: 148) describes the most typical errors—often produced under pressure of time and without any quality checks—as follows: formal errors (e.g. repetition or omission of a section of the ST), incorrect figures and measurements, typographical errors, lack of correspondence between graphics and verbal text, discrepancy between text and reality, errors of expression (e.g. incorrect terminology), and lack of comprehensibility across all text levels. Genres which, according to Schmitt, are the least likely to contain errors are those which are subject to rigorous quality checks, often for legal reasons, such as standards (*Normen*) and patent specifications (*Patentschriften*).

The level of quality checks in a professional context—according to what is agreed by the translator and the client—should be included in the specifications for the job in order to avoid later misunderstandings. These typically include provision for revision by another suitably qualified or experienced translator, and a further check, this time of the TT, by a person qualified to judge the appropriacy of the register, terminology, genre conventions and so on for the stated communicative purpose in the relevant subject field/s. This is called a 'review'; no reference is made to the ST. In both cases—revision and review (see Chapter 16)—the translator is responsible for implementing any recommendations for correction. Proofing is usually the final stage. Further details of the complete professional requirements for handling translation services can be found in the British Standards Institute (BSI) document BS EN ISO 117100:2015 (*Translation Services—Requirements for translation services*). Another relevant standard—*Translation Projects—General guidelines*—consists of a comprehensive professional-level checklist for items which should be considered when a translation job is contracted, including: ST profile, subject-field specification and terminology requirements, TL information, layout, permissions, delivery and payment details (BSI: PD ISO/TS 11669: 2012). We mention these standards as a way of indicating that professional translation has moved from the kitchen table to an industry. But even if you are just beginning to learn about translation as a profession, it is useful to be aware that misunderstandings with clients about the translation brief need to be avoided, regardless of the area of translation. A truncated and accessible set of ten points to specify in the translation 'brief' (see also Chapter 2) can be found in Olohan (2016: 19).

Trainee translators might be surprised by the frequency of errors as, for instance, described by Schmitt, in technical texts. Indeed, we are reminded of a pithy aphorism by another well-known German scholar, Hans Hönig, that '*Defekte*' are a normal characteristic of living texts (as reported in Schmitt 1999a: 147). For reasons mentioned earlier (e.g. density of information), small ST errors can have significant effects. If plausible, they can pass unnoticed into the TT. In other cases, they can make a ST perplexing for an inexperienced translator—who nevertheless has to guard against the ready assumption that 'the ST must be wrong' in all cases.

In some cases, however, it might not even be appropriate to correct an error. Imagine, for instance, a translation of a journalistic article on a hot scientific topic which is commissioned by the scientist on whose work it is based but who does not understand the language in which the article is written. The reason for requesting the translation is to follow up on rumours that the journalist has misunderstood and therefore misrepresented the scientist's work. In such a case, the translator has a duty to provide a TT which truly follows the meaning of the ST, including any errors. This is why it is always important for the translator to establish the purpose of the translation.

One type of error that we haven't yet discussed is that introduced into the TT by the translator, raising the spectre of legal liability. A wise precaution taken by many professional translators is to invest in Professional Indemnity Insurance, as advised by professional associations (see, for instance, ITI n.d.).

Translating units of measurement

A common but not exclusive feature of sci-tech texts is the use of numbers. At first glance, 'translating' numbers of various kinds might seem straightforward. After all, they are factual and objective, are they not? Well, up to a point. In fact, numbers must be treated with caution and are often subject to cultural and contextual factors, especially dates, telephone numbers and currency, as well as the presentation of decimal figures. Contextual factors notably include genre and text type.

It is the translator's job to decide whether to convert the numbers in some way (e.g. from metric to imperial), to approximate them (is precision a priority?), or simply to transfer them. Numbers in literary texts are, according to Schmitt (1999b: 298), usually converted unless a different system of measurement would clash with the local situation e.g. converting imperial to metric in a Sherlock Holmes story would not ring true. In texts which are predominantly informative, however, the tendency is for numbers to be converted, especially in texts intended for use by customers e.g. in instructions for use and manuals, although Schmitt points out that this could result in a lack of coherence between the verbal text and the graphics, as diagrams, tables and so on, are rarely changed (1999b: 299). In such cases the translator needs to check with the client whether to convert or not.

Times are also often converted, regardless of the genre or text type. Persuasive texts such as tourist brochures often include opening times, for example. The 24-hour German clock is normally expressed as a.m. and p.m. in English: '*9 bis 12 Uhr*' becomes '9 a.m. to 12 p.m.'. The 24-hour clock is still used in English for information purposes—to avoid ambiguity—in airports and stations for departure/arrival times, and in military and medical language. In a literary text, such usage would probably not be converted if the context were military or medical, although other cases such as a description of when something happened, or when to meet for coffee, or when to leave for the airport would be.

Texts which deal with technical matters in everyday language tend to reflect more popular usage, as Schmitt (1999b: 298) points out, often lagging behind official policy on units of measurement. In some cases, mixed usage (metric and imperial) is permitted e.g. a 'pint' of beer in the now largely metric UK and '*Pfund*' for a half-kilo loaf (see Olohan 2016: 86–7 for more examples).

In the UK almost all metric data can be left in metric form, especially in expert-to-expert texts. Some cases are more complex: in technical texts for consumers, for example, 'litres per 100 km' needs to be converted to 'mpg', but as Schmitt notes (1999b: 298), the German system for measuring fuel economy is based on the fuel consumption in relation to the distance driven, the UK system reverses this, being based on the distance driven in relation to the fuel consumption. Therefore, when in German the fuel consumption rises ('*höherer Verbrauch*'), the measurement of mpg goes down ('lower mileage' per gallon). This is simply another example to highlight the need to think through the logic of what is being translated in terms of *both* numbers and words.

The use of commas and full stops to support the structuring of verbal text is very familiar. Certainly in English, there is considerable discretion in their use. Not so with numbers, as English and German practices differ. In the presentation of decimal markers, for example, German numerical expressions use a comma where the Anglophone countries use a point, e.g. 32,3% versus 32.2%. The point can also be used as a thousands separator (e.g. 1.075), but *not* in the Anglophone tradition where the comma is usually used: 1,075. Confusing the use of commas and points in an English TT could therefore lead to serious miscalculations. Indeed, in order to avoid confusion between, say, 1.075 as one thousand and seventy-five, and as one point zero seven five, the international system of units (SI: *Système International d'Unités*) recommends using a space as a thousands separator: 1 075. A detailed list of '*Maßeinheiten und Umrechnungsfaktoren*' can be found in the *Handbuch Translation* (Snell-Hornby et al. 1999: 401–16). Translators should also follow international standards for the unit of measurement e.g. kilometres per hour 'km/h', kilogram 'kg', second 's' (see the EU *Bureau International des Poids et Mesures* n.d.).

Another potential error facing trainee translators concerns the use of large numbers: in German a *Milliarde* and a *Billion* are a thousand million (10^9) and a million million (10^{12})—i.e. a 'billion' and a 'trillion'—respectively. The American understanding of 'billion' as 10^9 has been in use (although not uniformly) in UK English for around 50 years now: previously a 'billion' was 10^{12}. These correspondences can be summarised and extended as follows:

Table 14.1 Large numbers in German, UK English and US English

Numerical value	German	UK English	US English
10^6	*Million*	million	million
10^9	*Milliarde*	billion	billion
10^{12}	*Billion*	trillion	trillion
10^{15}	*Billiarde*	quadrillion	quadrillion
10^{18}	*Trillion*	quintillian	quintillian
10^{21}	*Trilliarde*	sextillion	sextillion

Mistaking a '*Milliarde*' for a 'million', not recognising an earlier UK use of 'billion', or translating *Billion* (10^{12}) as a 'billion' could fatally affect calculations for Science (e.g. space travel, particle accelerators in Physics) or for Economics (e.g. volume of oil production, the securities market) if readers are relying on an English translation for their information. Discussions on translators' forums or dictionary sites such as Leo still bear witness to the many possible confusions, most of which threaten to have serious consequences. It might also even be the case that the translator's close engagement with the ST highlights a numerical error for the first time.

What is less serious, but needs judgement, is when to be approximate and when to be precise in translating numbers. We pointed out in Chapter 3 when discussing the translation of a poem, that neither accuracy nor cultural issues are always a priority in the translation of numbers, depending on the genre of the source text and the purpose in translating it. Let's take another example, a headline in an online news publication about the dwarf planet Pluto. The headline reads: '*Raumfahrt: 5 Milliarden Kilometer. Pluto bekommt erstmals Besuch von der Erde*' which we could translate as: 'Space Travel: 5 Billion Kilometres. Pluto receives its first visit from Earth'. Whilst we can quickly establish that *Milliarde* is a 'billion', if the house-style rules of our client—who is publishing an English version online—require a conversion from kilometres to miles, we are immediately faced with a problem: a quick calculation shows that 5 billion kilometres is 3,106,855,960 miles, clearly inappropriate in terms of genre conventions for a magazine headline: too long and too much detail. A more acceptable translation would be: 'Space Travel: over 3 Billion Miles . . . '.

When we think of 'text', we are likely to think of words rather than numbers. But in informative texts in particular, numbers might be the most important component of the text. In a translation exercise, students were asked to translate from German into English an A4 information sheet to be distributed by Lufthansa at Frankfurt Airport on how to deal with an impending public-service strike. The top half of the text consisted of a heading ('*Lufthansa aktuell*') and a subheading ('*Der Streik trifft uns alle. Wir sind für Sie da*'.) and a large box containing contact helpline telephone numbers for a range of German cities printed in large bold font. The bottom half consisted of three columns printed in small font which aimed to assure customers of Lufthansa's assistance in coping with travel problems, followed by the company logo. This part of the text had a persuasive flavour. The relative importance of the two parts of the text was clearly signalled by the layout, and yet, some students omitted all the cities and telephone numbers from the translation, presumably assuming that the information could simply be transferred and so was not part of their translation assignment. Even if the information had been transferable in its ST form, it should still have been included in the assignment as a crucial part of the text. In fact, the numbers were not transferable in their ST form as many readers of the English version of the text—not just US and UK travellers—would not have German mobile phones. For instance, the number for Berlin in the German ST is '(030) 88 75 88', but if this number were to be dialled from a non-German mobile phone, as is likely in an international airport, the international code would need to be added: '+49 (0)30 88 75 88'. The alphabetical order of the cities would also need to be changed as '*Köln*' becomes 'Cologne'. And the spelling of some cities changes from German to English e.g. '*Hannover*' > 'Hanover', '*Nürnberg*' > 'Nuremberg'.

Concluding remarks

In this chapter we have aimed to give you some practical information on recommended research and translation procedures, as well as on some common pitfalls. We have also drawn attention to some of the differences between scientific and technical texts with implications for their conventional functions. Sci-tech texts are likely to be perceived as the biggest challenge to traditional modern-language students, but as with any other kind of text, the translator needs to carry out background and terminological research (albeit perhaps more in these subject areas), interpret the ST, make decisions according to the translation brief, and compare genre conventions for possible differences.

Further reading

Bowker, Lynne 2016. 'The need for speed! Experimenting with "speed training" in the scientific/technical translation classroom', in Vandaele, S. and Boulanger, P-P. (eds) *Sciences en traduction* [Special Issue], *META*, 61, pp. 22–36 [Online]. Available at: www.erudit.org/en/journals/meta/2016-v61-meta02902/ (Accessed: 26 March 2018).

Byrne, Jody 2007. 'Caveat translator: Understanding the legal consequences of errors in professional translation', *JoSTrans*, Issue 07/January 2007, pp. 2–24 [Online]. Available at: www.jostrans.org/issue07/issue07_toc.php (Accessed: 26 March 2018).

Practical 14

14.1 TRANSLATION: TECHNICAL TEXT (SPECIFICATION OF WORKS)

Assignment

i   The ST here is from a specification of works issued by a government agency for trunk road construction and aimed at prospective contractors. For a study visit by British planners and engineers, you are asked to provide an English translation. Bearing in mind the information supplied in this chapter with reference to the ST, discuss the decisions that you have to take before starting detailed translation of this ST, and outline and justify the approach you adopt.

ii   Translate the text into English.

iii What were the main problems which you encountered? Structural? Terminological? Judging the audience's level of specialist knowledge?

iv   Which terminology sources did you find most helpful and why?

v   Compare your translation with the professionally prepared TT that will be made available to you by your tutor.

Contextual information

The target audience, like the ST's users, should be thought of as professionals fully conversant with the technology and terminology of tunnelling. In addition to guidance given in the body of Chapter 14, the following terminology should be noted: '*Schalwagen*'—'jumbo'; '*Zuluftstollen*'—'air intake adit'; '*Abluftkamin*'—'ventilation shaft'.

ST

Tunnelauskleidung
Die Herstellung der Abdichtung und der Innenschale erfolgt abschnittsweise zwischen den jeweiligen Angriffspunkten Nordportal—Kehltal—Flößgraben—Südportal. Mit dem Ausbau der Innengewölbe der zweiten Röhre wird umgehend nach dem
5   Durchschlag des jeweiligen Abschnittes begonnen. Nach Betonierung der 2. Röhre wird der Baustellenverkehr umgelegt und die 1. Röhre betoniert.
  Mit dem Einsatz von 2 Schalwagen wird eine Betonierleistung von rund 500 m/Mo erreicht, sodaß die Innenschale der beiden Röhren in den Abschnitten Nordportal—Kehltal und Kehltal—Flößgraben nacheinander betoniert werden kann. Im Abschnitt
10   Flößgraben—Südportal werden die Innenschalen der beiden Röhren gleichzeitig betoniert.
  Gleichzeitig mit dem Betonieren der Innenschale erfolgt der Ausbau der Kaverne Kehltal und anschliessend der Kaverne Flößgraben mit den zugehörigen Zuluftstollen, Zuluftbauwerken und der rund 20 m hohen Abluftkamine, des Hochbehälters im Kehltal
15   sowie der Betriebsgebäude am Nord- und Südportal einschließlich Portalbauwerke.
                                                                          (DEGES 1998)

14.2 TRANSLATION: SCIENTIFIC TEXT (EXPERT JOURNALISTIC ARTICLE)

Assignment

i   The ST comes from an article published online by *Die Welt*. The brief is to translate it for an equivalent-quality English-language newspaper. Discuss how the readership for this text differs from that of the previous text and its translation. What implications might this have for your translation?
ii   Translate the text into English.
iii   Explain the main decisions that you took.

Contextual information

The article's opening section explains that malaria is on the increase worldwide, and that for over 30 years scientists have been struggling in vain to find an effective vaccine. The extract is reproduced as it was printed.

ST

Jetzt will eine kolumbianisch-schweizerische Forschergruppe um den Immunologen Manuel E. Patorroyo einen viel versprechenden Ansatz entdeckt haben. Ausgangspunkt für den neuen Impfstoff war die Beobachtung, dass die Parasiten eine Art molekulare Achillesferse haben. Um in die roten Blutkörperchen
5 einzudringen, in denen sie sich vermehren, benötigen die Einzeller ein MSP-1 genanntes Eiweiß, dass sie wie ein Schlüssel auf ihrer Oberfläche tragen. Dieser öffnet das zugehörige 'Schloss' in der Membran der roten Blutkörperchen, so dass der Parasit eindringen kann.

    Den Forschern ist es gelungen das MSP-1-Proteinmolekül im Reagenzglas
10 nachzubauen und die so genannte Bindungsstelle—also den alles entscheidenden 'Schlüsselbart'—so zu modifizieren, dass ein ringförmiges Peptid entstanden ist. Ein solch zyklisches Molekül hat eine bestimmte räumliche Struktur und wird von Eiweiß abbauenden Enzymen nur sehr langsam verdaut. Beides Merkmale, die für die Wirksamkeit eines Impfstoffs ausgesprochen günstig sind. Tatsächlich ließ sich
15 im Tierversuch zeigen, dass das künstliche dreidimensionale Peptid Antikörper in hoher Konzentration erzeugt, die sich an die MSP-1-Moleküle heften und somit den Eintrittsschlüssel wirkungslos machen. Ob sich aus diesem Ansatz einmal ein Impfstoff herstellen lässt, bleibt abzuwarten.

(Feldmeier 2001)

References

Primary

DEGES 1998. *Tunnelauskleidung (Rennsteigtunnel)*. Berlin: Deutsche Einheit Fern-straßenplanungs- und -bau GmbH.

European Commission's European Master's (EMT) in Translation Network n.d. Available at: https://ec.europa.eu/info/resources-partners/european-masters-translation-emt/european-masters-translation-emt-explained_en (Accessed: 22 March 2018).

Feldmeier, Hermann 2001. 'Neuer Impfstoff bremst Vermehrung von Malaria-Erregern', *Die Welt*, 16 July [Online]. Available at: www.welt.de/print-welt/article463340/Neuer-Impf-stoff-bremst-Vermehrung-von-Malaria-Erregern.html (Accessed: 15 February 2018).

Goller, F. 1987. 'Der Gesang der Tannenmeise (*Parus ater*): Beschreibung und kommuni-kative Funktion', *Journal für Ornithologie*, 128, pp. 291–310.

Institute of Translation and Interpreting (ITI) n.d. Available at: www.iti.org.uk/ (Accessed: 26 March 2018).

Secondary

Byrne, Jody 2012. *Scientific and Technical Translation Explained: A Nuts and Bolts Guide for Beginners*. London and New York: Routledge.

Markel, Mike 2004. *Technical Communication*. 7th edn. Boston and New York: Bedford St. Martin's.

Mossop, Brian 2014. *Revising and Editing for Translators*. 3rd edn. London and New York: Routledge.

Olohan, Maeve 2016. *Scientific and Technical Translation*. London and New York: Routledge.

Rogers, Margaret 2015. *Specialised Translation. Shedding the "Non-Literary" Tag*. Basingstoke: Palgrave Macmillan.

Schmitt, Peter A. 1999a. 'Defekte im Ausgangstext', in Snell-Hornby et al., pp. 147–51.

Schmitt, Peter A. 1999b. 'Maßeinheiten', in Snell-Hornby et al., pp. 298–300.

Snell-Hornby, Mary, Hönig, Hans, Kußmaul, Paul and Schmitt, Peter A. (eds) 1999. *Handbuch Translation*. 2nd edn. Tübingen: Stauffenburg.

Lexical and related resources

British Standards Institute (BSI) 2012. *PD ISO/TS 11669: Translation Projects—General Guidelines*. London: British Standards Institute.

British Standards Institute (BSI) 2015. *BS EN ISO 117100: Translation Services—Requirements for Translation Services*. London: British Standards Institute.

Bureau International des Poids et Mesures n.d. *Measurement Units: The SI*. Available at: www.bipm.org/en/measurement-units/ (Accessed: 1 March 2018).

DocCheck News 2012. 'Medizinische terminologie: Sprich oder stirb', 21 November. Available at: http://news.doccheck.com/de/223/medizinische-terminologie-sprich-oder-stirb/ (Accessed: 1 March 2018).

E&S Dictionary n.d. Available at: www.ernst-und-sohn.de/es-dictionary (Accessed: 1 March 2018).

IATE (InterActive Terminology for Europe) n.d. Available at: http://iate.europa.eu/ (Accessed: 2 March 2018).

Leo n.d. Available at: www.leo.org/ (Accessed: 2 March 2018).

Oxford-Duden German Dictionary 1999. 2nd edn. Oxford: Oxford University Press.

ProZ n.d. Available at: http//www.proz.com/ (Accessed: 2 March 2018).

15 Translating literary texts

Wo man am meisten fühlt, weiß man nicht viel zu sagen.

Annette von Droste-Hülshoff

In this chapter on literature and translation we have a number of aims. For students who do not have much experience in analysing literary texts, we wish to offer an introduction to thinking about the ways that literary texts function, and the issues that 'literariness' raises for translation. We also discuss the kinds of research that translating literature can entail, including some basic bibliographical orientation for background research into German authors, literary history and literary scholarship. At the same time, we hope that this discussion will also be of interest to those for whom literature forms the main channel of their engagement with German, in that we will ask how thinking about translation from the point of view of literature can raise questions about some accounts of translation.

What is at stake in literary translation?

The texts here are from *Faust I*, the 1987 translation by David Luke, and the 1999 translation by John Williams. The excerpts are from the '*Abend*' scene: Faust steals into Margarete's house shortly after having met her and looks around the room. Read both translations and analyse them comparatively, before reading them alongside the German, which you should be able to find easily, and before reading our commentary here. Try to think about a range of issues, such as the scene that is represented, the syntax, and the rhythm. Line numbers refer to the lines in the play.

1987 David Luke	1999 John Williams
FAUST [gazing up and about him]	FAUST [*gazing around him*]
Welcome, sweet twilight, shining dim all through	The gentle light of evening falls
This sanctuary! Now let love's sweet pain	Into this sanctuary. Within these walls
That lives on hope's refreshing dew	Love's pangs clutch at your heart, but you
2690 Seize and consume my heart again!	Must still your cravings with hope's meagre dew.

1987 David Luke	1999 John Williams
How this whole place breathes deep content And order and tranquillity! What riches in this poverty, What happiness in this imprisonment! [He sinks into the leather armchair by the bed.]	This peaceful homestead seems to breathe A sense of order and content. Such poverty is wealth indeed, And there is bliss in such imprisonment. *He throws himself into the leather chair by the bed.*

1987 David Luke	1999 John Williams
2695 Oh let me rest here: long ago, among Their joys and sorrows, others sat on you, Embraced and welcomed! Ah, how often too Round this, their grandsire's throne, the children clung! My love herself, at Christmas time, a young 2700 Rosy-cheeked child, glad at some gift, knelt here Perhaps, and kissed his wrinkled hand so dear. What order, what completeness I am made To sense in these surroundings! It is yours, Dear girl, your native spirit that ensures 2705 Maternal daily care, the table neatly laid, The crisp white sand strewn on the floors! Oh godlike hand, by whose dear skill and love This little hut matches the heavens above! And here! [He draws aside a curtain from the bed.] What fierce joy seizes me! I could 2710 Stand gazing here for ever! Nature, you Worked this sweet wonder, here the inborn angel grew Through gentle dreams to womanhood. Here the child lay, her tender heart Full of warm life, here the pure love 2715 Of God's creative forces wove His likeness by their sacred art! And I? What purpose brings me? What Profound emotion stirs me! What did I Come here to do? Why do I sigh? 2720 Poor wretch! Am I Faust or not? Is there some magic hovering round me here? I was resolved, my lust brooked no delay— And now in dreams of love I wilt and melt away! Are we mere playthings of the atmosphere? 2725 If she came in this instant, ah, my sweet, How she would punish me! How small The great Don Juan would feel, how he would fall In tears of languor at her feet! (Goethe 1998: 84–5, trans. Luke)	How many generations has this seat Borne through all the years of joy and care! Her forebears sat upon this very chair, A throng of children playing at their feet. Perhaps my love, when Christmastime was near, With pious thanks and childish cheeks so sweet Would kiss the feeble hand that rested here. Dear child, I sense your presence all around me, Integrity and order everywhere. The traces of your daily tasks surround me; The table that you set with loving care, The sand you scattered on the flagstones there. One touch of your dear hand, and in a trice This humble dwelling is a paradise. And here! [*he raises the curtain round the bed*] Ah, what a shiver of delight! Here I could sit for hours and dwell On dreaming nature's magic spell That fashioned that angelic sight. As she lay here, the glowing surge Of life pulsed in her gentle breast, And here a pure creative urge God's image on the child impressed. And you! What brought you to her door? What do you want? Why is your heart so sore? What feelings hold you in their sway? Ah Faust, poor fool, I fear you've lost your way. Is there some magic spell around me? I lusted for her, and I find A dream of love comes to confound me. Are we the playthings of a breath of wind? And what if she should come while you are here? You'd answer for your recklessness, and all Your bold bravado would just disappear— Abject and sighing at her feet you'd fall. (Goethe 1999: 84–5, trans. Williams)

In these two translations, a number of seemingly small changes work together to give the reader different impressions of who the character Faust is, and what has gone on in his mind during the scene. There are perhaps two major differences that strike us. Firstly, the two texts have quite different rhythms: Luke's translation is overall faster, and, from the beginning is marked by a sense of restlessness; Williams's translation is calmer at the beginning, more hesitant, and in general gives the impression of greater control. Secondly, the object of address is different. In Luke's text, Faust addresses the twilight and objects in the room (the chair) in the second person. In Williams' translation, Faust reports as he observes and reflects, the 'address' becoming situational and implied.

The first line sets the pace in both texts: Luke's first line is divided, it begins with an affirmative 'welcome', and the two unstressed syllables in 'welcome, sweet twilight'(-vv-v), create a sense of movement. Williams's first line, a statement rather than an exclamation and one stress shorter, creates a different feel, not only because of its regularity, but also because of the longer first noun phrase 'the gentle light of evening'. We sense this same difference in line 2691, where Williams's translation favours, as in the first line, disyllabics with falling rhythms (peaceful (-v), homestead (-v)), where Luke's exclamation employs a line of monosyllabics. Notably, Luke's anaphoric 'what riches . . . what happiness' contrasts with Williams's chiasmus, or 'crossed' pattern. Both rhetorical figures underscore parallel sets of relationships, but with his chiasmus (again, a declarative sentence rather than an exclamation), Williams's Faust pronounces a composed maxim; Luke's makes an enthusiastic outburst. This observation leads us to another point which has significant rhythmical implications: Luke's translation (as he states in his foreword) frequently avoids end-stopped lines; it has frequent enjambment. This is especially notable from 2695 onwards. There is a breathlessness, a sense of tumult about this writing. Williams, too, certainly evokes Faust's sense of wonder at Margarete's house, but the word order is more straightforward, the relationship between the lines and the syntactic units is stronger, and the lines work as couplets more frequently (e.g. 2717–20). A reader unfamiliar with the original is meeting two rather different Fausts here: Luke's perhaps more immature, more 'poetic' in a conventionally romantic sense, Williams's more 'classical', more intellectual, more composed. In short, Williams's Faust seems like an older man, or at least it becomes difficult to imagine Williams's Faust exclaiming 'ah, my sweet' as Luke's does at the end of the monologue. These are not criticisms: both these translations are good, and written by translators who knew the texts, the author and the period extremely well. Both translations are also relatively close; but these Fausts do not speak the same language, and are not the same man because of it.

Not only that, but these two translations present different scenes: in Luke's translation, Faust addresses the twilight in the manner of Klopstock's poem 'Die frühen Gräber' (1764): '*Willkommen, o silberner Mond*'. Williams's Faust describes, articulating what he observes; his is closer to the interior monologue of a novel. It is the place—within these walls—that causes Williams's Faust to experience the pangs and clutches of love, a love that endures despite hope's meagre sustenance. Luke's Faust invites the pain of love, a pain that endures because of hope. Perhaps inevitably then, there is a greater change of pace in Williams's version when his Faust begins to perceive Margarete's presence more directly.

A further significant difference which stems from this distinction in setting or object of address occurs near the end: in Williams's version, as in fact in the initial monologue, Faust addresses himself in the second person (as in Goethe). On the one hand this is a natural manner of speaking—one can say 'what have you done' to oneself—on the other it underscores Faust's sense of self-alienation. Luke's Faust's questions turn around his *ego*, the 'and I' of course contrasts with the earlier addresses to objects ('Oh godlike hand!') but also gives Faust's question a different sense of direction, and conclusion: where Williams's Faust, bitterly half laughing surely, says 'I fear you've lost your way', Luke's Faust seems more alarmed, assertive almost, in his essential question about his identity: 'Am I Faust now or not?' Again, the reader comes away from these two texts not only with two Fausts but also with rather different impressions of what has gone on: Williams's Faust is 'confounded' by the experience he has undergone, where Luke's Faust 'wilts and melts away'.

Faust is a useful example to begin with when we think about what is 'at stake' in translating literature, simply because it is so famous and belongs, rightly, to what we can call world literature. Faust has been seen as embodying the German spirit, Goethe's *Faust* has been adapted and translated countless times; these are texts even readers relatively unfamiliar with German literature are likely to have heard of. It is very clear that it *does* make a difference what the Faust we read about is like as a person, and what the reading experience of *Faust* is like. Because *Faust* has been translated, performed, adapted so many times, it is a representative example of translation and retranslation as part of a broad and continuous engagement with a text as part of that text's reception history, even as part of the way that text lives and dwells among us. But it is also useful to begin with this translation comparison because these are both good translations. Both are also 'close', and respect the formal characteristics of the text too—and yet the differences that occur in them cumulatively have significant repercussions for the meaning of the text. It will be the purpose of the next section to ask why this is so.

Language and literariness

We began this book by framing translation as text production, as a kind of writing which is different of course from 'free' or 'original' writing, but in which nonetheless good writing skills, the ability to write with and for a purpose, to think critically about, edit and make decisions about your own text, are the core skills, alongside, of course, being able to understand the source text. In this sense, literary translation is not essentially different from other kinds of translation in terms of the processes, problems or strategies of translation—you have certainly translated lots of literature in each of the chapters where we have focussed on specific problems of translation, many of which one might consider to be more the concern of literary texts, but which, as we have seen, can affect a whole range of writing: cultural problems, metaphor, prosody, genre conventions, etc.

One reason for this is that literary language is not inherently different from non-literary language; certainly it is not the presence or absence of 'poetic diction' that makes a piece of writing into a linguistic work of art. When translating, say, a novel, the reader and translator may encounter a kind of writing which is highly stylised, but it is not that alone that makes it literature: the beginning of Thomas Mann's *Joseph* tetralogy is fearful in its syntactic complexity, but the same author begins his equally impressive *Zauberberg* with a disarmingly simply statement: '*Ein junger Mann reiste im Hochsommer von Hamburg, seiner Vaterstadt, nach Davos Platz in Graubünden*' (Mann 1974: II, 7). If anything, literature is characterised by its ability to imitate other forms of writing, that might include the language of diplomacy in an historical novel, or scientific language as we see in the following excerpt from Brecht's *Furcht und Elend des III. Reiches* where Brecht imitates the language of theoretical physics:

> Für ruhende, inkohärente, nicht durch Spannungen aufeinander einwirkende Materie ist $T = \mu$, die einzige von 0 verschiedene Komponente der tensoriellen Energiedichte.
>
> (Brecht 2005: I, 547)

The particular issues that arise in and as a result of literary translation are thus less the product of a special kind of language; rather the problems of literary translation are to do with the way that language creates meaning in the text, a text's 'literariness', that hard-to-define quality that makes a poem a poem, that makes a poem like a novel and like a play, and unlike an essay, or an instruction, or a speech, however well written or elegant they may be.

Literariness describes the special semantic density that is proper to literature and which is the product of the way literary texts construct meaning and their relationship to extra-textual reality. Every text, including a literary text, is a historical document or event: Goethe sat down over a specific length of time and wrote *Iphigenie*. As we have seen in Chapter 1 he rewrote it in Italy in discussion with others and under specific influences. Many authors may well have particular aims in mind when they write. Literary works can, like other texts, however, create meanings their authors did not foresee or intend: such is probably the case with Adalbert Stifter, who had a strong sense of Christian morality, but whose literary worlds can be seen as underlining the futility of man's attempts to pierce the mysteries of cold, indifferent nature. Literary texts can also speak to us and have meanings well beyond the lifetimes of their authors and intended readership: in the case of Stifter, he achieved moderate success in his lifetime, only to be an '*Entdeckung*' for the author and critic Hermann Bahr following the First World War (Bahr 1919). What makes a text work as literature is that for the reader it functions autonomously of its contexts and creates symbolic meanings of its own. This is what makes great literature live beyond its time, what allows us to engage with it, and what makes us return to it. It creates those meanings by internal reference. We have already mentioned in Chapter 8 the painting of Christian VII in *Unwiederbringlich*. If Fontane had mentioned that painting in a travelogue (which he also wrote), then what would interest us would be the painting's existence in reality: the words would point outside the literary world and would gain meaning through reference to the empirical world. In a literary text, what 'Christian VII' means as a sign is determined not solely, but primarily by the relationship of that sign to other aspects of the literary work itself, such as the representation of Holk's character.

Finally, literary works establish patterns of association so that everything achieves meaning within the context of the rest of the text's other features. If it can be said that the fundamental property of language is to create and express meaning through arbitrary signs which gain their significance as a result of their structural relationship to each other rather than to reality, then literature can be seen as an intensification of this process. Literary works are those which, when read with attention to these patterns of internal association, reveal themselves as complex but organically coherent structures of meaning. These meanings however, because they are created by association, are ambiguous, implicit and often unresolved. Interpreting literary texts involves a careful balancing act between our knowledge of the text's genesis and of the author, our awareness of our own circumstances as readers, but above all an acknowledgement of the primacy of the meanings created by the text on its own terms. This is important because it is tempting to associate literary translation primarily with the imitation of style. Clearly, a challenge for a translator of literature is indeed to imitate an author's style rather than imposing their own. But that is a challenge in many types of translation, and in translating the many different types of text a single author might write; the reason stylistic choices are important in literature is because they contribute to the creation of meaning in a way that is more significant than in most other texts.

In closing this section, we need to qualify the foregoing remarks by underlining that many texts, and many kinds of translation require interpretation of some kind (legal texts, Biblical texts, historical texts), and that most translation involves deciding on meanings which are often implicit and unresolved even in non-literary texts. What is more, as with any genre, the boundaries of what constitutes 'literature' not only evolve over time and are different in different cultures, but even in the West they are fluid: the extent to which a text may be said to be literary varies, and of course the oeuvre of any given author may well include not only literary texts but non-literary genres, such as essays, diaries, letters, journalism, etc. Whether something is literature or not is, in the final analysis, often as much part of a reader's interpretation as the overall meaning of the text.

Translations as meta-texts

One useful way of thinking about literary translation is to see it as a meta-textual activity, translations as meta-texts, that is texts which are part of the engagement with and around a literary work and through which the multifaceted meanings of that work are explored. James Holmes, in a 1970 paper on translation, placed translations of poetry on a scale of such meta-texts which ranges from critical essays to prose translations (paraphrase), verse translation, imitation, to poems inspired by another poem. Translation in this sense is a way of engaging with a text, part of a much broader activity of textual interpretation. This model is appealing, not least because it bridges the gap between properly literary texts and their translations, and other text forms which are variously discussed, analysed, interpreted and transmitted.

The relationship between translation and other forms of cultural production inspired by or that engage with a source text is a question that surfaces here. Many classic texts are translated and retranslated, often because a translation ages and a new translation is sought for a new generation of readers; more often, perhaps, because translation is an attentive reading, a way of entering a tradition. Translation is thus part of the ongoing reception history of a work, as Rudolf Kloepfer writes: '*Übersetzung ist eine Art der Progression. Für die Übersetzung gilt, was für die Dichtung gesagt wurde, sie ist nie abgeschlossen*' (Kloepfer 1967: 126). One difficult question is the extent to which the translation can be said to have its own status as a literary work, after all, if it 'works', it will function aesthetically itself. One important early scholar, Levý, argues clearly that the aim of translation is to preserve and communicate the meaning of the original but not to produce a new work, literary translation being unproductive. Kloepfer, whom we have just cited, sees translation as a properly literary activity, '*nicht irgendeine Dichtung, nicht Umdichtung, sondern die Dichtung der Dichtung*' (Kloepfer 1967: 126). Rather more polemically, Lawrence Venuti has criticised the 'invisibility' of literary translators (Venuti 2005). In reality, what a translation is, or should be, or how it is received depends on the culture of translation at a given epoch, the person translating, and what the translation means for them and their readers (see Albrecht 1998 for an historical discussion).

In many, perhaps most cases, readers wish to have the feeling that they are reading the author's work. Translations themselves however, such as Schlegel's translations of Shakespeare in German, can become canonical in their own right. Indeed, a modern German reader of *Hamlet* can choose between Schlegel's version, Erich Fried's version or a number of others, a plurality which makes the translator's choices and individual style all the more evident and an object of critical enquiry in itself. Retranslation poses interesting questions for scholars, readers and writers interested in translation, because previous translations, if they are known to the translator, can enter into the composition process—promoting some solutions, excluding others, so that translations of previously translated works effectively have several STs (White 2015).

Translation of literature can thus be seen as something which is closely linked to the engagement with and production of texts more broadly. Literary works, like all texts, have sources, influences, sources of inspiration, antecedents and followers, and the boundaries between 'translation', 'imitation' and 'poetic response' can be hard to draw. But it is ultimately this varied engagement that makes literary texts live and uncovers their rich and ever-changing meanings for us as communities of readers.

Specialism and literary translation: research and resources

We can usefully divide research in literary translation into two areas: the first encompasses what we might call the 'facts' of the world that is represented in the literary text: under this heading we might understand all sorts of objects or references that can occur as part of the represented world, especially in novels, whether that is the '*Pferdebahn*' in a nineteenth-century Berlin novel, or the names of illnesses and their treatments as they appear, say in Thomas Mann's *Zauberberg*. Here we can refer you back to the literary case study in Chapter 12. The second area of knowledge that can require research is more properly covered by literary studies itself: that is research on literary motifs and symbols, research on authors, research on periods of literary history, genres, style, etc.

The amount of research in literary scholarship a translator is likely to need to undertake will depend very heavily on the status of the TT and the purpose of the ST: if the translation itself is almost a work of scholarship and will require detailed notes, then obviously the translation needs to be informed by, and seen as part of a broader scholarly reception; in most cases, a literary translator needs both some general orientation and then punctual research to solve local problems. In any case, being able to find out what research and resources are available in an efficient way is essential. The following two overviews are very well known and provide guidance on how to conduct bibliographical research, with special reference to literary and language studies: Johannes Hansel and Lydia Kaiser, *Literaturrecherche für Germanisten* (2003); Paul Raabe, *Einführung in die Bücherkunde für Germanisten* (1994); and there are other similar 'bibliographies of bibliographies' on the market. Getting to know one of these books can save you a lot of time, as they list for the most part valuable reference works under classified headings. The first, Hansel/Kaiser also includes a valuable section on online resources, in particular it lists catalogues of university libraries and other specialist search engines, many of which now can provide access to digitalised materials. This can be particularly helpful for historical sources. Importantly, they also list reference works, including historical ones like those we used previously, relating to topics as might be encountered in literature, such as the *Handwörterbuch zur deutschen Rechtsgeschichte* we mentioned in Chapter 12.

Before even embarking on a translation, however, a translator, as a specialist in texts, has to consider the text on the page. The fundamental point of departure of all literary interpretation is the text, and this thus needs to be dependable. In the case of, say, a contemporary novel, there is likely to be (a) only one version and (b) the possibility of contacting the author through the publisher should inconsistencies or problems arise. With older texts, this is not as straightforward. Michael Hofman's English translation of Hans Fallada's *Jeder stirbt für sich allein* (*Alone in Berlin*) is considerably shorter than the newly published German paperback in the Aufbau publishing house; the English text uses the text as it appeared in the late 1940s, but the recent success of the novel in new translations abroad created a new internal market for the novel in Germany, and so the more recent German edition prints Fallada's novel without the cuts made by the publisher at the recommendation of initial reviewers (Giesecke 2014). With an author like Goethe, there may be several versions of his texts, as he amended them throughout his life. In these cases, we can decide whether we take the '*Ausgabe letzter Hand*' (i.e. the last one to have the author's seal of approval) as definitive, or an earlier one, more representative perhaps of the author and literature at an earlier period. While a translator is unlikely to need a critical historical edition (which lists all the amendments made to a text in order to show how it developed into its final form), recourse to a good '*Leseausgabe*' or '*Studienausgabe*' is important. An entry in the excellent multivolume Kosch, *Deutsches Literatur-Lexikon* (1968) which lists entries by author, will list scholarly editions in the bibliography, as will the *Kindler Literatur Lexikon* (now in electronic format). Reference works of this kind inevitably focus on canonical authors or authors from the past, and systematic presentations of '*Gegenwartsliteratur*' are harder to find. One resource worth mentioning here is the *Kritisches Lexikon zur deutschen Gegenwartsliteratur* published by Edition Text + Kritik since 1978, initially as a loose-leaf catalogue, and now in an online version. It presents short biographies and bibliographical information.

Not least, using a good edition of the ST or having reference to one where possible is important because they often contain useful background and notes. While this is obviously not the case for contemporary literature, it is the case for canonical texts. For volumes in the Reclam Universal-Bibliothek, the separate series of green volumes *Erläuterungen und Dokumente* are cheap and invaluable sources of ready information. Check these sorts of sources *before* spending time redoing others' work with your own research. Finally, we should note the *New Books in German* magazine, published by the Goethe Institut in collaboration with a number of other partners; this lists recent publications and older 'forgotten gems' in German and gives details of rights.

Concluding remarks: literary translation in Translation Studies

What we hope to have shown throughout this book and certainly in these closing chapters is that although translating literary texts and other texts is different, it is more productive and informative to see them as different facets of related activities. This has not always been the case in scholarship on translation as it has developed in the twentieth and twenty-first centuries. The beginnings of modern scholarship on translation saw in part a reaction against older accounts of translation which had been dominated by thinking about literary texts, so that literary texts were seen as lying outside what a linguistic theory of translation could accommodate. This division is arguably less antagonistic today, but the perception remains that literary and linguistic approaches of translation are poorly integrated (Tymoczko 2014: 11). The independent status of literary texts does not fit easily into models of translation based on communicative models where the idea of an intended message dominates, so that Mary Snell-Hornby, who sought to present an 'integrated approach' in the 1980s, contrasts literary texts with 'pragmatic' texts in terms of their autonomy: literary texts are relatively autonomous of their background situations *and* their target readership, in that the function of the translation is less definable (Snell-Hornby 1988: 119); Jörn Albrecht similarly rejects Hans Vermeer's purpose-focused Skopos theory because it concentrates too acutely on an identifiable, intended message, with the successful communicative purpose of the translation foregrounded (Albrecht 1998: 255–61). As translation began to become a greater object of scholarly enquiry from the 1970s, a range of scholars interested in literary translation, such as Jiří Levý, André Lefevere and Susan Bassnett, found the then linguistic models inadequate for a description of literary translations and, simultaneously, that the object of literary analysis in universities and in scholarship was too narrowly defined as national literature, leaving the influence of translations as texts and translating as an activity in accounts of literary history insufficiently examined (see Bassnett 2014: 25 for a summary of this perspective). They proposed that translation and translations could be studied descriptively, focusing on the characteristics of translations as a kind of text, and the embeddedness of translation in cultural systems of power, patronage, publishing, etc. In our view, the study of translation and translations is inevitably multifaceted, in the same way that language and textual study more broadly engenders a proliferation of specialisms, from *Goethe-Philologie* to *Dialektforschung*. We remain optimistic that these various branches of endeavour can remain mutually informing.

Further reading

Albrecht, Jörn 1998. *Die literarische Übersetzung: Geschichte, Theorie, kulturelle Wirkung*. Darmstadt: Wissenschaftliche Buchgesellschaft [Particularly useful for the history of translation practice. Provocative and informative.].

Apel, Friedmar and Kopetzki, Annette 2003. *Literarische Übersetzung*. Stuttgart: Metzler [This introduction to scholarship on literary translation contains an excellent bibliography.].

Bassnett, Susan 2014. *Translation*. London: Routledge [See esp. Chapter 1, pp. 16–36. This short introduction has a good bibliography particularly oriented to cultural approaches and literary translation. It presents a historical overview of the discipline from a similar perspective.].

Boase-Beier, Jean, Fisher, Lina and Furukawa, Hiroko (eds) 2018. *The Palgrave Handbook of Literary Translation*. London: Palgrave Macmillan.

Classe, Olive (ed.) 2000. *The Encyclopedia of Literary Translation into English*. 2 Vols. London and Chicago: Dearborn.

Horton, David 2013. *Thomas Mann in English*. London: Bloomsbury [Presents a study of translations of Mann both historically and with chapters focusing on specific issues, such as the translation of dialogue and terms of address.].

Lefevere, André 1977. *Translating Literature: The German Tradition from Luther to Rosenzweig*. Amsterdam: Van Gorcum.

Lefevere, André 1998. *Translating Literature: Practice and Theory in a Comparative Literature Context*. New York: MLA.

Peeters, Regina 2012. *Eine Bibliothek für Babel: Maßstäbe einer Spezialbibliothek für literarische Übersetzter*. Berlin: Logos [A recent study of how literary translators use resources.].

Wagner, Jan and Lendle, Jo (eds) 2017. Nachdichten. *Akzente*, 64(2) [A special edition of the literary journal with a focus on poetic imitation, including versions and drafts with final versions and discussions.].

Practical 15

15.1 TRANSLATING POETRY

Assignment

Because so much depends in literary translation on a sense of the whole, we begin here with two verse translations.

i   For a translation workshop open to the general public at a theatre and cultural centre, you have been asked to translate the following two texts. They are canonical German poems, Eduard Mörike's 'Auf einer Lampe' (1846) and Georg Trakl's 'Verfall' (1909).

ii   Translate the poems into English.

iii   Putting the originals to one side, analyse your translations along with others in the class *on their own terms*. How do they work as poems in their own right? What changes might you make to make your poems better poems? What changes might you make to move your translation closer to the original, in terms of individual lines or overall effect?

iv   To what extent does the act of translating lead you to an understanding of how the poems function as structures of meaning?

Auf einer Lampe

1   Noch unverrückt, o schöne Lampe, schmückest du,
    An leichten Ketten zierlich aufgehangen hier,
    Die Decke des nun fast vergeßnen Lustgemachs.
    Auf deiner weißen Marmorschale, deren Rand
5   Der Efeukranz von goldengrünem Erz umflicht,
    Schlingt fröhlich eine Kinderschar den Ringelreihn.
    Wie reizend alles! lachend, und ein sanfter Geist
    Des Ernstes doch ergossen um die ganze Form —
    Ein Kunstgebild der echten Art. Wer achtet sein?
10 Was aber schön ist, selig scheint es in ihm selbst.
                        (Mörike 1964: 85)

Verfall

1 Am Abend, wenn die Glocken Frieden läuten,
   Folg ich der Vögel wundervollen Flügen,
   Die lang geschart, gleich frommen Pilgerzügen,
   Entschwinden in den hersbtlich klaren Weiten.

5 Hinwandelnd durch den dämmervollen Garten
   Träum ich nach ihren helleren Geschicken
   Und fühl der Stunden Weiser kaum mehr rücken.
   So folg ich über Wolken ihren Fahrten.

   Da macht ein Hauch mich von Verfall erzittern.
10 Die Amsel klagt in den entlaubten Zweigen.
   Es schwankt der rote Wein an rostigen Gittern,

   Indes wie blasser Kinder Todesreigen
   Um dunkle Brunnenränder, die verwittern,
   Im Wind sich fröstelnd blaue Astern neigen.

(Trakl 1969: I/59)

15.2 TRANSLATING DIALOGUE

Assignment

Here is an excerpt from Hugo von Hofmannsthal's *Der Schwierige* (1920). You have been asked to produce a dual-language version of the play with minimal notes and a short introduction which can be used both in schools or university programmes, but can also be read by an English-speaking readership without German. Here is the first half of the opening scene. We are told it takes place in a '*mittelgroßer Raum eines älteren Stadtpalais, als Arbeitszimmer des Hausherrn eingerichtet*'. Lukas is '*erster Diener*' for Hans Karl Bühl, the main character, Vinzenz is a new servant.

i Translate the extract into English, giving notes where you think absolutely necessary.
ii Give an account of (a) your overall approach; (b) decisions of detail; (c) your research which informed both your overall approach and your local decisions.
iii What aspects of this first scene would be relevant for your introduction in the context of your reading on Hofmannsthal?

---

1 **Lukas** Hier ist das sogenannte Arbeitszimmer. Verwandtschaft und sehr gute Freunde werden hier hereingeführt, oder nur wenn speziell gesagt wird, in den grünen Salon.
   Vinzenz (*tritt ein*) Was arbeitet er? Majoratsverwaltung? Oder was? Politische Sachen?
5 **Lukas** Durch diese Spaltetür kommt der Sekretär herein.
   Vinzenz Privatsekretär hat er auch? Das sind doch Hungerleider! Verfehlte Existenzen! Hat er bei ihm was zu sagen?
   Lukas Hier geht's durch ins Toilettezimmer. Dort werden wir jetzt hineingehen und Smoking und Frack herrichten zur Auswahl je nachdem, weil nichts Spezielles
10 angeordnet ist.

Vinzenz (*schnüffelt an allen Möbeln herum*) Also was? Sie wollen mir jetzt den Dienst zeigen? Es hätte Zeit gehabt bis morgen früh, und wir hätten uns jetzt kollegial unterhalten können. Was eine Herrenbedienung ist, das ist mir seit vielen Jahren zum Bewußtsein gekommen, also beschränken Sie sich auf das Nötige; damit meine ich
15 die Besonderheiten. Also was? Fangen Sie schon an!
Lukas (*richtet ein Bild, das nicht ganz gerade hängt*) Er kann kein Bild und keinen Spiegel schief hängen sehen. Wenn er anfängt, alle Laden aufzusperren oder einen verlegten Schlüssel zu suchen, dann ist er sehr schlechter Laune.
Vinzenz Lassen Sie jetzt solche Lappalien. Sie haben mir doch gesagt, daß die
20 Schwester und der Neffe, die hier im Hause wohnen, auch jedesmal angemeldet werden müssen.
Lukas (*putzt mit dem Taschentuch an einem Spiegel*) Genau wie jeder Besuch. Darauf hält er sehr streng.
Vinzenz Was steckt da dahinter? Da will er sie sich vom Leibe halten. Warum läßt
25 er sie dann hier wohnen? Er wird doch mehrere Häuser haben? Das sind doch seine Erben. Die wünschen doch seinen Tod.
Lukas Die Frau Gräfin Crescence und der Graf Stani? Ja, da sei Gott vor! Ich weiß nicht, wie Sie mir vorkommen!

(Hofmannsthal 1966: 39–40)

References

Primary

Brecht, Bertolt 2005. *Ausgewählte Werke in sechs Bänden*. Frankfurt am Main: Suhrkamp.
Fallada, Hans 2009. *Alone in Berlin*. Translated by Hofmann, Michael. London: Penguin.
Giesecke, Almut 2014. 'Nachwort', in Fallada, H. *Jeder stirbt für sich allein*. Berlin: Aufbau, pp. 687–97.
Goethe, J.W. von 1998. *Faust Part One*. Translated by Luke, David. Oxford: Oxford University Press.
Goethe, J.W. von 1999. *Faust: The First Part of the Tragedy*. Translated by Williams, John R. Ware: Wordsworth.
Hofmannsthal, Hugo von 1966. *Der Schwierige*. Edited by Yates, W.E. Cambridge: Cambridge University Press.
Klopstock, Friedrich Gottlieb 1962. 'Die frühen Gräber', in Klopstock, F.G. *Ausgewählte Werke*. Edited by Jünger, Friedrich G. Munich: Hanser, p. 108.
Mann, Thomas 1974. *Romane und Erzählungen*. Berlin: Aufbau.
Mörike, Eduard 1964. *Sämtliche Werke*. Edited by Göpfert, Herbert G. Munich: Hanser.
Trakl, Georg 1969. *Dichtungen und Briefe*. Edited by Walter Killy and Hans Szklenar. Salzburg: Müller.

Secondary

Albrecht, Jörn 1998. *Die literarische Übersetzung: Geschichte, Theorie, kulturelle Wirkung*. Darmstadt: Wissenschaftliche Buchgesellschaft.
Arnold, Heinz Ludwig et al. (eds) 2009. *Kindlers Literatur Lexikon*. Stuttgart: Metzler.
Bahr, Hermann 1919. *Adalbert Stifter: Eine Entdeckung*. Zürich, Leipzig and Vienna: Almathea.

Hansel, Johannes and Kaiser, Lydia 2003. *Literaturrecherche für Germanisten*. Berlin: Schmidt.

Kloepfer, Rudolf 1967. *Die Theorie der literarischen Übersetzung*. Munich: Fink.

Korte, Hermann (ed.) 1978 ff. *Kritisches Lexikon zur deutschsprachigen Gegenwarts-literatur*. Munich: text + kritik. Available at: nachschlage.net.

Kosch, Wilhelm et al. (eds) 1968. *Deutsches Literatur-Lexikon*. 3rd edn. Berne and Munich: Francke.

Raabe, Paul 1994. *Einführung in die Bücherkunde für Germanisten*. Stuttgart: Metzler.

Snell-Hornby, Mary 1988. *Translation Studies: An Integrated Approach*. Amsterdam and Philadelphia: John Benjamins.

Tymoczko, Maria 2014. 'Why literary translation is a good model for translation theory and practice', in Boase-Beier, J., Wilson, P. and Fawcett, A. (eds) *Literary Translation: Redrawing the Boundaries*. London: Palgrave Macmillan, pp. 11–31.

Venuti, Lawrence 2005. *The Translator's Invisibility: A History of Translation*. 2nd edn. London and New York: Routledge.

White, Michael 2015. 'Herder and Fontane as Translators of Percy's *Reliques of Ancient English Poetry*: The Ballad "Edward, Edward"', in Robertson, R. and White, M. (eds) *Fontane and Cultural Mediation: Translation and Reception in Nineteenth-Century German Literature*. Germanic Literatures. Vol. 8. Oxford: Legenda, pp. 107–19.

16 Revising, reviewing and proofing TTs

Throughout this book, we have considered translation sometimes as a product (such as the assessment of existing TTs in practicals), but more often as a process in the form of rewriting. This chapter looks at what is usually regarded as the final stage of translation as a process—the stage during which the proposed TT is actually examined as a near-finished *product*. However, we will also be analysing a range of checking tasks which occur during the translation process. The procedures outlined here are neither new nor confined to certain genres. We only need look to the history of the early seventeenth century King James translation of the Bible to find reference to 'every word pass[ing] through the hands of the whole body of revisers' (Bobrick 2001: 246). Nevertheless, proofing errors were still reported—apparently one for every ten pages, including a famous confusion of pronouns: 'and he went into the city' where 'she' is correct (*ibid.*: 260).

Frequent reference will be made along the way to *Revising and Editing for Translators* (2014) by Brian Mossop, a Canadian translation scholar and practitioner. You are also referred back to the chapter on Research and resources (Chapter 12), as research is part of the overall checking process, as also practised by the seventeenth-century teams of Bible translators who 'consulted every known text, commentary, and translation, ancient or modern' (Bobrick 2001: 245–6).

As a first step, some of the key terms used in relation to 'checking' are clarified, before we move on to two case studies intended to introduce you to the kind of issues which arise in different types of TT checking. The second part of the chapter goes into more detail on the actual procedures which you need to carry out.

The terminology of 'checking'

Many terms are used to describe the various types of checking task that are carried out when producing a TT. We will deal with the most common ones in this section in order to do two things. Firstly, we need to establish which terms we will be using and how we will be using them in the rest of this chapter. Secondly, in any dealings with clients (or your tutor) you need to know what is expected of you in terms of the final product: so, for example, if you agree that the translation will be 'proofed', does this mean that you will also edit for ST content errors? In order to contextualise the various checking tasks, we will adopt here the three-phase model of the *whole* translation process set out in Mossop (2014: 182): 1. Pre-drafting (reading the ST, conducting research, noting ideas); 2. Drafting (e.g. sentence by sentence); 3. Post-drafting (checking tasks). We will be dealing with the third phase, but also with the second, particularly when considering '*self*-revision'.

'*Revision*'/'*self-revision*', '*review*'

We have already mentioned in Chapter 14 on sci-tech translation that according to published standards, 'revision' is usually understood as checking the TT for errors against the ST, whereas 'reviewing' is checking without reference to the ST. The former task is carried out by a second translator, the latter by a subject expert. Alternative terms make explicit the differences: 'comparative re-reading' for 'revision' and 'unilingual re-reading' for 'review' by a translator rather than a subject expert (see Mossop 2014: 222–9 for a glossary of terms). Revision assumes a particular importance when, for example, there are insufficient native speakers of the TL. In the former GDR, the state foreign language service, *Intertext*, used German native speakers to translate into English, relying on rare English native speakers temporarily living in the GDR to revise the texts.

While 'revision' and 'reviewing' occur at a late stage in the TT production and involve a second translator or specialist reader, 'self-revision' can be integrated in all three phases (Mossop 2014: 184). In fact, 'self-revision' will be key to this chapter as it is the procedure which most closely characterises the classroom-based situation. It can also be referred to as 'checking', defined as the translator's 'overall self-revision' or responsibility to check for 'possible semantic, grammatical and spelling issues, and for omissions and other errors' (BS EN ISO 17100:2015, *Translation Services—Requirements for translation services*). In this book we will stick to 'revision' as specified in the relevant standards, but mostly prefer the more transparent 'self-revision' rather than 'checking'. For the review process, we will use 'review' or 'unilingual re-reading' with no implied difference of meaning.

'*Editing*', '*mental editing*'/'*transediting*' and '*post-editing*'

'Editing' is sometimes used as a synonym for both reviewing and revision. However, it is not mentioned in the relevant translation standards because, as Mossop points out (2014: 224), 'editing' is generally understood to be carried out on a text that is not a translation. Nevertheless, derived terms incorporating 'editing' can and often do refer to translated texts. For example, our attention is usefully drawn to a process that is called 'mental editing', i.e. 'correcting or improving the writing quality while translating it' (Mossop 2014: 226). In this book we will refer to this as 'transediting', a 1980s term coined in order to deal with the 'similarities and differences between editing and translating', as professional translators frequently need to ' "clean up" poorly expressed thoughts and ideas' (Stetting 1989: 371–2), usually in non-literary texts. Transediting is an integral part of the translation process (including pre-drafting and drafting) and hence an important part of 'self-revision'. Our last 'editing' term—'post-editing'—refers rather confusingly to the process of *revising* Machine Translation output, sometimes aiming for a low not-for-publication level of quality, in which case the finished product must be labelled 'rapidly revised machine translation' for the client (see Mossop 2014: 199–201; Olohan 2016: 45–6 for more details).

'Proofing'/'proofreading'

This is often designated as the final stage in the production process and cannot be performed until all other post-drafting tasks have been carried out. It is generally agreed to refer to final orthographical and layout corrections to the post-drafting TT such as punctuation, spelling, capitalisation, numbering, heading levels and so on, often using a 'style guide' setting out the client organisation's 'house style' (for more details, see Byrne 2012: 142–3; Mossop 2014: 43–4). Failing that, other style guides can be called upon such as the *Guardian and Observer style guide* (n.d.), *The Economist Style Guide* (Wroe 2018), the Modern Humanities Research Association *Handbook for Authors and Editors* (2013) or the European Commission Directorate-General for Translation's *English Style Guide* (2016).

Moving on

Any form of post-drafting task is an operation carried out in writing on a pre-existent text—on-screen or on paper, although error spotting is said to be more efficient on paper (Mossop 2014: 107). But don't forget that much can be done to mitigate changes in the last phase by careful self-revision in the preparation phase (e.g. good research on terminology, background and subject matter; making sure you are familiar with the brief and your target audience) and the drafting phase (e.g. following the relevant style guide as you translate; checking that no sentences or negatives are omitted, although this is sometimes easier to spot during re-reading when non-sequiturs or plain nonsense emerges). Revision in the post-drafting phase is concerned with ensuring accuracy by eliminating remaining errors and inconsistencies.

Errors of accuracy can be relatively minor, such as spelling mistakes or punctuation (especially when meaning can be changed: watch out for defining *versus* non-defining relative clauses, see paragraph 2.14 of the DGT *English Style Guide* 2016), but they can also include ungrammatical or misleading constructions. And it is not only the language of the TT that may be wrong or unfit for purpose: the concepts themselves may have been distorted in transmission. In a professional situation, an ethical decision would have to be made regarding your competence to accept and carry out the job, as well as a commercial decision about whether the job would be uneconomic if extensive research is required. In a classroom situation, however, the trainee translator has a chance to research a new subject area and to learn from this experience as well as from the tutor's and classmates' feedback.

In order to understand the scope of revision and of reviewing, two case studies follow, before we set out the details of the procedures which you need to undertake.

CASE STUDY 1:   Revision

Except in the case of clear factual errors, it is usually easier to correct someone else's work (given a certain level of competence) than your own, but if you *are* revising someone else's work, you need to focus on identifying and correcting errors, not rewriting the text 'so that it looks like one of your translations' (Byrne 2012: 147; see also Mossop 2014: 171–2). Nevertheless, some translations might be of such poor quality that they are not worth revising. Mossop advises accordingly: 'If a translation is full of unidiomatic word combinations, if the sentence structures are so influenced by the source text that the result is unreadable, and of course, if the translator has misunderstood numerous passages of the original text, the solution is to retranslate, not revise' (2014: 27). One criterion for the assessment of translations by trainees is that the translation will fail if the tutor concludes that it would be quicker to retranslate than to revise the submitted work.

As a preliminary exercise, it will be useful to assess the quality of the translation reproduced below and to point out where the faults lie as a post-drafting exercise incorporating revision and proofing. The ST and TT were issued in parallel by the German government-supported *Inter Nationes* organisation as '*Sonderthema*' information leaflets before the organisation was amalgamated with the *Goethe Institut* in 2000. The ST's title is '*Privatisierung und Deregulierung in Deutschland: Der Fall Telekom*'. We can assume that the English text was intended to be of publishable quality as *Inter Nationes* was a respected international organisation associated with the government.

The target audience is presumably readers who are well educated with an interest in German culture and society but who do not understand German, nor are they necessarily native speakers of English. We print here an extract from early in the document:

ST

Die Privatisierung verschiedener deutscher Unternehmen, die sich bisher im Besitz des Staates befanden, erfolgt aus prinzipiellen Gründen: Die deutsche Bundesregierung will den Staat auf seine Kernaufgaben zurückführen. Im Vordergrund stand und steht der ordnungspolitische Ansatz,

5   den Staat aus der Wirtschaft zurückzuziehen. Bundeskanzler Helmut Kohl hat diese Überzeugung in seiner Regierungserklärung so formuliert: 'Eine Wirtschaftsordnung ist um so erfolgreicher, je mehr sich der Staat zurückhält und dem einzelnen seine Freiheit läßt. Wir wollen nicht mehr, sondern weniger Staat'. Und Bundesfinanzminister Theo Waigel, in dessen Ressort

10 die Verwaltung und Privatisierung der Bundesunternehmen fällt, ergänzt: 'Privatisierung bedeutet für uns Investition in Wettbewerb, Effizienz und Innovation zur Sicherung des Wirtschaftsstandortes Deutschland'. Deshalb ist nach den erfolgreichen Privatisierungen der fünfziger und sechziger Jahre, als sich der Bund von einem Teil seines Aktienbesitzes an den Firmen VW, VEBA,

15 und Preussag trennte, in den achtziger Jahren eine neue Privatisierungswelle eingeleitet worden. [. . .] Der genaue Preis für die T-Aktie wird in einem Bieterverfahren erst kurz vor dem Börsenstart festgelegt. Zunächst wird eine Preisspanne veröffentlicht. Interessenten können Angebote machen, nach denen der Ausgabepreis ermittelt wird. Auch der Preisnachlaß für

20 Privatanleger wird erst kurz vor dem Verkauf festgelegt. Bislang haben sich rund anderthalb Millionen Interessenten in einem eigens dafür eingerichteten 'Aktien-Informations-Forum' registrieren lassen.

(Zawadsky 1996a: 1–2)

The English of the published TT is conspicuously awkward and unidiomatic and also includes a number of mistranslations, even though the ST is written in language distinctly more lucid and accessible to the layperson than many German business texts. Figure 16.1 shows some changes which a reviser might make. The reasons for these changes—which you might like to think about yourself—can be discussed with your tutor. You might disagree or have other changes to suggest.

The corrections to the TT in Figure 16.1 are so extensive that any reviser would need to question whether retranslation would be a more economic option. For obvious reasons, the examples we use in this chapter tend to be translations that raise plenty of issues. However,

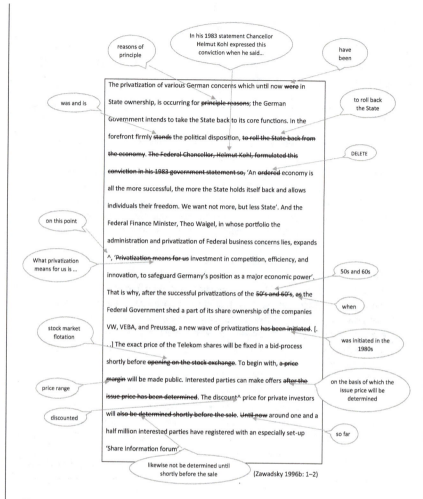

The privatization of various German concerns which until now ~~were~~ in State ownership, is occurring for ~~principle reasons~~; the German Government intends to take the State back to its core functions. In the forefront firmly ~~stands~~ the political disposition, ~~to roll the State back from the economy. The Federal Chancellor, Helmut Kohl, formulated this conviction in his 1983 government statement so,~~ 'An ~~ordered~~ economy is all the more successful, the more the State holds itself back and allows individuals their freedom. We want not more, but less State'. And the Federal Finance Minister, Theo Waigel, in whose portfolio the administration and privatization of Federal business concerns lies, expands ^, '~~Privatization means for us~~ investment in competition, efficiency, and innovation, to safeguard Germany's position as a major economic power'. That is why, after the successful privatizations of the ~~50's and 60's~~, a̶s the Federal Government shed a part of its share ownership of the companies VW, VEBA, and Preussag, a new wave of privatizations ~~has been initiated~~. [...] The exact price of the Telekom shares will be fixed in a bid-process shortly before ~~opening on the stock exchange~~. To begin with, ~~a price margin~~ will be made public. Interested parties can make offers ~~after the issue price has been determined~~. The discount^ price for private investors will ~~also be determined shortly before the sale~~. ~~Until now~~ around one and a half million interested parties have registered with an especially set-up 'Share Information forum'.

(Zawadsky 1996b: 1–2)

reasons of principle

In his 1983 statement Chancellor Helmut Kohl expressed this conviction when he said…

have been

was and is

to roll back the State

DELETE

on this point

What privatization means for us is …

50s and 60s

when

stock market flotation

was initiated in the 1980s

price range

on the basis of which the issue price will be determined

discounted

so far

likewise not be determined until shortly before the sale

Figure 16.1 TT as published but showing suggested revision and proofing changes. The full colour figure is available online at www.routledge.com/9781138920989.

much revising and proofing work is done on high-quality TTs involving complex subject matter and typography in which errors may well be rare and unobtrusive. In sci-tech texts, of course, unobtrusive errors can be major errors (see Chapter 14). Even in the post-drafting phase (after the first translator's self-revision) TT errors might still persist, and this is why some translation companies require that the work of every translator is passed to another team member for further revising and proofing with fresh eyes. One well-known German translation company was known to

present their available levels of service—with associated price adjustments and depending on the purpose of the translation—in terms of the
number of 'eyes' that would peruse the TT, starting from zero for 'raw',
i.e. unedited MT output.

CASE STUDY 2:   Review

In our earlier text about telecommunications deregulation, it was hard to
tell whether the TT deficiencies lay in the command of English only, or
also in the subject knowledge. We now present an example of a text that
simply needs attention from a native speaker of English familiar with the
special language and genre conventions of recruitment advertisements:
in other words, a review or 'unilingual re-reading'. The TT is shown in
Figure 16.2 with suggested changes and queries.

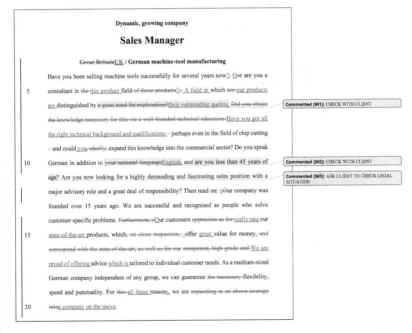

Figure 16.2 Suggested review of draft TT (previously translated from German). The full colour figure is available online at www.routledge.
com/9781138920989.

Whether the rather stilted draft TT is fit for purpose—i.e. would it still recruit high-quality candidates—is a moot point. On balance, we think that the need to sustain a successful corporate image outweighs any relatively minor cost implications of revision. In the contemporary global market, good English can help to signal success. As one guide to buying translations points out with reference to what is called 'accurate yet unpolished work', often referred to as 'for-information' translations (cheaper and quicker): 'if you're trying to sell or persuade, or if image is important to you, that probably won't be enough' (Durban/ITI 2014: 9). What is needed, it is argued, is a 'for-publication' translation which is appropriately 'polished'.

In what follows we elaborate on some of the problems with the published TT, only one of which—the dangling adjective-phrase 'high grade'—is a formal error, aside from some minor punctuation issues. A number of recommended changes e.g. shorter and/or simpler sentences, reflect the way in which such texts are rapidly skimmed. The second person mode of address is engaging and often regarded as good practice in job advertisements.

line	Comment on review of published TT
l.3	'Great Britain' has for some years been less in use than 'UK', whereas *Großbritannien* is still widely used in German-speaking countries.
ll.4–6	The opening sentence consists of three clauses: now changed to three sentences as a punchier beginning. The relative clause at the end of the first sentence, 'which are distinguished . . . ', is clumsy, especially as the 'products' are 'distinguished' not, as one might expect, by some special excellence they possess, but by 'a great need for explanation'. An alternative has been proposed, referring to the quality of the products. As this is a potential change of content, it is being referred back to the client for approval.
l.10	'your national language' has been replaced by 'English'; this is an assumption and is therefore referred back. Also, 'national language' is not the same as 'first language or 'mother tongue'.
ll.10–11	The reference to age has also been marked up for referral back as it might contravene employment regulations, certainly in the UK.
l.12	English punctuation rules usually require a lower-case initial letter after a colon, although this is changing in some circles.
l.14	The conjunction 'Furthermore' is formal and more suited to legal and academic parlance; its use—particularly in isolation at the head of the sentence—is not consistent with the conventions of the genre, as a check of online templates for job adverts can easily demonstrate.
l.16	The hyphenated 'state-of-the-art' is certainly genre-appropriate, but only when used adjectivally, not as a noun. The phrase has been incorporated into a simplified version (see l.15) of the sentence originally beginning 'Furthermore'.

line	Comment on review of published TT
ll.14–17	The sentence in which 'state-of-the-art' appears is also structurally complex. The sentence starts with a main clause, in the middle of which is embedded a relative clause, itself consisting of two co-ordinated components ('which . . . offer value for money and correspond with . . . '). Easy for the skim-reader to lose track. Splitting the sentence into two, maybe adding some intensifying words such as 'really' and 'rate' for 'appreciate' (*schätzen*?), removing 'on close inspection' (adds nothing), 'competent' (what else? the English reader might ask) and the dangling adjective phrase 'high grade', are suggested.
l.19	'For this reason' is not a dated expression, but its placing is faintly unidiomatic. A less formal expression such as 'That's why . . . ' or 'And so . . . ' or even 'For all these reasons' would be better.
ll.19–20	The final clause of the piece—' . . . we are expanding at an above-average rate'—is perfectly sound grammatically, but has the effect of a damp squib, given that the genre requires an up-beat tone. The phrasing is more reminiscent of an economic report intended for shareholders. The proposed substitution (' . . . we are a company on the move') aims at a less formal tone designed to capture the attention of enterprising applicants.

Procedures—'how to . . . ' or 'how could *I* . . . ? '

Producing a translation of any kind is a complex cognitive activity. It is therefore not surprising that there is no single way of achieving your goal, which is a fit-for-purpose translation. Your translation journey can take various paths depending on a number of factors. These include: the nature of the brief, the time available, the length of the ST, your familiarity with the genre and subject matter, access to resources (human, paper and online) and to tools (basically, technology, ranging from word-processing functions such as spellcheckers to Translation Memory or Machine Translation). But there is another important factor, and that is *you*, the translator and how you prefer to work. There is no single way of checking (i.e. self-revising) your translation or someone else's: what we are aiming to do here is to present you with some possible ways of working; we leave you to decide which suits you best. In what follows, we are assuming that the translation is not supported by either TM or MT. The focus will be on self-revision, as this is applicable to all translation work and is expected of any professional, whether or not the TT is subsequently revised by another translator or reviewed by a subject expert.

We continue here with the three-phase model of the translation process outlined earlier in the chapter and have already indicated that various types of checking can take place at any time during the three phases. It is therefore useful on occasion to distinguish between the checking *tasks* which need to be carried out and the *phases* of production, as different translators will conduct these tasks at different times in the production process (Mossop 2014: 183).

We already suggested in Chapter 12 that translators have different styles when researching information: our examples were the 'economical' researcher or the 'explorer' (Gough 2017). Different 'styles' have also been suggested for how translators approach the task of composing the TT. The different distributions of tasks across the three phases of translation production result from what Mossop calls 'strategies' for self-revision. Since the late 1980s, many attempts have been made to characterise a range of styles in translation, often based, as here, on how the translator's time is distributed between the three phases. Mossop adopts and adapts some of the labels developed to describe styles of writing (see Chandler 1993): some translators invest a lot of time in research in the pre-drafting phase ('architects'), others very little ('steamrollers'). Some revise as they translate during the drafting phase, layering revision upon revision ('oil painters'), others do most of their revision in the post-drafting phase ('steamrollers', by necessity). There is, of course, some connection between the amount of pre-drafting planning and post-drafting checking. The following table summarises and slightly adapts Mossop's approach (he only applies what we have called 'styles'—'architect', 'steamroller' and 'oil painter'—to the composition stage on a sentence-by-sentence basis). This characterisation is not without its critics (e.g. Pym 2009) but could help to give you some clues about your own style of producing a translation.

Table 16.1 A model of TT production (sentence by sentence) according to three proposed 'styles' after Mossop (2014)

Style	Pre-drafting	Drafting	Post-drafting
Architect	Detailed planning: • Read through ST • Mark difficult passages • Do considerable conceptual research • Note possible TL wordings	• Consider several TL possibilities before typing out • Move immediately to next sentence	Minimal residual revision

Steamroller	Little if any planning:	• Type out something straight away:
		  o Leave gaps
		  o Note alternative translations
		  o Guess solution and mark with question mark
		  o May conduct some research while composing
		• Move immediately to next sentence
			Considerable revision usually needed, including some composition

Oil painter	Some basic planning e.g. quick glance at ST:	• Type out something quickly—often a fairly literal translation • Immediately revise (possibly several times) • Move on to next sentence	Minimal residual revision

Even if you turn out to be an architect or an oil painter, given sufficient time, it is worth doing a thorough final check on your translation. The following section deals with post-drafting checks, which could also be applied to another translator's work if you are the reviser.

From style to mechanics

The translator (as part of self-revision) and the reviser both need to consider a wide range of issues before delivering a finished translation. In this section, we deal briefly with a 'macro-level' issue, namely the 'style' of the text, and then with specific linguistic features usually covered by proofreading, or 'mechanics' (Mossop 2014: 147–8). There is no rule book for choosing an appropriate textual style, but there are many guides which are concerned with the so-called 'mechanics'. These are confusingly called 'style sheets' or 'style guides', as noted earlier.

Style

'Style' is a tricky issue when considering the properties of any text, as understandings of 'style' vary considerably, from degrees of linguistic formality, to 'personal' style, to a value judgement of writing quality. In literary translation, the TT is a new piece and in a sense the translator's own—normally to be judged in terms of the stylistic character of the original ST, whether it is a work of literary merit or pulp fiction. Most commercial, legal, technical and other specialised texts are written in a way which do not require attention to a personal style. As we have mentioned earlier in this book, such texts sometimes—as indeed the current volume— have multiple authors. For such texts, we have emphasised that it is important for the translator to consider the genre conventions in the target culture. In most cases, as long as the message is accurate, clear, and genre-compliant, a reviser or a reviewer will as far as possible leave the 'style' to look after itself.

Completed translations are occasionally passed on to an editor before publication, with the translator or reviser being consulted about changes to the TT. Treating the text as any other text for publication—not necessarily as a translated text—an editor may wish to prune perceived irrelevancies, or to reduce the length of the text due to typographical or pagination constraints. This is a common factor in editing, as well as in translation for the print media.

Proofing

Reading is an activity which takes us years to learn. Our fluency and speed depend on developing skills of anticipation in terms of both words and structures in an attempt to construct meanings. It is therefore rather challenging to read a text for other purposes, such as checking for errors in formal characteristics. Quite naturally, we tend to gloss over such errors, focusing on meaning, and reading what we think is there instead of what actually is, especially if we have written the text ourselves. It is therefore useful to develop ways of countering this tendency. One way, suggested by Mossop (2014: 180), is to read the text backwards, sentence by sentence. Another way is to compile a list of items to check (e.g. 'from' versus 'form'), possibly based on an analysis of your own past translation drafts. As an example, we reproduce here part of a checklist of common error types caught at the proofing stage from the Translation Bureau of the Canadian Public Works and Government Services (n.d.):

- Misspelling
- Misprints
- Punctuation errors
- Incorrect capitalisation
- Erroneous compounding or word division
- Failure to ensure that, when first used, an abbreviation follows the full name of the entity it represents, unless the abbreviation is well known
- Incorrect form of an abbreviation
- Inconsistency in presenting numbers (as numerals or words)
- Erroneous or inconsistent use of decimal point
- Inconsistency in presenting SI/metric symbols, including spacing between symbols and figures [SI: *Système International d'Unités*, see Bureau International des Poids et Mesures n.d.]
- Inaccurate transcription of numbers from one draft to the next
- Arabic in place of Roman numerals, and vice versa
- Non-agreement of subject and verb and use of singular noun where plural is required

For spelling/typo errors, always use the spell checker in your word-processing package (both as you are drafting and in the post-drafting phase) but make sure that you have set the tool to the relevant language *and* language variety. Be prepared for spelling conventions—especially in English e.g. hyphenation, '-ise' *versus* '-ize', 'History' versus 'history'—to differ from those in the relevant style guide, so always double-check any automatic corrections. In our experience, grammar checkers are of little help.

Concluding remarks

Regardless of whether you know your work is to be revised, reviewed or edited, you still have a responsibility for 'quality control', tedious though you may find it. But how you organise this, is—as we hope to have shown—up to you.

Further reading

Künzli, Alexander 2014. 'Die Übersetzungsrevision—Begriffsklärungen, Forschungsstand, Forschungsdesiderate', *trans-kom*, 7(1), pp. 1–29 [Online]. Available at: www.trans-kom.eu/ihv_07_01_2014.html (Accessed: 27 March 2018) [Provides a more recent view of research conducted into revision for translation than Mossop (2007), dealing also with the related terminology in German.].

Landers, Clifford E. 2001. *Literary Translation: A Practical Guide.* Clevedon: Multilingual Matters [See section on 'The crucial role of revision', pp. 159–61; concrete advice from a practising literary translator.].

Maier, Carol (ed.) 2000. 'Evaluation and translation' [Special Issue]. *The Translator*, 6(2) [A collection of papers by well-known researchers on Translation Quality Assessment.].

Mossop, Brian 2007. 'Empirical studies of revision: What we know and need to know', in Brunette, L. (ed.) *Revision and Technical Translation* [Special Issue]. *JoSTrans*, Issue 08/July 2007, pp. 5–10 [Online]. Available at: www.jostrans.org/issue08/issue08_toc. php (Accessed: 27 March 2018) [An early contribution to a growing topic, but the discussion of issues which might impact on the quality of revision is still useful. Other articles in this Special Issue are also of interest.].

Practical 16

For all these exercises, we suggest that you adopt a style guide for proofreading. Your university department may refer you to a standard style guide, such as the *MHRA* (2013), or you can choose another available online such as the European Commission's *English Style Guide* (2016), mentioned previously: both are rather long but you can focus on the sections on punctuation, spelling, capitalisation, names and titles, numbers, abbreviations/symbols/units of measurement, and currencies.

16.1 REVISION (INCLUDING PROOFING): CRITICAL ANALYSIS (INFORMATION LEAFLET—ECONOMICS)

Assignment

Your task here is to consider the proposed revisions of the published translation of the text extract in the main chapter: '*Die Privatisierung verschiedener deutscher Unternehmen* . . .' from the *Inter Nationes* 'Special Topic' information leaflet on *Privatisierung und Deregulierung in Deutschland: Der Fall Telekom* (see Figure 16.1). The text from which the extract has been taken will appear in a new edited collection of articles—to be published in English—tracking the development of deregulation in the economies of the EU. The editors—political economists—will add a scholarly commentary in English to each contribution, once the revised English translation is available. Please think about the following—maybe together with a fellow student or as advised by your tutor.

i   Can you reconstruct the reasons for the proposed changes resulting from the revision process?

ii   Do you agree with the proposed changes?

iii Would you propose any further changes?

iv   How long do you think such revisions would take?

v   Is time an important factor here? How would you set priorities for revision/ proofing given a tight deadline?

16.2 REVISION (INCLUDING PROOFING): INFORMATION LEAFLET—ECONOMICS

Assignment

i   You have now been asked to revise from scratch the following extract from the same information leaflet mentioned in Assignment 16.1 and in the main chapter. Discuss the main types of revision challenges the TT poses.

ii   Revise the TT, or a part of it.

iii Report on your revisions, saying what criteria you adopted for assessment of the TT, and explaining the main changes you made.

Contextual information

As for Assignment 16.1.

ST

1995 sind 15 Milliarden DM an Schulden getilgt worden; für 1996 ist ebenfalls eine Verringerung in zweistelliger Milliardenhöhe geplant. Zusammen mit einem weiteren Personalabbau bis zum Jahr 2000 von derzeit über 200.000 auf 170.000 Mitarbeiter und dem Ende der hohen Investitionen in Ostdeutschland läßt diese Sanierung
5 steigende Gewinne erwarten.
    Die Privatisierungspolitik ist auch für den Bund erfolgreich. Denn die Bundesregierung hat über zehn Milliarden DM aus dem Verkauf des staatlichen Unternehmensbesitzes eingenommen. Rund ein Drittel davon haben die VW-Stiftung und die Deutsche Bundesstiftung Umwelt erhalten. Über sechs Milliarden DM aus
10 dem Privatierungserlös sind in den Bundeshaushalt geflossen.
    Hinter der Telekom wartet eine Reihe weiterer Privatisierungskandidaten des Bundes. So wird über den Verkauf der Postbank bereits verhandelt; auch die Deutsche Siedlungs- und Landesrentenbank soll verkauft werden. Die Tankstellen und Rasthäuser an den Autobahnen will der Bund ebenso privatisieren wie die Brief-
15 und Paketpost, staatliche Wohnungsbaugesellschaften und Flughäfen sowie eine Wirtschaftsprüfungsgesellschaft und das Regierungs-Gästehaus Petersberg bei Bonn.
    Das Ziel ist der schlanke Staat, der sich auf das konzentriert, was durch private Initiative nicht zu leisten ist. Indem der Staat nicht länger unternehmerisch tätig ist, erweitert er die wirtschaftlichen Handlungsfelder für die Bürger, die als Unternehmer
20 in aller Regel dynamischer und erfolgreicher sind als der Staat. Damit ist die Privatisierung aber nicht nur für die privaten Unternehmer und Investoren von Vorteil, sondern sie ist wegen der privatwirtschaftlich zu erzielenden Effizienzsteigerungen, Wettbewerbszunahmen und Innovationen für die Volkswirtschaft insgesamt ein Gewinn.

(Zawadsky 1996a: 4–5)

TT

During 1995, fifteen thousand million DM's of debt were repaid; for 1996 an eleven figure debt reduction is also planned. With a further work force reduction from presently over 200,000 down to 170,000 by the year 2000, together with the end of the high investment levels in Eastern Germany, this restructuring will allow climbing
5   profits to be expected.

The privatization policy has also been a success for the Federal Government, as the Federal Government has had takings of over ten thousand million DM's out of the sale of State company property. About one third of which has gone to the VW Foundation and the German Federal Foundation for the Environment. More than six
10 thousand million DM's of privatization proceeds have flowed into the coffers of the Federal budget.

Behind Telekom further Federal privatization candidates are waiting in line. Negotiations over the sale of Postbank are already in progress; the Deutsche Siedlungs- und Landesrentenbank (German housing, credit, and finance, bank)
15 should also be sold. The Federal Government wants to privatize the petrol stations and service stations on the motorways, as well as the letter and parcel post, State housing-construction companies and airports, also an accounting company, and the government's Petersberg guest house near Bonn.

The objective is the slim State, which concentrates upon that which cannot be
20 managed through private enterprise. In so far as the State is no longer active in business, it expands the business manœuvrability of the citizen, who as business people are usually more dynamic and successful than the State. Privatization is not just advantageous for private business people and investors, but rather, through the increases in efficiency, competition and innovation, which can be achieved by
25 private business, it is a gain for the national economy as a whole.

(Zawadsky 1996b: 4–5)

16.3 REVISION (INCLUDING PROOFING) *OR* REVIEWING: HOLIDAY COMPANY MAGAZINE

Assignment A (Revision)

i   You have been asked to revise the following translation of the German ST below. Discuss the main types of revision challenges it poses.

ii   Revise the published TT, or a part of it.

iii Report on your revisions, saying what criteria you adopted for assessment of the TT, and explaining the main changes you made.

OR

Assignment B (Reviewing)

i   Ignoring the German ST, read through the TT below and start thinking about its fitness for purpose in the context of a promotional text for an upmarket holiday company. Make a note of some possible improvements. How would you characterise these?

ii   Compare the published English TT with the alternative version which will be made available to you by your tutor.

Contextual information

The texts are from a summer issue of *Holiday*, the client magazine of the upmarket Swiss timeshare company Hapimag, and are part of a long, illustrated feature on a new Hapimag holiday village that opened that summer in the Algarve. The magazine is published in German and English editions. As a company which aims for higher-end clients, it values its image: hence the importance of a polished English text. (At Hapimag's request we edited out one minor (outdated) detail from ST and TT. The German ST is presented first. The texts have been reproduced as published.)

ST

Wir spazieren auf einer ersten Besichtigungstour durch die Anlage. Wohnhäuser, wohltuend niedrig, nur zweistöckig gehalten, verteilen sich auf dem 11 Hektar grossen Gelände, das sich gegen das Meer und die Küste hin neigt: eine Reverenz an die für viele Reisende schönste Küste unseres europäischen Kontinents. Locker
5   verteilt stehen die Wohnhäuser, die 9 bis 26 Wohnungen umfassen. Insgesamt sind es 196 Partnerwohnungen, aufgeteilt auf 30 Studios, 137 Zwei- und 29 Dreizimmer-Ferienwohnungen. Alles in allem teilen sich 13 Wohnhäuser und das Hauptgebäude das grossflächige Grundstück: da bleibt für alle reichlich Platz. Der Resort Manager begleitet uns. Ein kreisrunder Platz zu unserer Linken, erkennbar alt, irritiert.
10 Lachend klärt uns der Resort Manager auf: wir befinden uns auf einem ehemaligen Landgut, die Fläche sei der damalige Dreschplatz und bleibe erhalten. Ebenso wie eine Zisterne, aus ockerfarbenen Steinen gefügt. Knorrige, verwachsene Feigenbäume wurden nicht gefällt, werden im Herbst, wohl zur Freude der Kinder, ihre süsse Frucht tragen. Gegen die Tennisplätze hin fällt das Gelände steiler ab, ein
15 Olivenhain säumt die aus groben Steinen gemauerte Stützwand, vereinzelte Mandelbäume stehen in Blüte, das Meer immer in Sichtweite.

(Hapimag 1995a: 7)

TT

We take a first tour of inspection through the village. Pleasantly low buildings, just two storeys high, spread over the 27 acre1920 grounds that incline themselves to the sea and coastline in reverence to a coast that by many travellers is considered the most beautiful on our European continent. The buildings, consisting of 9 to 26 apartments,
5   are loosely scattered. In all there are 196 Member apartments, divided into 30 studios, 137 two-room and 29 three-room holiday apartments. All in all the extensive grunds 2122are shared by 13 apartment buildings and the main building, so there's enough room for everyone. We are accompanied by the resort manager. To our left, a circular patch, obviously old, sticks out conspicuously. The resort manager
10 laughingly explains we are on an old country estate and this is the former thrashing spot which will remain intact, as will the ochre coloured 2324stone well. Gnarled, stunted fig trees have not been felled, but left to bear their sweet fruit in autumn, to the certain delight of the children. In the direction of the tennis courts the terrain slopes more steeply, an olive grove lines a coarse stone retaining wall and the odd almond
15 tree is in blossom with the sea in the background.

(Hapimag 1995b: 7)

16.4 POST-EDITING MT OUTPUT: UNIVERSITY WEBSITE

Choose a text (or text extract) of around 300 words about a German-speaking university from its website which is not yet available in English. An English-speaking Chinese friend of yours is interested in taking a beginners' German course in the summer but would like to know something about the university before making a decision. Copy and paste the chosen text into an online MT system (e.g. Google Translate or Babelfish) and then rapidly post-edit the raw MT output (on paper? on screen?) so that your friend can get the gist of the ST. How comprehensible is the raw output?

i   What types of error did you identify?
ii   Which errors did you choose to correct and why?
iii How long did the rapid post-editing take you and would you do anything differently next time?

You could also try running the ST through two different online MT systems in order to compare and evaluate the outputs.

16.5 REVISION (INCLUDING PROOFING): TRANSLATION BY FELLOW STUDENT

Choose a translation which you and your fellow students have recently completed. Swap paper or electronic copies of your translations with a classmate and revise the translation. If you are working with an electronic copy, try using Microsoft Word Comment and Track Changes (under the Review tab) to provide written feedback. Return the revised translations to each other, digest the feedback and discuss.

i   What did you learn about your own strengths and weaknesses as (a) a translator and (b) a reviser?
ii   What is different about revising your own work and revising that of others? Which do you find easier and why?
iii Did you manage to be tactful and diplomatic in the way you carried out any revisions? Were you irritated or offended by any of the revisions proposed to your translation? How can you develop your interpersonal skills in order to get the job done without conflict?

References

Primary

Hapimag 1995a. *Holiday*, June.
Hapimag 1995b. *Holiday*, June.
Zawadsky, K. 1996a. *Privatisierung und Deregulierung in Deutschland: Der Fall Telekom.* Bonn: Inter Nationes.
Zawadsky, K. 1996b. *Privatization and Deregulation in Germany: The Telekom Case.* Bonn: Inter Nationes.

Secondary

Bobrick, Benson 2001. *The Making of the English Bible*. London: Weidenfeld & Nicolson.

British Standards Institution 2015. *BS EN ISO 117100:2015 Translation Services—Requirements for Translation Services*. London: British Standards Institution.

Byrne, Jody 2012. *Scientific and Technical Translation Explained: A Nuts and Bolts Guide for Beginners*. London and New York: Routledge.

Chandler, Daniel 1993. 'Writing strategies and writers' tools', *English Today*, 9(2), pp. 32–8.

Durban, Chris/Institute for Translation and Interpreting (ITI) 2014. *Translation: Getting It Right: A Guide to Buying Translation* [Online] Available at: www.iti.org.uk/attachments/article/242/English.pdf (Accessed: 12 May 2017).

Gough, Joanna 2017. *The Patterns of Interaction Between Professional Translators and Online Resources*. PhD Thesis. University of Surrey, UK [Online]. Available at: www.surrey.ac.uk/library/ (Accessed: 13 February 2018).

Mossop, Brian 2014. *Revising and Editing for Translators*. 3rd edn. London and New York: Routledge.

Olohan, Maeve 2016. *Scientific and Technical Translation*. London and New York: Routledge.

Pym, Anthony 2009. 'Using process studies in translator training: Self-discovery through lousy experiments', in Göpferich, S., Alves, F. and Mees, I.M. (eds) *Methodology, Technology and Innovation in Translation Process Research*. Copenhagen: Samfundslitteratur, pp. 135–56.

Stetting, Karen 1989. 'Transediting—A new term for coping with the grey area between editing and translating', in Caie, G., Haastrup, K., Jakobsen, A. L., Nielsen, J. E., Sevaldsen, J., Specht, H. and Zettersten, A. (eds) *Proceedings from the Fourth Nordic Conference for English Studies*. Copenhagen: University of Copenhagen, Department of English, pp. 371–82.

Lexical and related resources

Bureau International des Poids et Mesures n.d. *Measurement Units: The SI*. Available at: www.bipm.org/en/measurement-units/ (Accessed: 1 March 2018).

Directorate-General for Translation/European Commission January 2016. *English Style Guide: A Handbook for Authors and Translators in the European Commission*. 8th edn. (last updated January 2020). Available at: https://ec.europa.eu/info/sites/info/files/style-guide_english_dgt_en.pdf (Accessed: 2 February 2020).

Guardian and Observer Style Guide n.d. [Online]. Available at: www.theguardian.com/guardian-observer-style-guide-a (Accessed: 12 February 2018).

Modern Humanities Research Association 2013. *MHRA Style Guide: A Handbook for Authors and Editors*. 3rd edn. London: Modern Humanities Research Association. Available at: www.mhra.org.uk/style (Accessed: 27 March 2018).

Translation Bureau of the Canadian Public Works and Government Services n.d. *The Canadian Style* (Section 16: Revision and Proofreading). Available at: www.btb.termiumplus.gc.ca/tcdnstyl-chap?lang=eng&lettr=chapsect16&info0=16# (Accessed: 2 March 2018).

Wroe, Ann 2018. *The Economist Style Guide*. 12th edn. London: Profile Books.

Postscript

A career in translation?*

Having completed the course, you may feel you wish to know more about becoming a translator. This final part of the book aims to provide some preliminary information and advice for those seeking entry to the profession. We cannot cover the situation across the globe, but the website of the FIT, the Fédération Internationale des Traducteurs/International Federation of Translators, has links to a very wide range of professional associations, including those in English-speaking and German-speaking areas. The FIT also publishes a newsletter on its website—*Translatio*—with news about associations and events.

Translators are usually either 'in-house' or 'freelance'. The in-house translator is employed by a business in a dedicated translation department or section to provide translations in the workplace, on either a permanent or a fixed-term basis. Over the last 20 years or so, the number of in-house opportunities of this kind has reduced as companies have developed different business models to meet the requirements of a rapidly changing and sometimes unpredictable global language market, and as the possibilities to work remotely have increased. More work is now outsourced to freelancers—sometimes ex in-house staff—with fewer posts available as employees. In fact, most translators now work as freelancers, which was not the case even 20 years ago (more on setting up as a freelancer later). The advantage of being in-house for a newcomer to the profession is the opportunity to gain experience quickly, in an environment where mentoring and feedback are usually supplied. Another way of getting access to mentoring and feedback is to work for what is now usually called a Language Service Provider (LSP); the terms 'translation company' or 'translation agency' are less favoured in the modern market. The organisation delivers translations (often in various media) and sometimes other services such as interpreting, multilingual web set-up and maintenance, and multilingual desktop

---

*Note: We are very grateful to Eyvor Fogarty, MA, FITI, LLCM, FRSA for her expert guidance and advice on many issues covered in this Postscript. As an experienced translator, interpreter, teacher and writer, she is a former Chairman of FIT Europe and a distinguished holder of the Pushkin Gold Medal from the Russian Union of Translators and the John B. Sykes Prize for Excellence from the Institute of Translation and Interpreting, UK. Any errors or oversights in the Postscript remain, of course, our own.

publishing. Project Management (PM) has become an additional career path for some translators as LSPs often take on large-scale projects requiring translation of documentation into many languages on tight schedules. The project manager's job includes sourcing suitably qualified and experienced translators and revisers, often from a network of suppliers, as well as marshalling resources and ensuring the client's requirements are met. Some Master's programmes now include training in PM.

A crucial role in the UK professional field is performed by two major players: the Institute of Translation and Interpreting (ITI) and the Chartered Institute of Linguists (CIoL). We enumerate later a few of the items which you can find on their websites (please see list later on and on the course website at www.routledge.com/9781138920989, but the best advice is to browse and see for yourself).

The ITI was established in 1986, describing itself on its website as 'the UK's only dedicated association for practising translation and interpreting professionals'. The CIoL has a longer history, starting in 1910, with a broader profile as 'the leading UK-based membership body for language professionals', according to its website. Neither the ITI nor the CIoL make explicit mention of literary translation. Instead, the Society of Authors, which describes itself online as 'a trade union for all types of writers, illustrators and literary translators', has included the Translators Association (TA) since 1958, in order to 'provide literary translators with an effective means of protecting their interests and sharing their concerns'. Nevertheless, many of the issues which arise in the professional practice of translation will be shared, as we have tried to indicate throughout this course, whether the assignment is literary or specialised.

The ITI and CIoL websites provide a wealth of information which is regularly updated. The ITI, for instance, offers guidance on how to become a translator, and, more specifically, on setting up as a freelancer, including an online course. The CIoL also offers good advice on Continuing Professional Development (CPD) strategies and opportunities, as well as publishing job adverts. Both organisations publish professionally relevant magazines—*The ITI Bulletin* and *The Linguist*—and promote networking to foster personal contact between translators at different stages of their careers, including students as aspiring translators. A wide range of membership categories is available in the ITI and in the CIoL, starting in both cases with student membership or affiliation as one of the 'Non-Qualified' categories or the 'Pre-professional grades'.

In the German-speaking area the largest organisation is the *Bundesverband der Dolmetscher und Übersetzer*, covering the whole of Germany. In addition to the many useful items on topics also covered by the ITI and the CIoL, there is a useful short piece on the skills needed for translation as well as a profile of the profession (see list of websites presented later). Here you will find arguments to counter the assumptions made by some clients that an online machine-translation system is adequate for any job, based on the misconception that translation is a straightforward word-substitution exercise rather than a profession which requires extensive knowledge, judgement and training, as well as bilingual language competence. Unfortunately, such assumptions can be used as an attempt to depress rates of pay.

Other professional associations in Germany can be accessed through the FIT website, as also the Austrian and Swiss associations (see also list of websites later). They differ in various ways, including geographical coverage and type of specialism.

When working as a professional translator, you are likely to have questions about what constitutes professional behaviour in many respects, including relations with clients and other translators, the rights of text authors, your own level of competence to accept particular assignments, ethical issues regarding the nature of some assignments, and so on. It is therefore important to be aware of and follow such advice as is given in professional codes of conduct.

In the USA, every American state has its own translators/interpreters association, affiliated to the American Translators Association (ATA). The ATA website pages contain similar information to those of the ITI and the CIoL, as do those of the main Canadian professional organisation, as well as the Australian and the New Zealand associations (see list of websites). All are affiliated to the FIT.

With very few exceptions, there is no legal requirement for you to have a qualification in order to be able to work as a 'translator': clearly not the case if you want to work as a doctor or a lawyer, for instance. However, whatever the legal situation, there are clearly competence-related and ethical reasons why a qualification is advantageous: being competent in two languages is necessary but not sufficient to be a competent translator. Relevant qualifications come in different shapes and forms. As noted, some modern-language Bachelor's degrees offer specialisms in translation, and possibly in introductory interpreting. However, even with an undergraduate qualification, you might not be so successful in an increasingly competitive international jobs market. The Institute of Linguists Educational Trust offers its own well-established Diploma in Translation or 'DipTrans', a postgraduate-level qualification for which preparation is available at a number of institutions around the world (see website). Since the 1980s, postgraduate programmes in translation offered by universities have grown in number to provide a very wide choice to prospective students. The ITI provides a useful list of available programmes offered by ITI Corporate Members (which includes educational institutions). You can narrow down the sometimes bewildering range according to a number of filters, including:

- the translation pairs on offer, as well as the translation direction
- the breadth of the programme (generalist or focused on a particular specialism)
- a particular focus e.g. on specialised translation or on literary translation or on audio-visual translation
- the availability and use of up-to-date professional-level translation technology
- the balance in the curriculum between translation practice and more discursive modules
- the experience and qualifications of the programme tutors responsible for the practice-based modules
- membership of the European Master's in Translation Network of the European Commission's Directorate-General for Translation (presupposing successful post-Brexit negotiations)

- the research profiles of the academic staff
- the engagement of the department with professional translation organisations and the availability of placements

Other ways in which you can improve your chances of succeeding in the translation profession include getting a 'Europass' to present your experience and qualifications for jobs in Europe. Another European organisation which can help is ESCO, which aims to connect people and jobs online using 'big data'. It specifies skills and competences for nearly 3,000 occupations, including translation and related professions, which are being increasingly recognised.

You can also do some background research into the profession by looking at surveys conducted by authoritative bodies: these will help to map out the subject areas and environment in which translators work; they provide an assessment of the market and document trends and concerns. Two surveys are included in our list of websites. Annual surveys of the language services market are also available online, produced by Common Sense Advisory, a US-based market research company.

If you do decide that you want to make a career in translation, bear in mind that you need not just enthusiasm, but the motivation and self-belief to carry you through difficult patches. Freelancing, in particular, is not for the faint-hearted. Although you will need to be in contact with other translators and informants— as well as your clients—to solve translation problems, working freelance can be rather isolating compared to working in a busy office. It is here that the professional network meetings and contact with local universities become particularly important. Work flows can be erratic, at least until—having established your language profile and your specialism/s—you become established and have several work-providers. Most translators stick with a particular area of expertise e.g. financial, sci-tech (or even narrower), medical, legal. If necessary, rather than expand their range of specialisms, most translators prefer to expand their range of languages, often to one in a cognate relation to their existing languages e.g. adding Norwegian or Dutch to German. Some literary translators do, however, cross over to non-literary topics, and vice versa, whether out of interest or financial necessity is unclear (see Rogers 2019: 162). If you can become successfully established and acquire competence in your field, you are unlikely to want to return to a routine job: there can be real interest in the endlessly varied real-life or imaginative material that passes through your hands, and real delight in using language to earn your living.

Websites

English-speaking translators' associations

American Translators Association (ATA): www.atanet.org/
Australian Institute of Interpreters and Translators (AUSIT): https://ausit.org/
Chartered Institute of Linguists (CIoL): www.ciol.org.uk/
   Code of Professional Conduct: downloadable from https://www.ciol.org.uk/

Continuing Professional Development: https://www.ciol.org.uk/cpd

Jobs: https://www.ciol.org.uk/search/node/jobs

Membership categories: https://www.ciol.org.uk/grades

Networks (Translating Division): https://www.ciol.org.uk/td

Qualifications (the CIoL's own): https://www.ciol.org.uk/ciol-diptrans

The Linguist: https://www.ciol.org.uk/the-linguist#ufh-c-1251-the-linguist-archive

Conseil des Traducteurs, Terminologues et Interprètes du Canada/Canadian Translators, Terminologists and Interpreters Council (CTIC): www.cttic.org/mission.asp

Institute of Translation and Interpreting (ITI): www.iti.org.uk/

    Code of Professional Conduct: downloadable from https://www.iti.org.uk/about-iti/professional-standards

    Continuing Professional Development: https://www.iti.org.uk/professional-development/cpd

    How to Become a Translator: https://www.iti.org.uk/professional-development/career-development/

    ITI Bulletin: https://www.iti.org.uk/about-iti/iti-bulletin

    Membership Categories: https://www.iti.org.uk/membership/categories

    Networks: https://www.iti.org.uk/professional-development/networks-regional-groups

    Qualifications (list of universities with Corporate ITI Membership offering postgraduate or equivalent qualifications): https://www.iti.org.uk/professional-development/career-development/universities-courses

    Setting Up as a Freelancer: https://www.iti.org.uk/more/iti-blog/1114-the-recipe-for-a-successful-start-to-a-freelance-translation-career

New Zealand Society of Translators and Interpreters/Te Rōpū Kaiwhakamāori ā-waha, ā-tuhi o Aotearoa (NZSTI): www.nzsti.org/

Translators Association (a 'Group' within the Society of Authors): https://societyofauthors.org/Groups/Translators

German-speaking translators' associations

Association Suisse des Traducteurs, Terminologues et Interprètes (ASTTI): www.astti.ch/

Assoziierte Dolmetscher und Übersetzer in Norddeutschland e. V. (ADÜ Nord): https://adue-nord.de/

Austrian Association of Literary and Scientific Translators/Interessengemeinschaft von Übersetzerinnen und Übersetzern literarischer und wissenschaftlicher Werke (AALST): www.literaturhaus.at/index.php?id=6540 (available through the *Literaturhaus Wien* website).

Bundesverband der Dolmetscher und Übersetzer (BDÜ): https://bdue.de/der-bdue/

    Was machen Übersetzer und Dolmetscher eigentlich? https://bdue.de/aktuell/news-detail/was-machen-uebersetzer-und-dolmetscher-eigentlich/

    Berufsbild Übersetzer: https://bdue.de/der-beruf/uebersetzer/

Deutscher Verband der freien Übersetzer und Dolmetscher e.V. (DVÜD): http://dvud.de

Verband der Übersetzer und Dolmetscher e.V. (VÜD): http:// www.literaturuebersetzer.de

Other

Common Sense Advisory. *The Language Services Market: 2019.* https://insights.csa-research.com/reportaction/305013045/Marketing?SearchTerms=%22The%20Language%20Services%20Market%3A%202019%22 (annual updates available)

European Skills, Competences, Qualifications and Occupations (ESCO): https://ec.europa.eu/esco/portal

Europass: http://europass.cedefop.europa.eu/

European Master's in Translation (EMT): https://ec.europa.eu/info/resources-partners/european-masters-translation-emt_en

Expectations and Concerns of the European Language Industry 2019: https://ec.europa.eu/info/sites/info/files/2019_language_industry_survey_report.pdf (annual updates available)

Fédération Internationale des Traducteurs/International Federation of Translators (FIT): https://www.fit-ift.org/

Further reading

In addition to the websites listed previously, some print publications might also be of interest. Publications in the area of professional practice very quickly go out of date in this age of rapid change, so older items (anything over three years) need to be read with caution. Practices in literary translation are less likely to change so rapidly.

Olohan, Maeve. 2016. *Scientific and Technical Translation*. London and New York: Routledge.

Park, Catherine (ed.) 2018. *Where Are We Headed? Trends in Translation and Interpreting 2018*. Institute of Translation and Interpreting. Available at: https://www.iti.org.uk/more/news/1116-iti-trends-e-book-now-available

Rogers, Margaret 2019. 'From binaries to borders: Literary *and* non-literary translation', in Dam, H.V., Korning Zethsen, K. and Nisbeth Jensen, Matilde (eds) *Moving Boundaries in Translation Studies*. London and New York: Routledge, pp. 151–67.

Samuelsson-Brown, Geoffrey 2010. *A Practical Guide for Translators*. 5th edn. Clevedon: Multilingual Matters. [likely to be rather outdated by now but still worth dipping into]

Wright, Chantal 2016. *Literary Translation*. London and New York: Routledge.

Index